CANON POWERSHOT G16

THE EXPANDED GUIDE

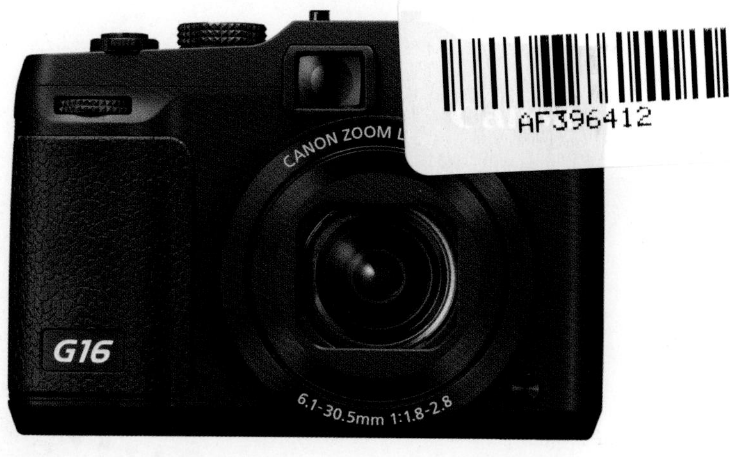

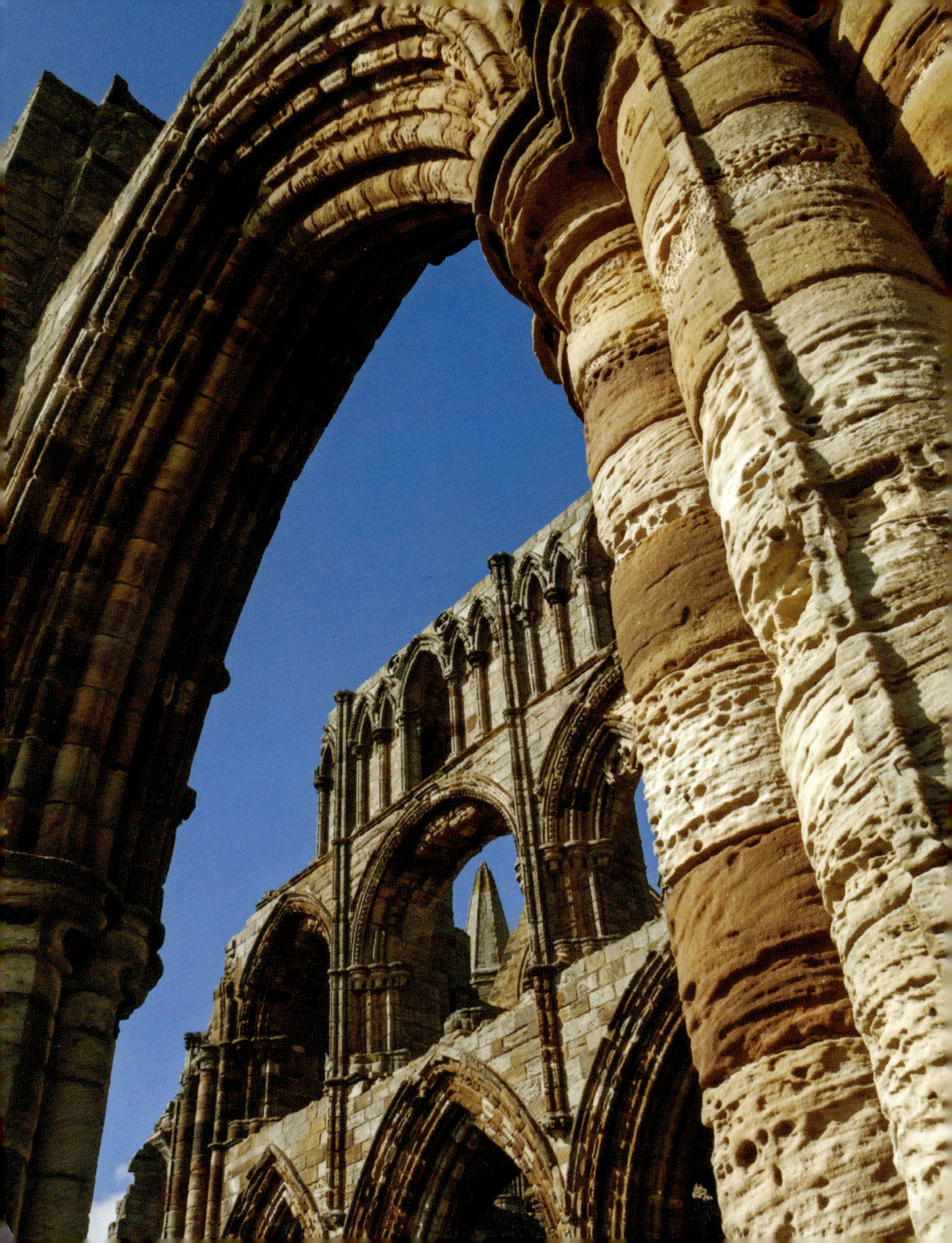

CANON POWERSHOT G16

THE EXPANDED GUIDE

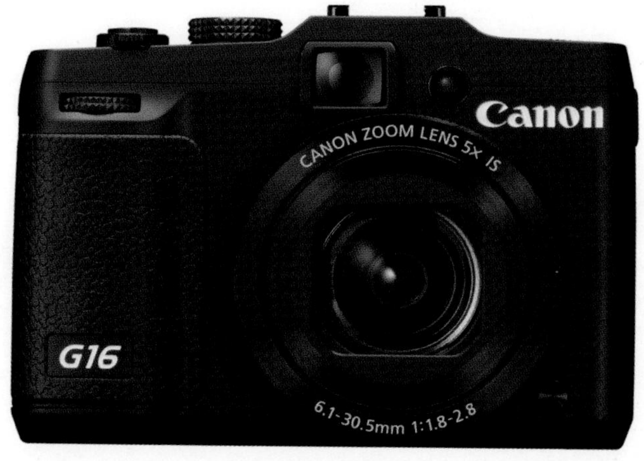

David Taylor

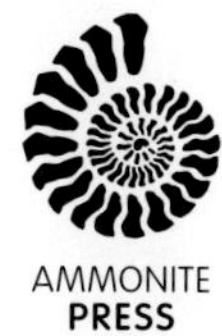

AMMONITE PRESS

First published 2014 by
Ammonite Press
an imprint of AE Publications Ltd
166 High Street, Lewes, East Sussex, BN7 1XU, UK

Text © AE Publications Ltd, 2014
Images © David Taylor, 2014 (unless otherwise specified)
Copyright © in the Work AE Publications Ltd, 2014

ISBN 978-1-781450-82-6

All rights reserved

The rights of David Taylor to be identified as the author
of this work have been asserted in accordance with the
Copyright, Designs, and Patents Act 1988, Sections 77
and 78.

No part of this publication may be reproduced, stored in
a retrieval system, or transmitted in any form or by any
means without the prior permission of the publishers
and copyright owner.

While every effort has been made to obtain permission
from the copyright holders for all material used in this
book, the publishers will be pleased to hear from anyone
who has not been appropriately acknowledged, and to
make the correction in future reprints.

The publishers and author can accept no legal
responsibility for any consequences arising from the
application of information, advice, or instructions given
in this publication.

British Library Cataloging in Publication Data: A catalog
record of this book is available from the British Library.

Editor: Chris Gatcum
Series Editor: Richard Wiles
Design: Belkys Smock

Typefaces: Giacomo
Color reproduction by GMC Reprographics
Printed in China

‹‹ PAGE 2
Whitby Abbey,
North Yorkshire, UK.

» CONTENTS

1

OVERVIEW

The Canon PowerShot G16 was announced on August 22nd, 2013, less than a year after its predecessor, the PowerShot G15. This is a relatively short time for a product to be refreshed and in many ways this is apparent in the specifications: it's fair to say that the G16 is an evolutionary camera, rather than a revolutionary one.

However, this is not meant as a criticism. Canon has concentrated on improving an already excellent camera, leaving what worked alone and refining any remaining rough edges. The focusing is one area that has been improved, and it is noticeably "snappier" than previous G-series cameras. This is mainly due to the use of the latest Canon Digic image processor: Digic 6.

The headline feature of the G16 is the inclusion of Wi-Fi. This seems to be a necessity in new cameras, although it's notable that the Wi-Fi implementation in the G16 doesn't allow remote shooting. You can, however, transfer images between a variety of different devices quickly and easily (once Wi-Fi has been set up).

Perhaps the most intriguing addition to the G16 is the Star Mode. This offers several options that allow you to use your G16 long after the sun has gone down, to capture the night sky in all its glory. A spin-off of that facility is the extension of the maximum shutter speed to 250 seconds when shooting in Manual (**M**) exposure mode. As a result, low-light photography is now a pleasure rather than a frustrating experience on a G-series camera.

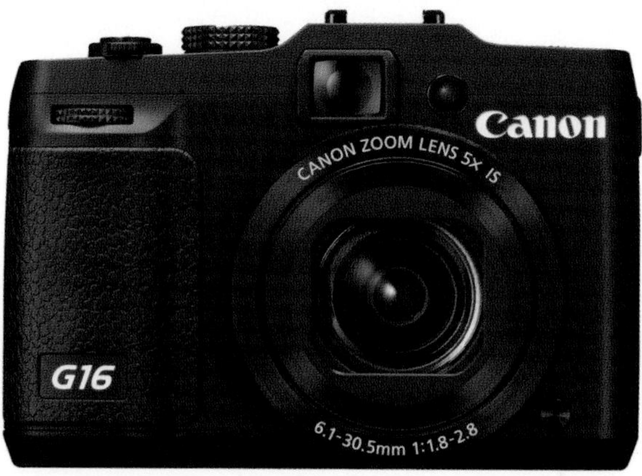

TIMING »
One of the joys of a small camera like the G16 is that it can be kept with you at all times, so you are ready to capture any photographic opportunity that presents itself.

EVOLUTIONARY «
If you've used one of the previous G-series cameras you will find the G16 is easy to get to grips with.

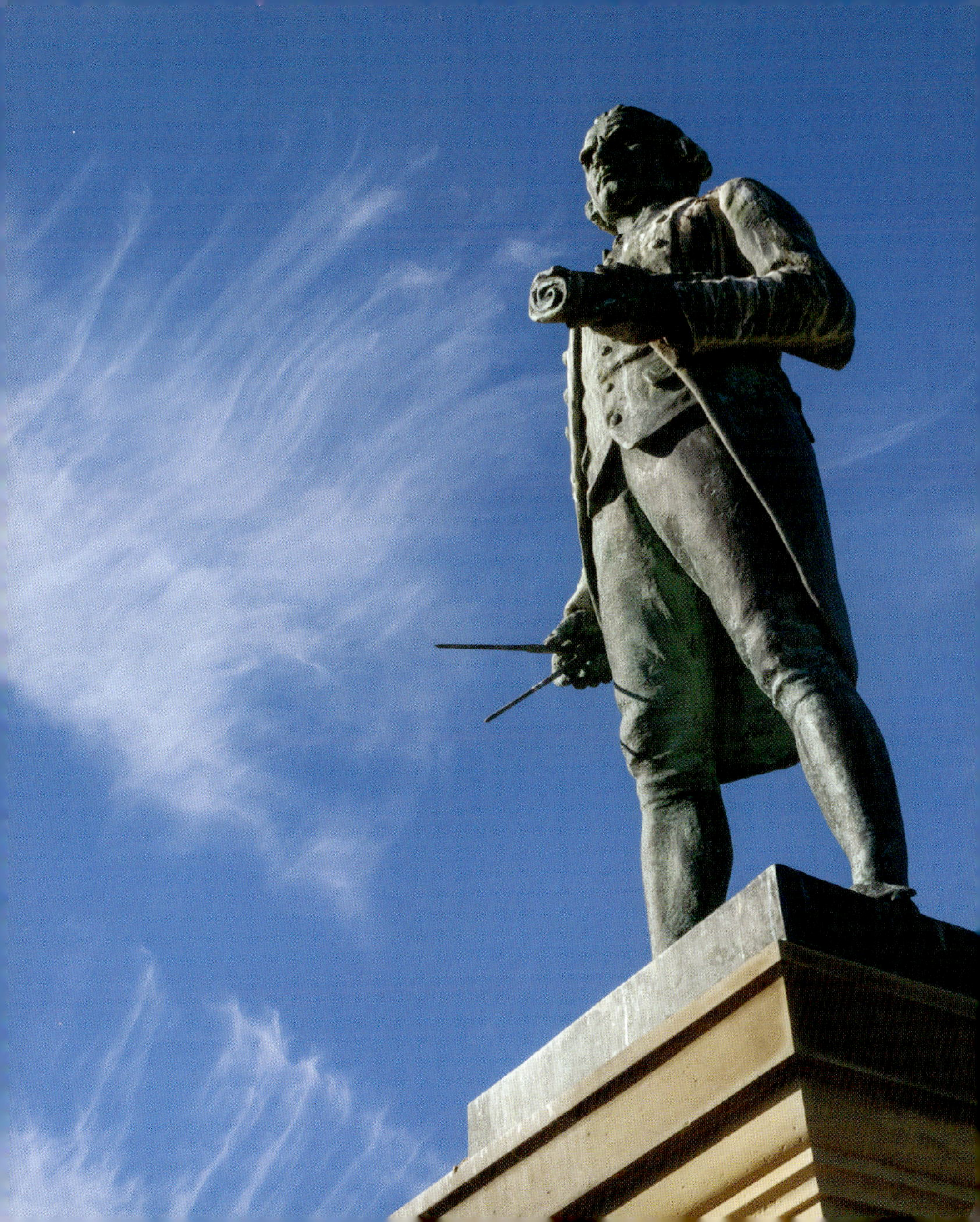

» MAIN FEATURES

Body

Dimensions (W x H x D):
4.28 x 2.99 x 1.58in./108.8 x 75.9 x 40.3mm
Weight: 12.56oz./356g with battery and
memory card

Sensor and processor

Sensor: 0.29 x 0.22in./7.44 x 5.58mm
RGB CMOS sensor
Effective resolution: Approx. 12.1
megapixels
Image processor: Digic 6

Still image file types and sizes

JPEG resolution (pixels):
4:3 aspect ratio: 4000 x 3000 (L),
2816 x 2112 (M1), 1600 x 1200 (M2),
or 640 x 480 (S)
16:9 aspect ratio: 4000 x 2248 (L),
2816 x 1584 (M1), 1920 x 1080 (M2),
or 640 x 360 (S)
3:2 aspect ratio: 4000 x 2664 (L),
2816 x 1880 (M1), 1600 x 1064 (M2),
or 640 x 424 (S)
1:1 aspect ratio: 2992 x 2992 (L) ,
2112 x 2112 (M1), 1200 x 1200 (M2),
or 480 x 480 (S)
4:5 aspect ratio: 2400 x 3000 (L),
1696 x 2112 (M1), 960 x 1200 (M2)
or 384 x 480 (S)
Raw resolution: 4000 x 3000 pixels
Raw format: .CR2

LCD monitor

Type: TFT LCD
Resolution: Approx. 922,000 pixels
Size: 3.0in./7.6cm diagonal

Viewfinder

Optical viewfinder: Yes
Coverage: Approx. 80%
Diopter adjustment: Yes

Lens and focusing

Lens: 5x optical zoom
Focal length range:
6.1–30.5mm (28–140mm equivalent)
Minimum focus distance:
0.4in./4cm (6.1mm); 2.8ft/40cm (30.5mm)
Digital zoom:
20x (when combined with Digital
Tele-Converter)
Image stabilization: Yes
Focus modes: Continuous; Servo AF/AE;
Tracking; Manual

Exposure

Metering patterns: Evaluative; Center-
weighted average; Spot
Aperture range: f/1.8–f/8 (at 6.1mm);
f/2.8–f/8 (at 30.5mm)
Shutter speeds: 1/4000 sec.–250 seconds
ISO range: ISO 80–12,800 (Manual); ISO
80–1600 (Auto) Exposure compensation:
±3 stops in $1/3$-stop increments
Automatic exposure bracketing:
±3 stops in $1/3$-stop increments

Drive modes

Drive modes: Single; Continuous;
Continuous Shooting AF;
Self-Timer
Continuous shooting: Max. 12.2fps
(frames per second)

Flash

Integral flash range:
1.6–23ft./50cm–7.0m at 6.1mm
focal length
3.3–14.7ft/50cm–4.5m at 30.5mm
focal length
Hotshoe: Yes (compatible with EX
Speedlite flashes)
Sync speed: 1/2000 sec.
Flash exposure compensation: ±2 stops
in $^1/_3$ -stop increments
Flash modes: Auto; Slow-Sync; Red-eye
reduction; 1st & 2nd curtain sync

Movies

Resolution: 1920 x 1080 pixels (Full HD)
at 60fps or 30fps
1280 x 720 pixels (HD) at 30fps
640 x 480 pixels (VGA) at 30fps
Format: .MOV format (H.264 compression
for image data and Linear PCM for audio)

Memory card

Type: Secure Digital (SD up to 2GB;
SDHC up to 32GB; SDXC 32GB+)

Connections

Remote terminal (for remote switch
RS-60E3); A/V OUT/Digital terminal (USB);
HDMI; Wi-Fi

Software

None supplied (Digital Photo Professional,
ImageBrowser EX, PhotoStitch, and
CameraWindow available as free
downloads from Canon's web site)

1 » FULL FEATURES & CAMERA LAYOUT

FRONT OF CAMERA

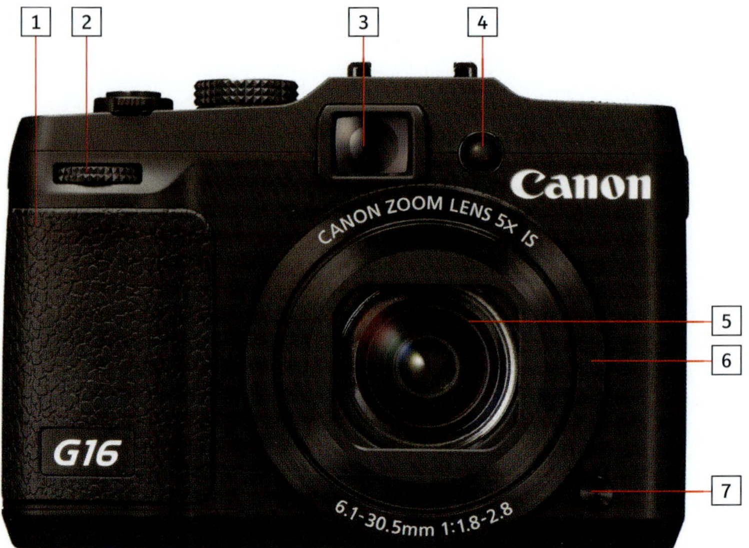

1	Handgrip
2	Front dial
3	Viewfinder
4	Lamp
5	Lens
6	Lens ring (removed when fitting optional lens accessories)
7	Lens ring release button

BACK OF CAMERA

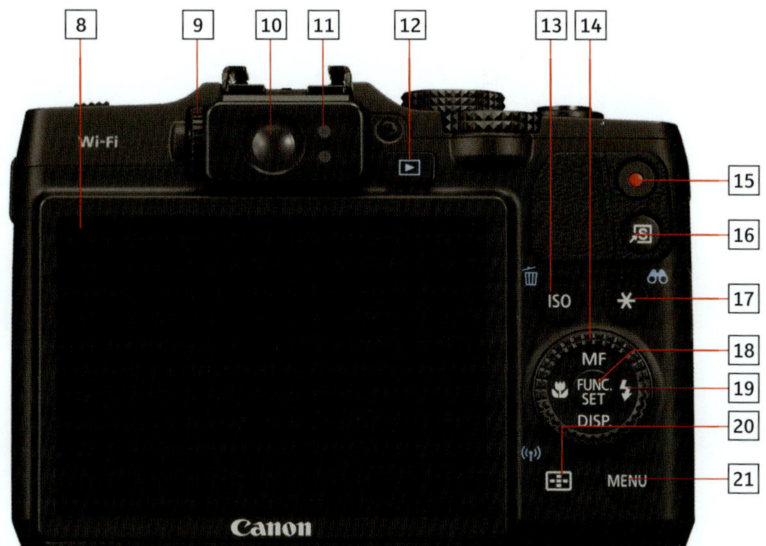

8	LCD monitor	16	Shortcut button
9	Viewfinder diopter adjust	17	AE/FE lock / Filtering image display button
10	Viewfinder		
11	Indicator lights	18	Function set button
12	Playback button	19	▲/Manual Focus / ▼/**DISP.** / ◄/Macro / ► /Flash buttons
13	ISO / Delete button		
14	Control dial	20	AF Frame select / Wi-Fi button
15	Movie record button	21	MENU button

» FULL FEATURES & CAMERA LAYOUT

TOP OF CAMERA

LEFT SIDE

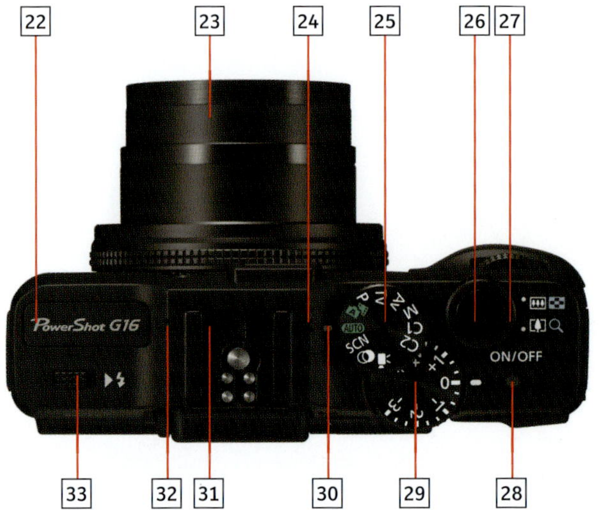

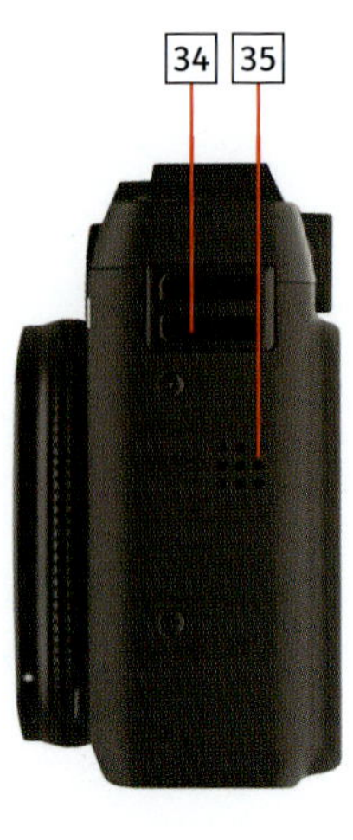

22	Flash	28	ON/OFF button
23	Lens (extended)	29	Exposure compensation dial
24	Right microphone		
25	Mode dial	30	Mode dial index mark
26	Shutter-release button	31	Flash hotshoe
27	Lens zoom rocker / Magnify images	32	Left microphone
		33	Flash release switch

34	Strap mount
35	Speaker

RIGHT SIDE

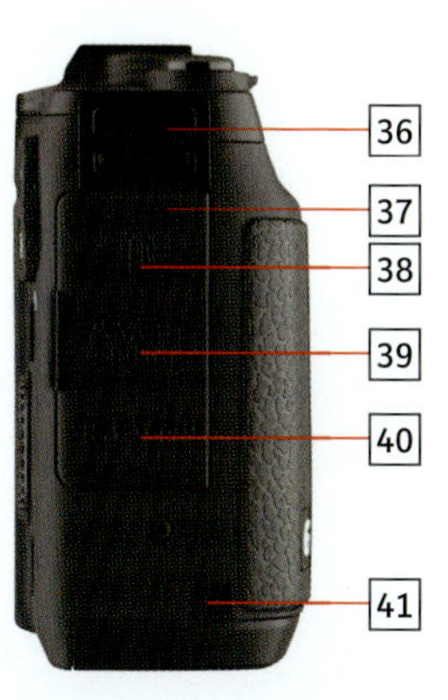

BOTTOM OF CAMERA

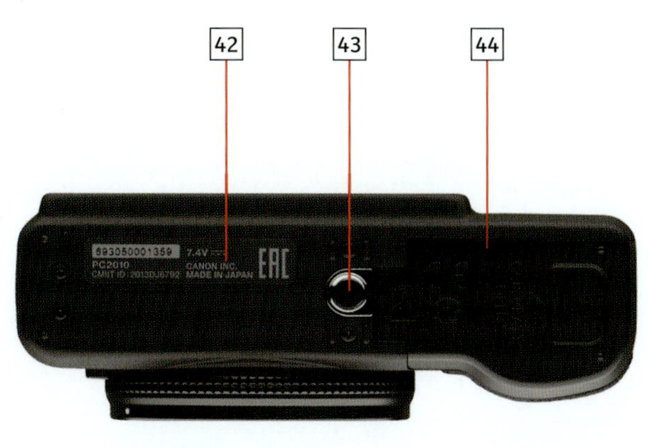

36	Strap mount	42	Information panel
37	Terminals cover	43	Tripod socket
38	Remote release terminal position	44	Battery / Memory card cover
39	Audio/Video output / Digital terminal position		
40	HDMI terminal position		
41	DC terminal cover		

» SHOOTING INFORMATION DISPLAY

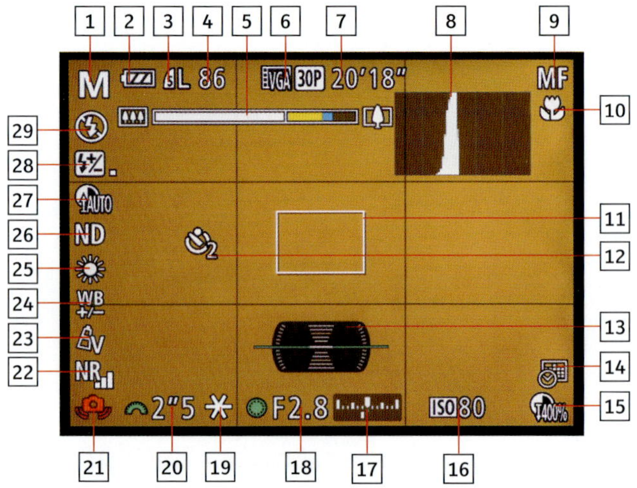

1 Exposure mode	**16** ISO speed
2 Battery charge status	**17** Exposure level indicator (Manual exposure only)
3 Compression (Image quality)	
4 Still images: Recordable shots	**18** Aperture value
5 Digital Zoom magnification / Digital Tele-Converter	**19** AEB lock (Not available in Manual exposure)
6 Movie quality	**20** Shutter speed
7 Available movie recording time	**21** Camera shake warning
8 Histogram	**22** Noise reduction
9 Manual focus mode	**23** My Colors
10 Macro focus mode	**24** White balance correction
11 AF frame	**25** White balance preset
12 Self-timer	**26** ND Filter
13 Electronic level	**27** Shadow Correction
14 Date stamp	**28** Flash exposure compensation
15 DR Correction	**29** Flash mode

» PLAYBACK SCREEN

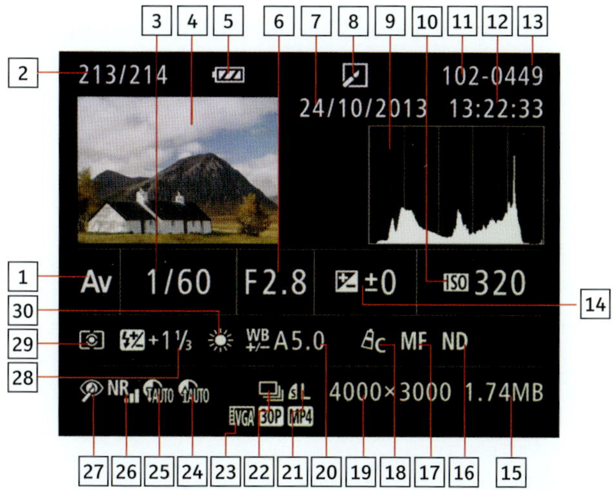

1	Shooting mode	16	ND Filter
2	Image number / Number of images on memory card	17	Manual focus
3	Shutter speed	18	My Colors setting
4	Image thumbnail	19	Image resolution
5	Battery charge indicator	20	White balance shift
6	Aperture value	21	File type / Quality setting
7	Shooting date	22	Continuous drive
8	Image editing	23	Movie setting (replaces 21 & 22 when viewing a movie)
9	Histogram	24	Shadow Correction
10	ISO	25	DR Correction
11	Folder number	26	Noise reduction
12	Shooting time	27	Red-eye reduction
13	File name	28	Flash exposure compensation
14	Exposure compensation / Exposure shift amount	29	Metering method
15	File size	30	White balance setting

2 FUNCTIONS

The Canon PowerShot G-series is a highly regarded line of cameras that is used by amateurs and professionals alike. The G16 is the latest model to join the range, offering a wide range of controls that will enable you to create high quality images.

Your G16 is effectively two cameras in one. On one level it can be set to act as a "point-and-shoot" camera: you press the shutter-release button and the camera does the rest. On another level, it is also a fully featured camera that allows you to take complete control over every stage in the making of an image. If you're so minded you can set your own exposure (either using the G16's internal exposure meter as a guide or using values obtained from a separate exposure meter), focus manually, and even use wireless flash. This level of control does require more effort and thought, but the pleasure of creation will be your reward. This chapter is a guide to getting to grips with your camera as a creative tool.

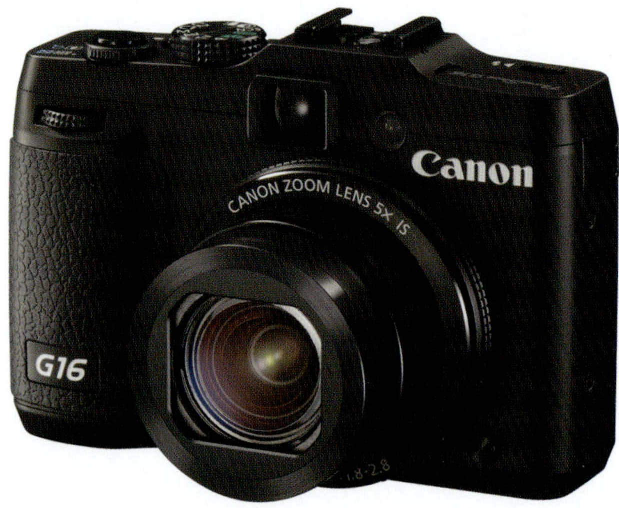

SIZE «
The G16's diminutive size belies the fact that it's a very capable camera with an impressive feature set.

VISION »
Although it's highly sophisticated, the G16 can't decide what photographs are made with it. It's merely a tool that allows you to show how you view the world.

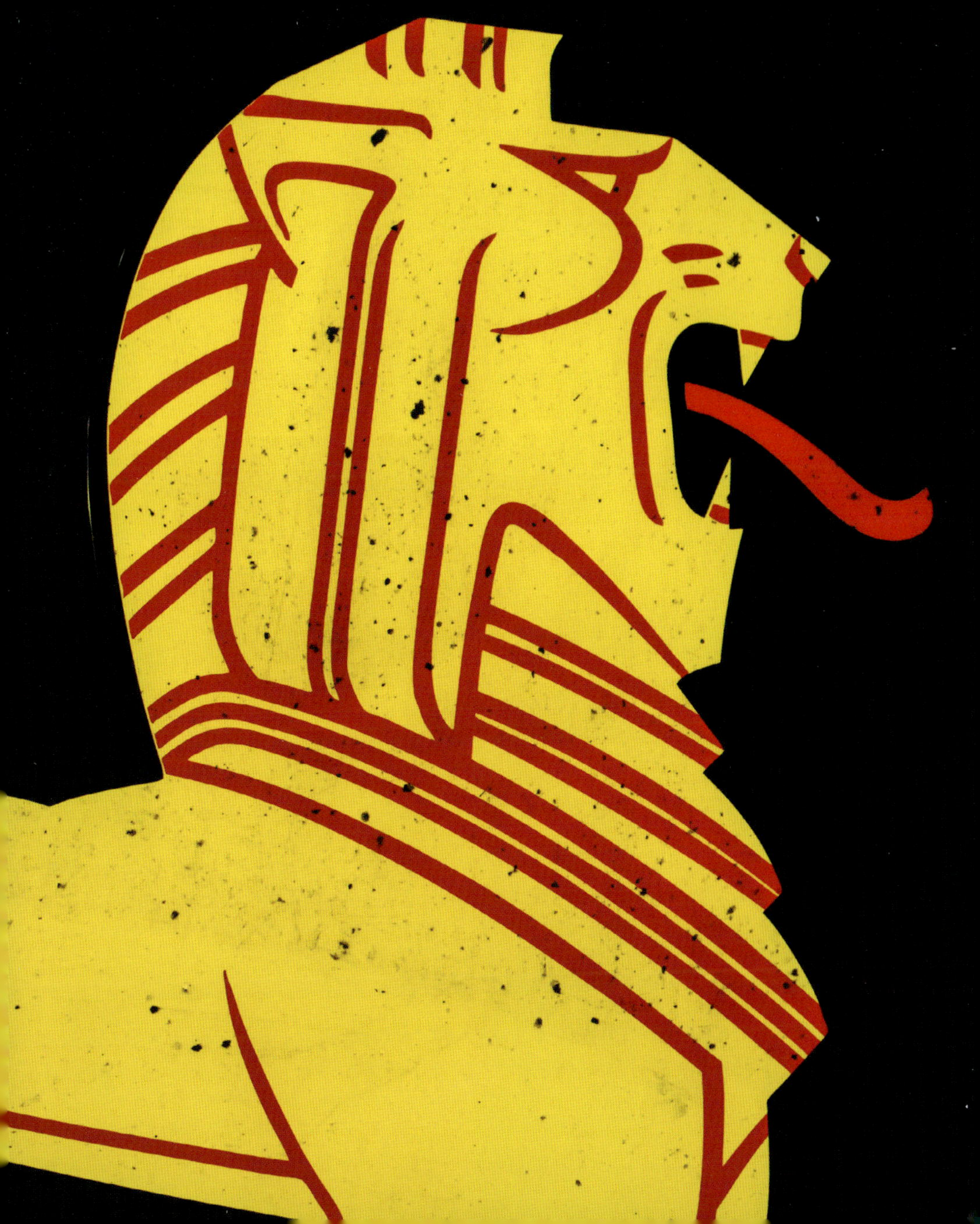

2

» CAMERA PREPARATION

› Attaching the strap

The G16 is supplied with a cloth neck strap and it's highly recommended that you attach it. Although the G16 isn't particularly large or heavy, having the camera hanging from your neck is far less tiring than holding it in your hand.

To attach the strap to your G16, pull one end out of the attached buckle and plastic loop and then feed it through either the right or left strap mount on the side of the camera. Feed this end back through the plastic loop and then under the length of strap still in the buckle. For safety, allow at least 2 inches (5cm) of strap to extend beyond the buckle. Repeat on the opposite side of the camera.

› Using the viewfinder

An expected feature of a G-series camera is an optical viewfinder, and the G16 is no exception. However, if you're used to the optical viewfinder of a DLSR, the one built into the G16 may come as a bit of a shock. For one thing, you don't see exactly what the camera "sees." The viewfinder shows approximately 80% of a scene compared to the view captured by the lens, and while the viewfinder zooms as you adjust the focal length of the lens, the two never match at any point on the zoom range.

As a result, relying on the viewfinder to compose a shot means you will include more of a scene in the final image than intended. There are two ways around this. The first is to crop your images afterward, so that the composition matches your original intentions. This can be achieved either in postproduction or using the G16's cropping tool.

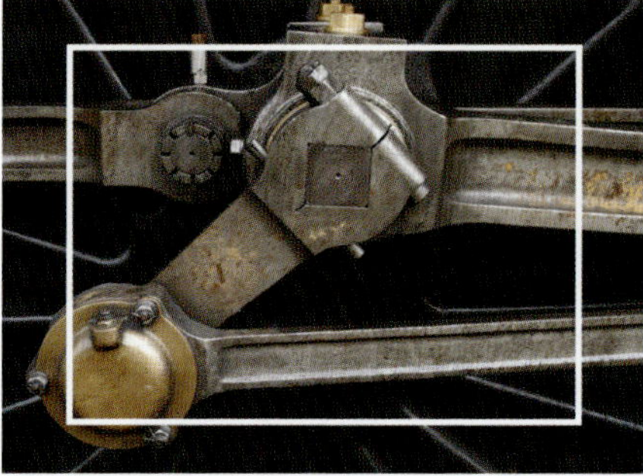

VIEWFINDER ⌃
When looking through the G16's viewfinder, the area outside the white rectangle wouldn't be visible, but it would be recorded when the shot was taken.

> **Tip**
>
> *If you intend to crop your images after exposure, shoot using the maximum resolution possible.*

The second method is to compose your shot using the viewfinder, and without moving position, increase the focal length of the lens using the zoom lever. This takes time to master, but with practice it is possible to achieve reasonable accuracy.

Another problem with the viewfinder is that no shooting information is shown, so you will not be able to see the exposure settings or the point of focus without looking at the LCD, which isn't convenient when you're just about to take a shot.

Given these limitations, you'd be forgiven for thinking that the viewfinder isn't worth using, but it's worth persevering with for three reasons. The first is that the LCD screen can be switched off, which conserves battery power. The second is that it's easier to keep a camera steady when it is pressed to your face than when

it is held at arm's length (a stance that is necessary when composing your shots using the LCD screen). Finally, in bright conditions it's often easier to see through the viewfinder than it is to see a clear image on the rear LCD screen.

If you plan to use the viewfinder you can adjust the diopter to compensate for any defects in your eyesight. The adjustment range is -3 to +1 m^{-1}. To adjust the diopter, look through the viewfinder and move the adjustment wheel to the left of the eyepiece up or down until the image appears crisp.

> **Notes:**
> Although autofocus (AF) is still available when using the viewfinder, you won't see what is in or out of focus through the viewfinder. Face detection focusing is not available either.
>
> The viewfinder shape matches the G16's standard 4:3 aspect ratio, so if you shoot using any other aspect ratio you will not see an accurate representation of the final image.

ADJUSTING THE DIOPTER ⌄

Adjusting the diopter of the viewfinder will not affect the autofocus.

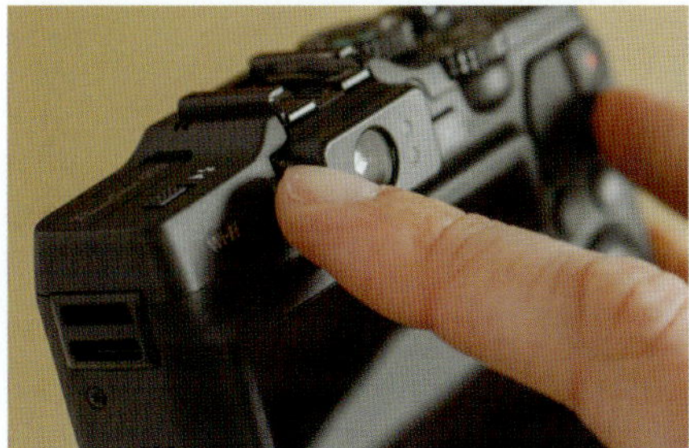

» POWERING YOUR G16

› The battery

The G16 uses a Canon's proprietary NB-10L lithium-ion battery (the same battery used in the G15). Canon's li-ion batteries are small and lightweight, yet they have a large power capacity for their size. The usable overall life of a battery is measured in charge cycles and the NB-10L battery is designed for approximately 300 charge cycles. A single charge cycle is when 100% of the battery's power is used and then recharged, but this doesn't mean that you need to deplete a battery entirely before you recharge it: using 20% of the battery's charge, recharging, and repeating this five times completes one charge cycle. Indeed, recharging the battery in this way, before it is depleted completely, is actually better for the "health" of a battery.

To make the most of the battery's power, it is a good idea to keep your use of the LCD screen to a minimum. Using the optical viewfinder is one way of doing this, while another option is not to spend time reviewing and editing your images as you shoot (a habit known as "chimping").

Cold and heat can also reduce the efficiency of a battery, so if you plan to be out in extreme cold or heat, it's a good idea to carry a fully charged spare battery with you. At normal temperatures, a battery should last for approximately 300 shots if you are using the LCD to frame your shots, or 770 shots if you are shooting using the viewfinder only.

› Battery charging

The battery must be charged fully before you first use it in your G16. To charge the battery, first remove the terminal cover. Slot the battery into the CB-2LC or CB-2LCE charger by aligning the ▲ symbol on the battery and charger and then pushing the battery in and down.

Connect the CB-2LCE battery charger to the supplied AC power cord and insert the plug into a wall socket or plug the CB-2C charger directly into a wall socket after flipping out the power terminals.

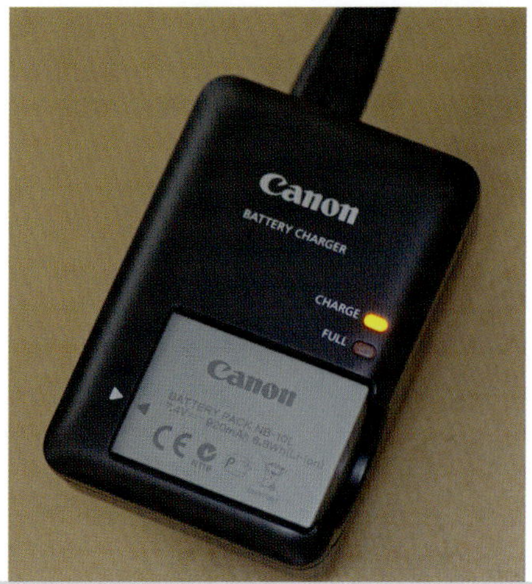

While charging, the Charge lamp glows orange, and when charging is complete the Full lamp glows green. The normal time taken to charge a fully depleted battery is approximately 110 minutes. Once the battery is fully charged unplug the charger from the wall socket and remove the battery by sliding it in and up from the charger.

> **Notes:**
> When you remove the battery from your G16, replace the terminal cover and keep it in a cool, dry place.
>
> The battery charger can be used anywhere in the world that uses a 100–240v AC 50/60hz power supply (although you may need to use a plug adapter if you travel abroad).

Battery charge indicator

▐▨▨▨	Battery sufficiently charged
▐▨▨	Battery slightly depleted
▐▨	Battery nearly depleted (flashes red)
Change the battery pack	Battery depleted fully

› Inserting and removing the battery

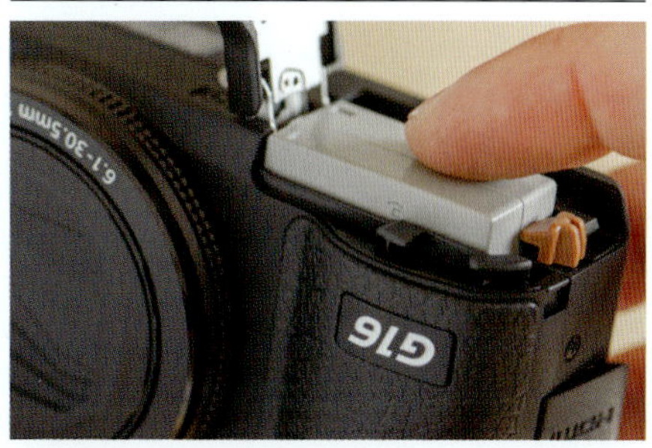

INSERTING THE BATTERY ≪
Push the battery into the compartment with the side of the battery pressing against the battery lock lever as you do so.

Turn your G16 upside down. Slide the battery cover door on the camera base across to release and open it—the door is spring-loaded and will pop open automatically. With the metal contact terminals of the battery facing down and toward the back of the G16, push the battery into the compartment with the side of the battery pressing against the battery lock lever as you do so. Once the battery has clicked into place close the battery cover. To remove the battery, push the lock lever away from the battery and gently pull it out. The battery charge indicator is shown at the top left of the LCD.

Although the G16's battery is remarkably long lasting, there are times when a continuous power supply is preferable. This could be when you're using your G16 to display a slideshow on a TV, for example, or when printing directly from the camera using the PictBridge facility. Canon produces the optional ACK-DC80 AC adapter kit for just these occasions, which will ensure that your camera doesn't come to a premature halt due to lack of power.

To fit the adapter, turn the G16 off and remove the battery (if fitted), leaving the battery cover open. Plug the adapter's power cord into the coupler, and then slide the coupler into the camera as you would with a standard battery. The coupler should click into place. Close the battery cover, slotting the power cable into the DC coupler terminal cover.

Plug the power cord into the AC adapter and then connect to a convenient wall socket. Turn the camera on and use as normal. Turn the camera off and reverse the process above to remove the adapter.

> **Note:**
> The G16 has a built-in backup battery that retains the time and date settings for up to three weeks when the NB-10L is removed. The backup battery is recharged every time a charged NB-10L is inserted into the G16 or when the camera is connected to an AC adapter. This charging process takes about four hours and will continue even if the G16 is turned off. When the backup battery is depleted the Date/Time menu screen will be displayed on startup.

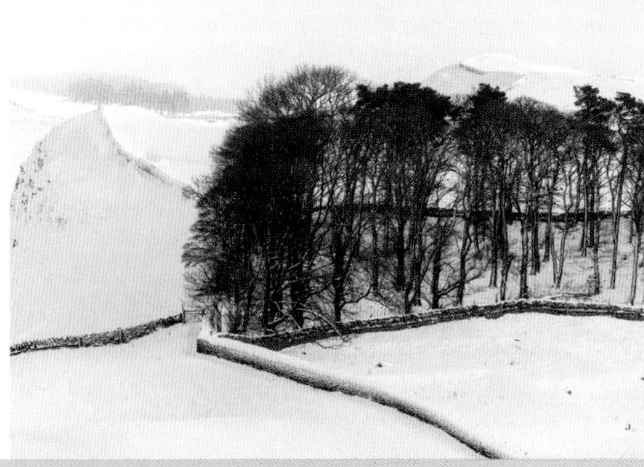

COLD «
Near-freezing conditions will deplete your battery more quickly. Carrying a fully charged spare is a good idea if you think you'll be outside for some time.

» BASIC CAMERA FUNCTIONS

Controlling your G16 means learning the functions of the buttons and dials on the body of the camera, as well as familiarizing yourself with the camera's comprehensive menu system.

To navigate around the menu system you use the Control dial, rear control buttons, and **FUNC./SET** button on the back of the camera. These will be represented by the following symbols in this book: Control dial / ⬤; the individual rear control buttons Up ▲ / Down ▼ / Left ◄ / Right ► (or ✛ if you have the choice of which button to use); and **FUNC./SET** / (FUNC. SET).

On the front of the camera, just below the zoom lever, is the Front dial, which will be shown in the book as ⬤. All the other buttons and controls will be referred to by their name. When a function in this book is shown in bold type, it is referring to an option on a menu.

Pressing ▼ / **DISP.** in shooting mode will cycle through a series of screens displaying different amounts of shooting information. How much information you need will depend on your shooting style. Pressing ▼ / **DISP.** in playback mode also cycles through a series of screens, which show different levels of information about the currently displayed image.

› Switching the camera on

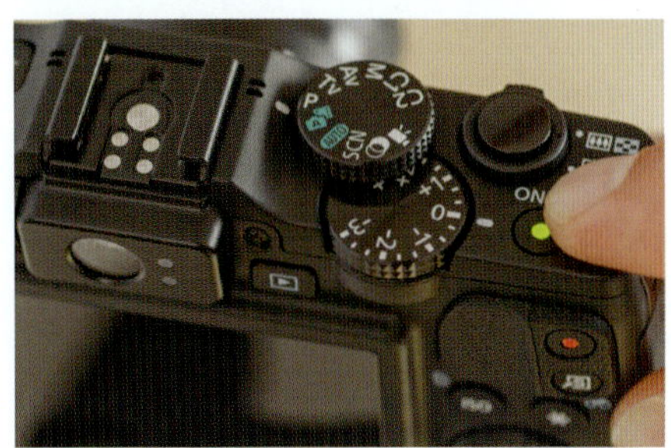

The power switch is found behind the shutter-release button. Switched on, the power light will turn green, the lens will extend, and the G16 will be ready for shooting. Press the button again to turn off the G16. If you just want to view images, pressing ▶ will turn the G16 on without extending the lens. Pressing ▶ again will turn the camera back off once more.

> ### *Tip*
>
> *By default, the G16 will automatically enter power save mode after a set period of time. Altering the settings on the 📱 / **Power Saving** menu screen allows you choose how quickly your G16 powers down and how long it takes the screen to turn off.*

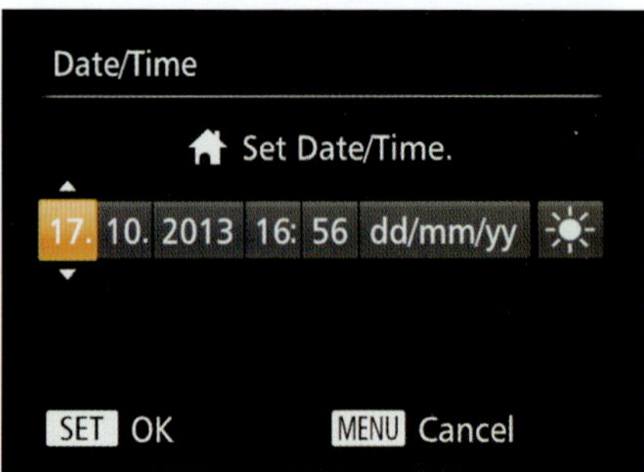

The first time you switch on your G16 you will be prompted to enter both the current time and date. Pressing **MENU** allows you to skip this and start shooting immediately, but until you set the time and date you will be prompted every time the camera is switched off and on again.

It's actually quite important to set the correct date and time. Every time an image is captured, the date and time is added to its metadata (metadata is information embedded into an image file that can be read by most imaging software). The date and time information can then be used to display or filter images when you review them in-camera, and can also be used to sort or search for particular photos when they are stored on your computer.

Setting the time and date

1) Turn on the G16.

2) Press ◀ / ▶ to highlight one of the time/date options; **Date**, **Time**, **Date format**, or **Daylight saving preference**. With the required option highlighted press ▲ / ▼ or turn ⬤ to make a change.

3) Once you've altered all the settings press ⬤ to save your changes and close the time and date screen. To exit the Date/Time screen without saving your changes, press the **MENU** button.

> *Notes:*
> Setting **Daylight Saving** to ☀ will advance the clock one hour.
>
> When the G16 is on, press and hold ⬤ and a digital clock will be displayed on the LCD. You can change the background color of the clock by pressing ◀ / ▶ or turning ⬤. When the camera is held vertically the display will change and the current date will be shown as well as the time.

› Using the menu system

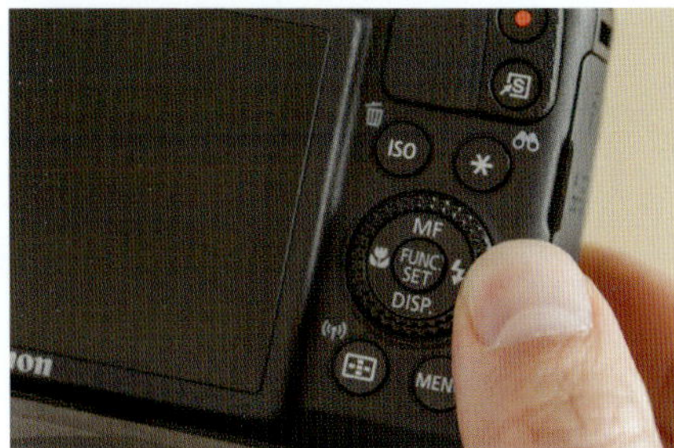

The G16's menu system allows you to control various functions of still and movie image shooting, playback, and other general camera settings. Related functions are collected together under five different menus, each distinguished by a unique icon: 📷 Shooting, 🔧 Set-up, ▶ Playback, 🖨 Print, and ★ My Menu.

The menus that are shown will depend on the camera mode you're using when you press **MENU**. The Shooting 📷 and My Menu ★ options only appear when you are in Shooting mode, for example, while Playback ▶ and Print 🖨 only appear when you're in Playback mode.

The options that appear on the menus are also mode dependant: any option that is not available will be ghosted out and will be skipped over as you move up and down the menu.

Altering menu settings

1) Press the **MENU** button.

2) Move the zoom lever left or right to highlight the icon of the required menu. Press ▲ / ▼ or turn 🔘 to move the highlight bar up and down the menu.

3) If the highlighted option has only two options shown (such as **ON** or **OFF**) use ◀ / ▶ to toggle between them. The option that is highlighted in dark orange is the one currently selected.

4) Some settings have more than two options. The currently selected option will be shown against a dark orange background: use ◀ / ▶ to skip between the different options.

5) If the option description is followed by "..." this means that there is a submenu with multiple choices. Press 🔘 to view the submenu. Press ◀ / ▶ or turn 🔘 to highlight the required option on the submenu. Where indicated press 🔘 to select an option. Press **MENU** to return to the main shooting menu screen.

6) Press **MENU** to return to your original camera mode or lightly press down on the shutter-release button to go directly to Shooting mode.

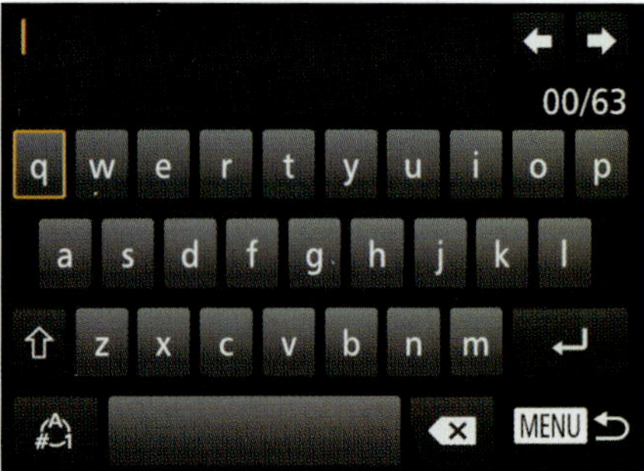

There are a number of options on the G16 that require you to enter text (such as **Wi-Fi Settings**) and this is done using the G16's keyboard screen. Unfortunately, the G16's LCD isn't touch-sensitive, even though it's tempting to start tapping away at the screen.

The keyboard screen uses a standard QWERTY layout, although you can switch between this and two numbers/symbols keyboard screens as well. The number of characters you have entered and the number it is possible to enter are both shown at the top right corner of the LCD below ← →.

Using the keyboard screen

1) Use ✛ or turn ⬤ to highlight the required character or symbol. Press (FUNC SET) to enter that character/symbol into the text entry box at the top of the screen.

2) If you want to move the cursor backward and forward in the text entry box, highlight ← or → and press (FUNC SET) to move the cursor left or right respectively.

3) To enter a line break (carriage return) highlight ↵ and press (FUNC SET).

4) To switch between upper and lower case letters highlight ⇧ and press (FUNC SET).

5) To switch between the three different keyboards highlight ⌨ and press (FUNC SET) repeatedly until the required keyboard is displayed.

6) To delete a character in the text entry box either highlight ⌫ and press (FUNC SET), or press 🗑 (keep it held down to delete five characters at a time).

7) Press **MENU** to finish.

› The shutter-release button

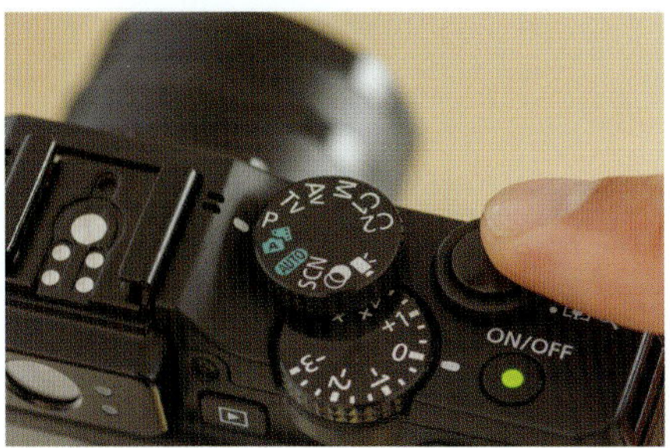

The G16's shutter-release button has two separate stages as you press down on it. Pressing lightly halfway down on the button activates the autofocus and metering systems, preparing the camera to expose a still image. If you're viewing previously shot images in Playback mode this is cancelled automatically and the LCD (if switched on) will display a live image of the scene in front of you.

Once the focus and exposure are established, pressing the shutter-release button down fully will take the shot. When Single Shot advance is selected the G16 will only shoot one image—to shoot another image you have to take your finger off the shutter-release button and repeat the process.

In Continuous shooting mode, the shutter will continue to fire at the maximum frame rate until you take your finger off the shutter-release button, or until the frame buffer or the memory card is full.

› Indicators

The G16 uses three separate colored lamps to show the status of the camera. A green Power lamp is housed in the ON/OFF button, while the other two lamps are found at the right of the viewfinder, green over orange. The functions of these lamps are shown in the table below.

	Color	Status	Operational message
Power lamp	Green	Lit	Power on
Indicator lamp	Green	Lit	Camera ready (with flash deactivated)
		Blinking	Reading, writing or transmitting images from memory card. Proximity warning / Unable to focus (with flash deactivated) / Connecting or transmitting to Wi-Fi
Indicator lamp	Orange	Lit	Camera ready (with flash activated)
		Blinking	Proximity warning / Unable to focus (with flash activated)

» MEMORY CARDS

SD memory cards are made by a wide variety of manufacturers and are ubiquitous. It's often possible to find them in supermarkets and other general (non-photographic) stores. The oldest type is known as SDSC and is limited to a maximum of 2GB. The most recent variant, SDXC, can theoretically be produced with a capacity of 2TB (or 2048GB), but to date no manufacturer has produced an SD memory card with this capacity.

The G16 is also compatible with Eye-Fi memory cards. These memory cards have a Wi-Fi transmitter built into them, which allows you to copy files from the G16 to a Wi-Fi enabled computer without needing a cable or card reader.

Although storage capacity is an important factor when choosing a memory card, it's not the only aspect to consider. SD memory cards also vary in the speed at which they can read and write data: the higher the read/write speed of a card, the faster files can be written to and from it.

The official way to show the speed of an SD memory card is with a Class Rating: the higher the Class Rating, the faster the read/write time. The Class Rating of a memory card is particularly important if you plan to shoot movies (Canon recommends a memory card with a Class Rating of 6 or higher when shooting movies).

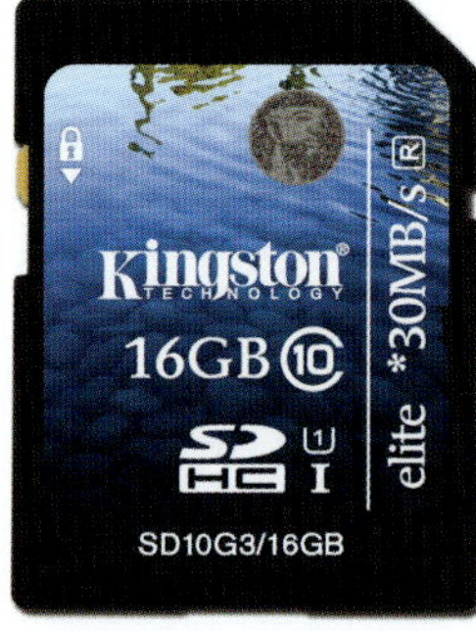

SPEED »
The faster your memory card, the less time you'll spend waiting for images to download to your computer.

© Kingston Technology

Speed	Read/write speed (Mb/s)	Class rating
13×	2.0	2
26×	4.0	4
40×	6.0	6
66×	10.0	10

Note:
The speed of an SD memory card is also often shown as a figure followed by an "x." This indicates the speed of a card in comparison to the read/write time of a standard CD-ROM drive. So a 66x (Class 10) memory card is able to read and write data 66 times faster than a standard CD-ROM.

Inserting a memory card

1) Ensure that the G16 is switched off and then open the battery cover door.

2) If your memory card has a write-protect tab, slide the tab to the unlocked position. If the card is locked, **Memory card locked** will be displayed on the LCD and you will not be able to shoot images. However, locking the card deliberately will ensure that images stored there will not be erased accidentally. If you use several memory cards over the course of a day, make it part of your shooting routine to lock each memory card as you fill it until you've had a chance to copy the files to your computer.

3) With the memory card contacts facing down and to the rear of the G16, push the card into the slot until it locks with a click.

4) To remove the memory card, push it down slightly until you hear a click. The card should now come free. Pull it out gently and close the battery cover door.

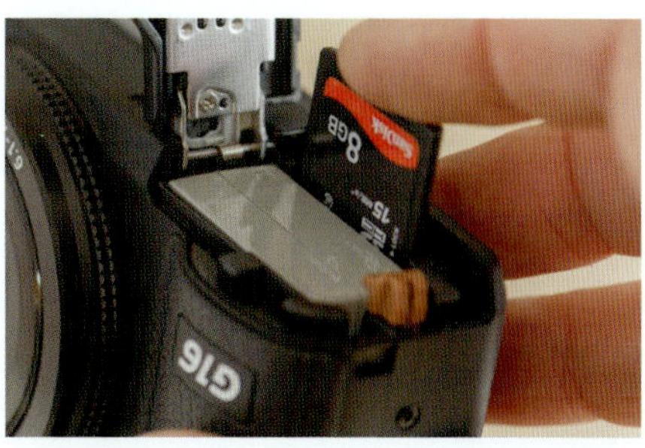

Notes:
When the top lamp next to the viewfinder is flashing green, the G16 is reading, writing, or erasing image data on the memory card. Do not remove the card or the battery when the lamp is flashing as this may corrupt the memory card data or even potentially damage the camera.

If there is no memory card in the camera, **No memory card** will be shown on the LCD. You will still be able to shoot pictures, but they will not be saved. **Cannot record!** will be displayed on the LCD screen to warn you of this.

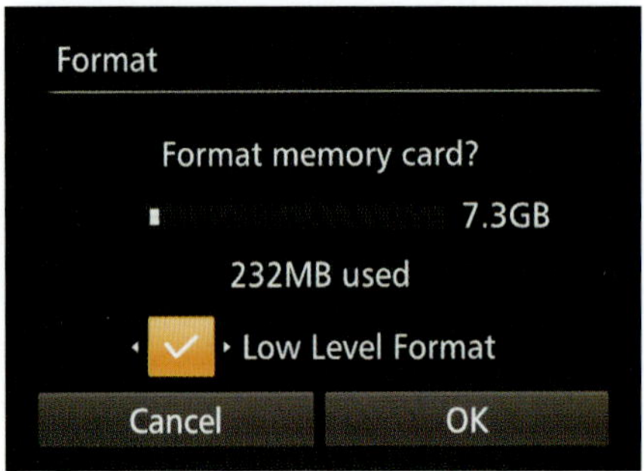

When you buy a memory card, you will generally find that it's been pre-formatted for immediate use. However, it's good policy to format a new card just in case. It's also recommended that you format a memory card if it's been used in another camera previously—as long as you've copied any images on the memory card to a safe place first!

Formatting a memory card

1) Press **MENU** and select **Format** from the ❗T menu.

2) You will now be asked **Format memory card?** Select **OK** to continue or **Cancel** to return to the ❗T menu without formatting the card.

3) On the **All data on the memory card will be erased** screen select **OK** to begin formatting the memory card or **Cancel** to go back to step 2.

4) Once formatting has finished, press ⓕ to return to the main menu.

> **Note:**
> When a memory card is formatted normally, only the file allocation table of the card is cleared. The file allocation table is a record of what files are stored on the memory card, a bit like the index in a book. With the file allocation table cleared your G16 ignores any files already on the memory card and overwrites them with new files, building up a new file allocation table in the process.
>
> However, because the old files are still on the card, it's possible to recover them after a normal format using commercially available data-recovery software. If you want to erase files permanently, highlight **Low Level Format** and press ▶. When ✓ is shown in the **Low Level Format** box, the time taken to format the memory card will increase and it will be impossible to recover any files on the card. You would typically only use a low level format when the record/read speed of the card drops, particularly when shooting movies.

» THE LENS

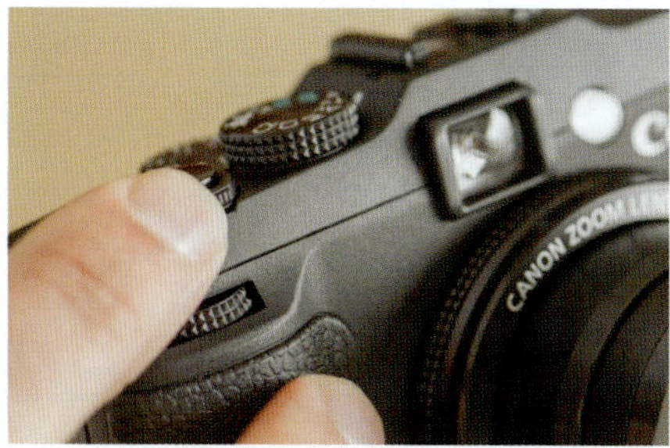

The lens fitted to the G16 is a zoom lens, which can be adjusted across a range of focal lengths from 6.1–30.5mm. At 6.1mm (W or ▲▲▲) the G16's lens is at its "widest," which means the lens is capturing the widest angle of view it can. The angle of view captured is roughly equivalent to a 28mm lens on a full-frame digital camera. At 30.5mm (T or ▲), the lens is at its longest and is equivalent to a 140mm lens on a full-frame camera.

As the lens is zoomed from ▲▲▲ to ▲, the angle of view decreases. This means the image is magnified, making your subject appear closer to the camera and larger in the frame.

Using the zoom lens

1) Turn on your G16 and select the Shooting mode you want to use.

2) When you first switch on your G16, the lens extends from the camera body to the 6.1mm / ▲▲▲ position. To increase the focal length of the lens (and zoom into the scene) push the zoom lever below the shutter-release button to the right. The lens barrel extends until it reaches the maximum optical zoom of 30.5mm / ▲. As you alter the focal length of the lens, the zoom bar on the LCD alters to show you where in the zoom range the lens is set. To zoom back out, push the zoom lever to the left.

3) When you are happy with the composition, press the shutter-release button down halfway to focus, and then down all the way to take the shot.

> **Note:**
> The G16 has the facility to jump to a series of set focal lengths (full-frame equivalent) when ⚙ is assigned to **ZOOM** (see page 134). The set focal lengths are 28mm, 35mm, 50mm, 85mm, 100mm, and 140mm; each click of the **ZOOM** jumps to the next focal length in the sequence.

› Digital Zoom

The lens' focal length range, from 🔍 to 🔍, is a 5x optical zoom. When shooting high-resolution JPEG images the G16 also offers a Digital Zoom function that allows you to extend the lens' reach. This increases the apparent focal length of the lens to 560mm at maximum zoom (full-frame equivalent), but it's important to appreciate that you don't get something for nothing.

Digital Zoom is achieved by cropping the image captured by the optical zoom and then resizing the cropped area back up to full resolution. The resizing is achieved by the interpolation of pixels. Interpolation is a method of filling in gaps in data by inserting values that logically bridge that gap. The greater the Digital Zoom factor you use, the more the image data is interpolated, which means there will be fewer "true" pixels in the image, resulting in a drop in image quality.

Note:
When the optical zoom is used, the zoom bar is white. When the zoom bar turns yellow, the digital zoom is activated, but the resulting image will not deteriorate noticeably. When the zoom bar turns blue, the image will be grainy and lower in quality.

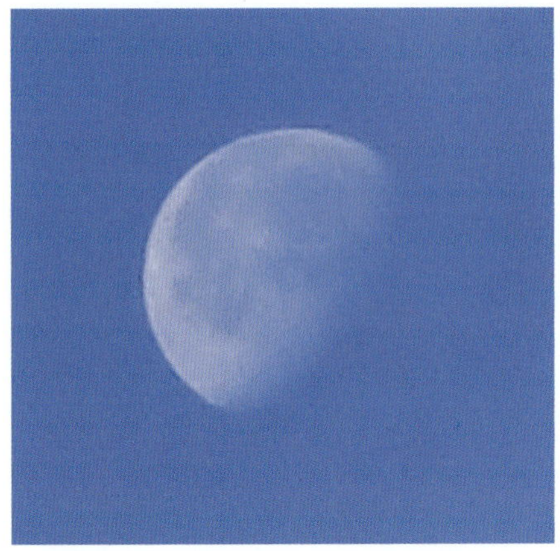

DETAIL ⌃
An image shot using maximum digital zoom will suffer a reduction in fine detail.

Turning on Digital Zoom

1) Press the **MENU** button and highlight **Digital Zoom** on the 📷 menu.

2) Set Digital Zoom to **Standard** and press **MENU** or lightly down on the shutter-release button to return to shooting mode.

3) Move the zoom lever to the right to zoom in. The zoom factor will be displayed on the LCD. When you reach the end of the optical zoom range the digital zoom will activate automatically and the scene on the LCD will continue to enlarge.

4) To turn Digital Zoom off set **Digital Zoom** to **Off**.

› Digital Tele-Converter

The Digital Tele-Converter is a subtle variation of the Digital Zoom, set using the same menu entry. A tele-converter is an optical accessory fitted between a camera and a lens that increases the focal length of the lens by a set factor, such as 2.0x (which would double the focal length).

However, the Digital Tele-Converter in the G16 isn't an optical solution: it creates a similar effect by "zooming" in on an area of a scene digitally and then resizing the resulting image. The main advantage with this is that the G16's lens has greater reach at every optical focal length, but unlike zooming you hold onto the maximum f/1.8 aperture for longer. This means that you can use a higher shutter speed, reducing the risk of camera shake. Unfortunately, this is compromised by the increased risk of the image quality deteriorating due to interpolation.

The Digital Tele-Converter has two settings: 1.5x and 2.0x. These settings will increase the focal length range of the lens to a full-frame equivalent of 42–210mm and 56–280mm respectively.

Using the Digital Tele-Converter
1) Press **MENU** and set **Digital Zoom** to **1.5x** or **2.0x**. Press **MENU** or lightly press down on the shutter-release button to return to Shooting mode.

2) The scene on the LCD will now be enlarged and the zoom factor displayed on the LCD.

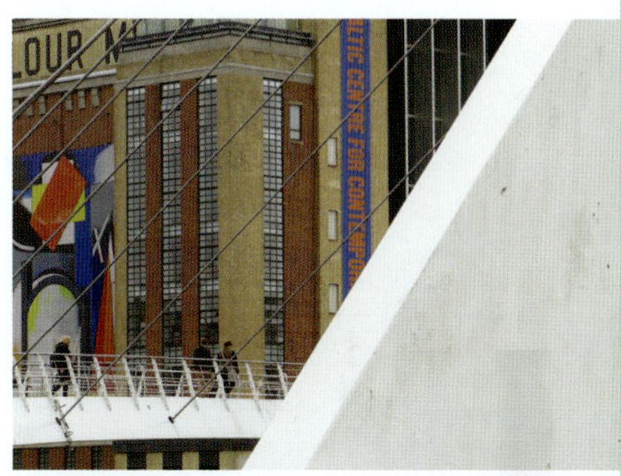

EXCLUDED
The Digital Zoom and Digital Tele-Converter allow you to exclude unwanted elements from an image—in this instance, a bland overcast sky.

Notes:
Digital Tele-Converter cannot be used in conjunction with **Digital Zoom** or with **AF-point zoom.**

You can achieve the same effect as using the Digital Tele-Converter by cropping and resizing an image in postproduction.

The G16's ▲▲▲ setting increases the angle of view to its maximum. This is particularly useful in tight places when you can't step back any further, but need to fit your subject entirely within the frame.

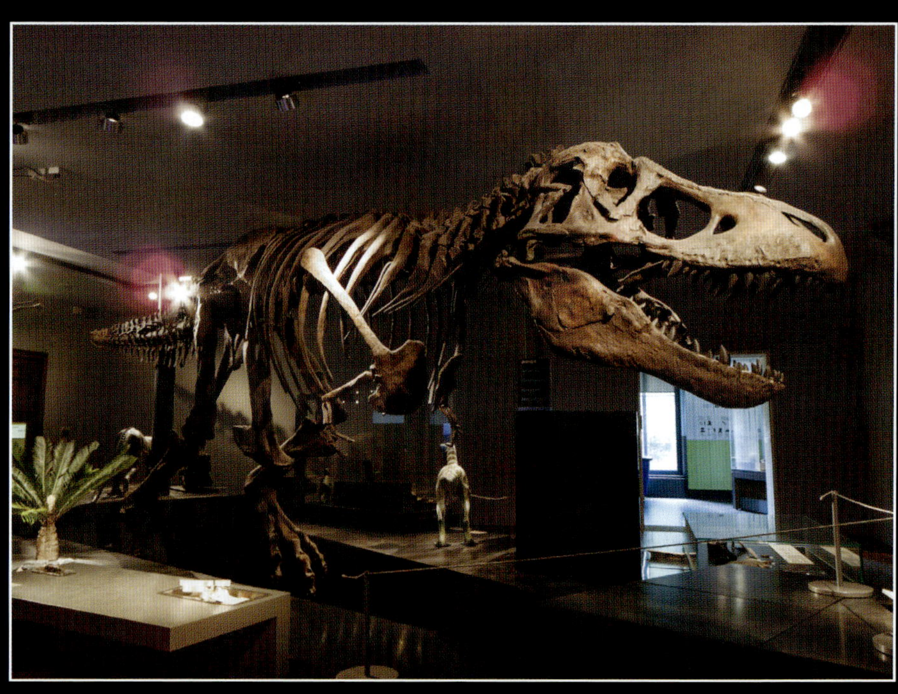

» ZOOMED

Using maximum zoom (image) reduces the angle of view, restricting the amount of a scene that's captured. It also has the visual effect of appearing to bring elements in the image closer together spatially.

Settings
> Focal length: 30.5mm (image)
> Exposure: 1/200 sec. at f/4.5
> ISO: 200

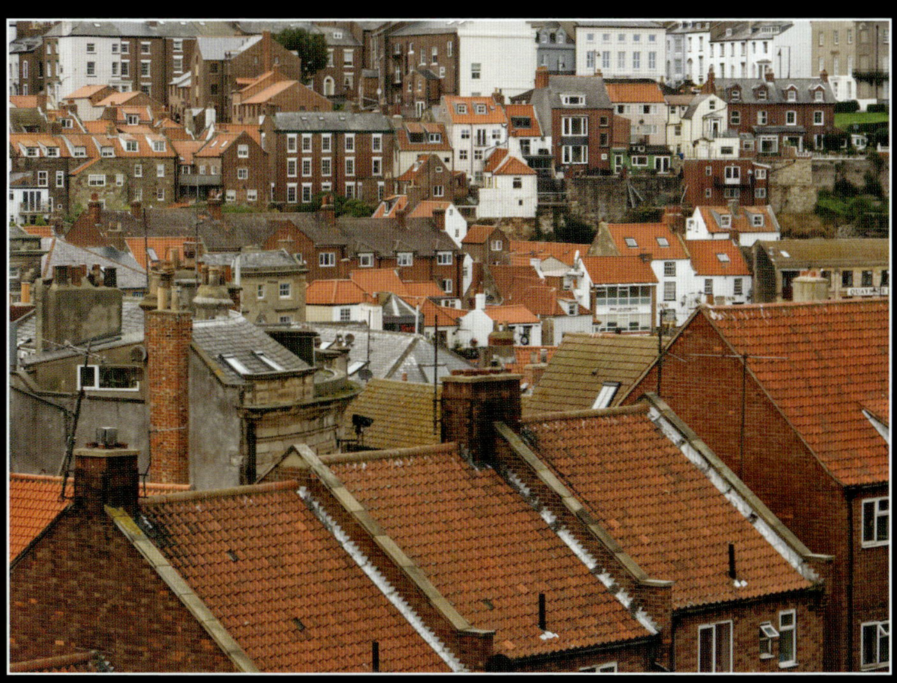

Once you've shot an image it will be displayed automatically on the LCD. During this initial review you can only view the image—it's not until you press ▶ that you have more freedom to view and zoom into the image or view previously shot images on the memory card.

To view other images press ◀ / ▶ (holding down either button to skip through your images more quickly). To speed things up turn ● to scroll through a stream of thumbnails of your images. Using this viewing method you can also press ▲ / ▼ to browse your images sorted by shooting date. Press (FUNC/SET) to view the image you're looking for full screen once you've found it.

Pressing ▼ / **DISP.** jumps between four different ways of viewing an image. The first view is a simple display showing the image only. The second view shows a limited amount of shooting information overlaid on the image. The third view displays more detailed information, including a luminance histogram of the image. The final screen adds an RGB histogram and any GPS information that is appended to the image.

› Magnify images

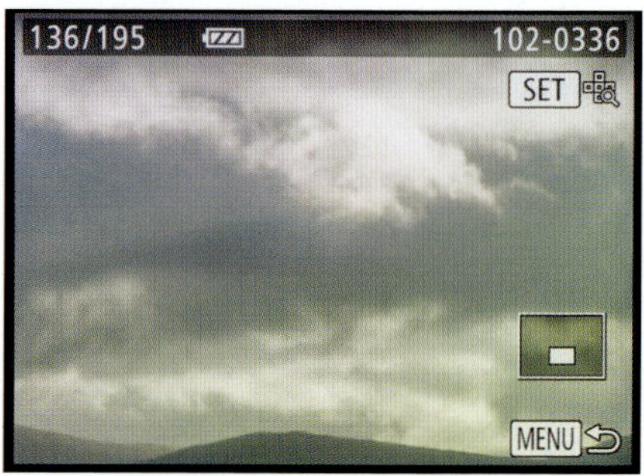

Still images can be magnified up to 10x to check aspects such as critical focus and composition.

Magnifying an image

1) In playback mode push the zoom lever to the right to increase the magnification of your image. The longer you hold the zoom lever, the greater the magnification. Push the zoom lever to the left to decrease magnification. Use ✤ to move around the magnified display. Your position and the current proportion of the image displayed are shown by a white box within a frame at the bottom right corner of the LCD.

2) If **SET** 🔍 is displayed on the LCD you can zoom into the AF frame position used at the moment of capture by pressing (FUNC/SET).

This is useful if you want to check that the focus at this point was accurate. Press (FUNC SET) to switch between other AF frames used at image capture.

3) Press **MENU** to restore your image to normal magnification.

> **Notes:**
> You can alter the length of time an image is displayed for after shooting by changing the **Review** function on the ◻ Shooting menu.
>
> In automatic review you can delete your image immediately by pressing the ISO / 🗑 button, selecting **Erase** and pressing (FUNC SET).

› Image index

You can display up to 100 image thumbnails on screen at any one time, enabling you to quickly find and select individual images on the memory card.

1) In playback mode, push the zoom lever once to the left to display four image thumbnails on screen. Keep pushing it to the left to display nine, 36, and then 100

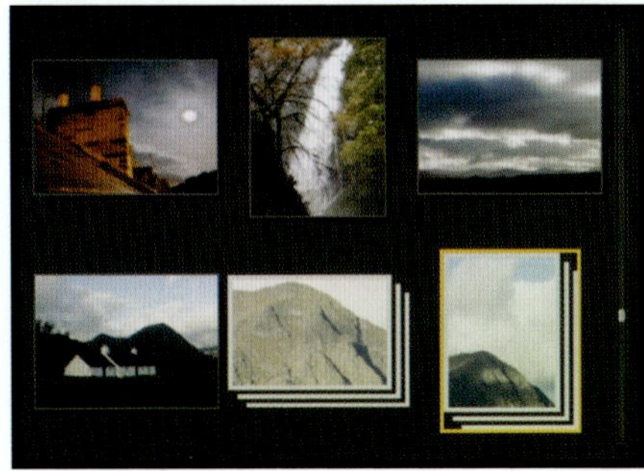

image thumbnails. An orange box will frame the currently selected image.

2) Use ✛ or ⬤ to highlight the required image. Press (FUNC SET) to view the currently selected image at normal magnification or push the zoom lever to the right to display fewer image thumbnails until you return to a single image.

> **Tips**
>
> *When still images are magnified you can still switch between them by turning ⬤.*
>
> *Turning your camera on its side will rotate the image to match the orientation of the camera (unless you are looking at the focus check screen).*

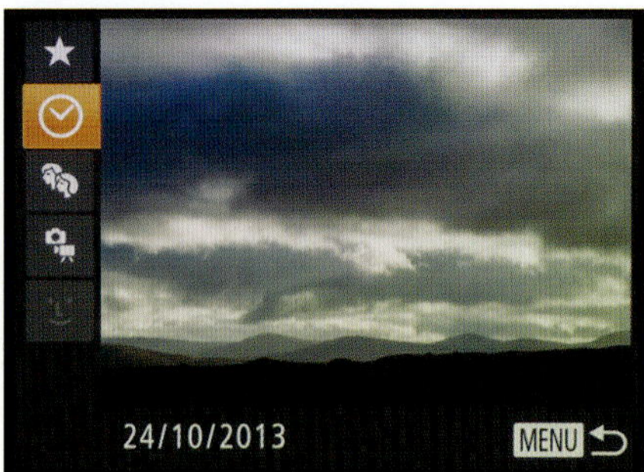

The photographs on a memory card can be filtered so that only specific images are shown. The filtering system is particularly useful when selecting a range of images to delete or protect.

> **Note:**
> If no images match a particular filtering condition, that filter will not be displayed.

Choose a target filter

1) In Playback mode press ✳/👓.

2) Press ▲ / ▼ to highlight either ★, ⊘, 👥, or 🎥 (see next page for 😊). Press ◀ / ▶ to select how images are filtered based on the filter target you've selected. As an example, if you've highlighted ⊘, pressing ◀ / ▶ highlights the different dates that images were created. Selecting one of those dates will show only images shot on that date.

3) Press (FUNC SET) to display the first image in the filtered selection. To display other images that match the filter conditions press ◀ / ▶ or turn ⚙. The filtered images will be displayed surrounded by a yellow frame, with the filter method shown at the top right corner.

4) Press ✳ / 👓 and then (FUNC SET) to revert to standard Playback mode display.

Filtering by registered person

1) In Playback mode press ✳ / 👓.

2) Use ▲ / ▼ to highlight 😊 and then press (FUNC. SET).

3) Press ✛ to highlight the required registered person and then press (FUNC. SET) once more.

4) Press (FUNC. SET) to display the first image in the filtered selection. To display other images that include the registered person press ◀ / ▶ or turn ●. The filtered images will be displayed surrounded by a yellow frame, with 😊 shown at the top right corner.

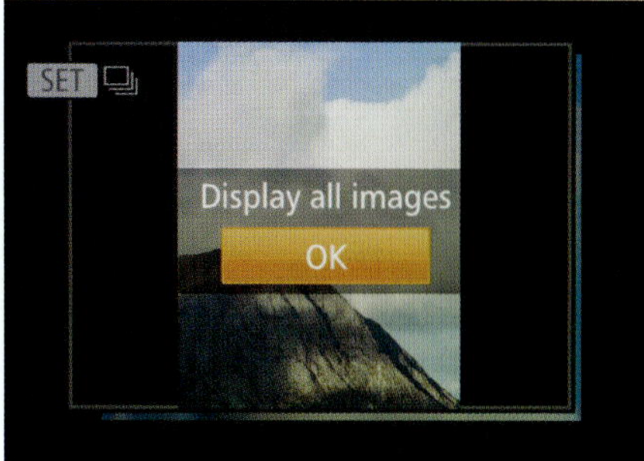

Grouped images

If you've used continuous shooting in **P**, **Tv**, **Av**, or **M** mode to shoot a sequence of images or ✨, they will normally be grouped together, with only the first image of the sequence displayed.

A group of images can be distinguished from a single image by SET 🗇 being displayed at the top left corner of the LCD. To display the individual images in a group, press (FUNC. SET) and then press ◀ / ▶ or turn ● to skip through the images.

Press ✳ / 👓 and then (FUNC. SET) to return to standard Playback mode.

Filter	Description
★ Favorites	Only displays images tagged as favorites.
⊘ Shot date	Only displays images shot on a specific date.
👥 People	Only displays images with faces that have been detected (but not necessarily registered).
📷🎥 Still image / Movie	Only displays still images or movies.
😊 Name	Only displays images of a registered person.

Getting a sharp image means focusing your G16's lens. You can either use the G16's autofocus (AF) system or focus manually for greater control (**MF**). The G16 also has a macro-focusing mode ✿— for more details about this see chapter 7.

By default, the G16 will use the AF system to focus. Focusing activates when you press the shutter-release button down halfway (unless **Continuous AF** on the ▣ menu is set to **On**). The focus point is shown on the LCD using an AF frame. There are three different AF modes, each with a different AF frame type. Which mode you choose is very much dependant on what your subject is and whether or not it's moving.

› Face AiAF

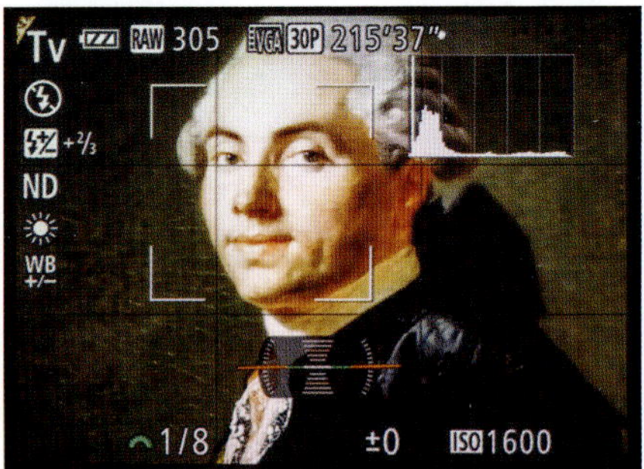

If portrait photography is your main interest, **Face AiAF** is the AF mode for you.

Face AiAF mode is specifically designed to help you achieve AF lock on people's faces quickly and reliably. If automatic white balance (AWB) is set, then the correct white balance for your subject(s) will be determined based on the light falling on their face(s).

Using Face AiAF

1) Press **MENU** and highlight **AF Frame** on the ▣ Shooting menu. Press ◀ / ▶ to set **Face AiAF**. Press **MENU** again or press lightly on the shutter-release button to return to Shooting mode.

2) Your G16 will automatically detect any faces in the scene. A white AF frame will be drawn around the face of the main subject and gray AF frames around any other faces. If your subjects move, the G16 will track the movement to a limited degree.

3) To select a new main subject, aim the camera at their face and press the ▦ button. **Face Select: On** will be displayed on the LCD and ⌐ ¬ will be drawn around your subject's face. Press ▦ to jump between the different faces in the scene. Once all the faces have been selected in turn, **Face Select** will be set to **Off**.

4) Press the shutter-release button down to take the shot. Green AF frames (▢) will be drawn around the faces in the scene that are in focus (up to a maximum of 9).

> **Notes:**
> The G16 will beep to confirm focus when **Mute** is set to **Off** on the ❏ Settings menu.
>
> Faces are not detected when **Servo AF** is set to **On**.

› Tracking AF

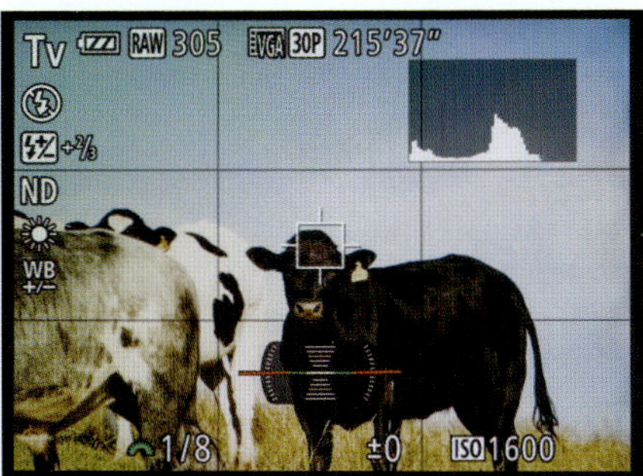

Tracking AF is the AF mode to use if either you or your subject is moving. It continually refines focus once the initial focus has been set, right up to the point when you press the shutter-release button down to take the shot. However, although it's impressive, it's not perfect: if your subject is moving particularly quickly, **Tracking AF** may struggle to keep up.

Using Tracking AF

1) Set **AF Frame** on the ◘ Shooting menu to **Tracking AF**. Press **MENU** or lightly down on the shutter-release button to return to Shooting mode.

2) The ⬚ AF frame will be displayed at the center of the LCD.

3) Aim your G16 so that the ⬚ AF frame covers the subject you want to focus on. Press ▣ to begin **Tracking AF** (and again to cancel **Tracking AF**). The AF frame will now change to ⬚ and the G16 will beep to confirm focus.

4) As long as your subject does not move too quickly or too close to the edge of the LCD, the G16 will continue to track its movement.

5) Press the shutter-release button down halfway. The AF frame will turn into a blue ☐. The G16 will continue to focus and set the exposure until you press the shutter-release button down fully to take the shot.

6) After making an exposure, the G16 will continue to track the subject.

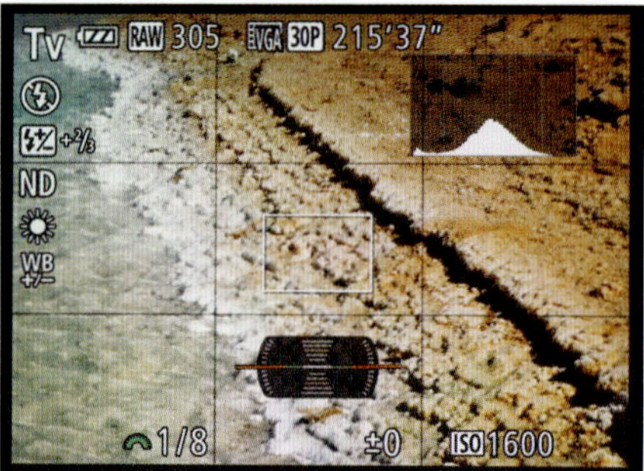

FlexiZone/Center AF allows you to resize and move the AF frame around the LCD screen to select the precise area of the scene that you want to focus on. If spot metering is used (and **Spot AE Point** on the ◘ Shooting menu is set to **AF Point**), the exposure metering will be measured from the position of the AF frame. In certain shooting modes FlexiZone is set to Center and the AF frame cannot be moved from the center of the LCD.

By default, the FlexiZone AF frame is a white rectangle located at the center of the LCD. Pressing halfway down on the shutter-release button focuses the lens. When focus has been achieved the AF frame will turn green. If the G16 can't focus, the AF frame will turn yellow and a yellow ❶ symbol will be displayed on the LCD. If this happens either move the AF frame to another part of the scene and try again, or switch to **MF**.

Setting, moving, and resizing the FlexiZone AF frame

1) Set **AF Frame** on the ◘ Shooting menu to **FlexiZone**. Press **MENU** or lightly down on the shutter-release button to return to Shooting mode.

2) Press ▣. The AF frame will turn orange. Use ✦ to move the AF Frame in small steps around the LCD or ⬤ to move it more coarsely. To quickly reset the AF frame to the center of the LCD press and hold down ▣.

3) Press **MENU** to toggle between a large (default) AF frame and a small AF frame.

4) When the AF frame is in the right position press ▣. Lightly press down on the shutter-release button to focus.

› Manual focus **MF**

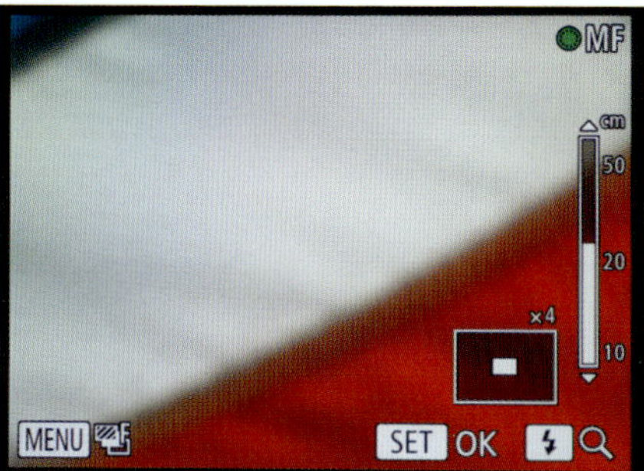

Generally, the G16's AF system is very reliable, but it's not perfect and can trip up occasionally. The G16 uses a contrast detection system to determine focus, so if your subject is flatly lit and has a very even texture you may find that the AF system can't lock on. Shooting in misty conditions can also prove problematic as mist reduces contrast. Fortunately, there's a backup: you. By switching your G16 to manual focus you can decide where the G16's lens focuses.

Setting manual focus

1) In Shooting mode press ▲. The **MF** indicator will be displayed at the top right of the LCD to show that manual focus has been activated.

2) Turn ⬤ or press ▲ / ▼ to begin focusing. Turning ⬤ to the left (or pressing ▼) will bring the focus point closer to the camera; turning ⬤ to the right (or pressing ▲) will move the focus point away. A bar at the right of the LCD shows the distance that the camera is focused at. If peaking is switched on, the area of the scene in focus will be edged with the peaking color (see chapter 4).

3) To increase the magnification of the focus point press ▶. To move the magnified focus point around the LCD press ▦ and then use ✥ to move the focus point in small steps or ⬤ to move it more coarsely. To quickly reset the focus point to the center of the LCD press and hold down ▦. When the focus point is in the right position press ▦ again.

4) Press down on the shutter-release button to take the shot.

5) Press ◀ to return to AF focus.

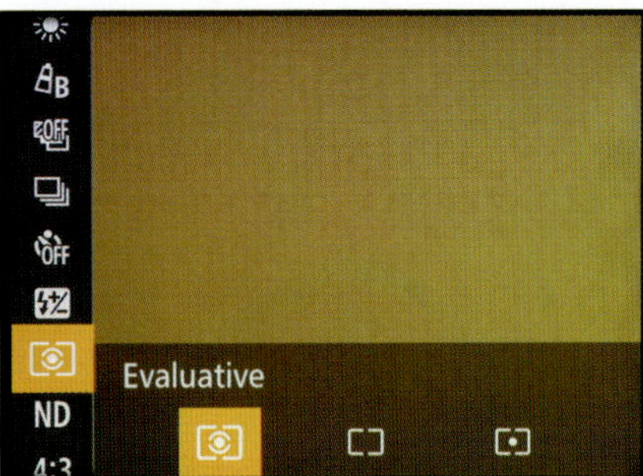

The G16 has three different exposure metering modes. Each has different advantages and disadvantages, so the one you use will depend on the type of scene you're photographing. The metering mode options are set via the FUNC. Menu.

Evaluative

Evaluative metering is the default setting and is generally accurate for most lighting conditions. It works by dividing the scene being measured into a series of zones. Each zone is assessed independently and the final exposure is calculated by analyzing these results in combination with information about the focus point and shooting conditions. Evaluative metering is generally very accurate, particularly when shooting in awkward lighting situations such as backlighting.

Center-weighted average

In this metering mode the exposure is calculated for the entire scene, but biased toward the center of the image. This is useful when your subject is central and the periphery of the image is less important.

Spot

Spot metering measures the exposure from a small area of a scene. When it is activated, metering is confined to the [ ] (Spot AE point) at the center of the LCD. However, you can also link the Spot AE Point to the AF Frame (see page 126). When linked to the AF Frame, the exposure will be calculated from the point of focus.

> **Notes:**
> When the G16 is set to **SCN** or Center-weighted average and Spot metering are not available.
>
> Spot metering can be linked to the AF Point on the menu except when autofocus is set to Face AiAF or Tracking AF.

› Exposure compensation

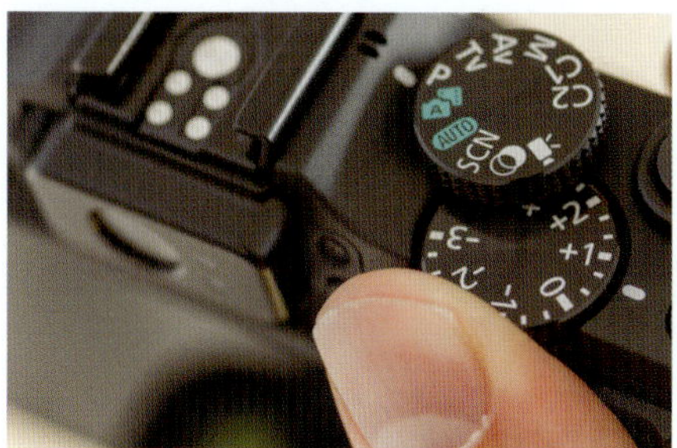

As good as the G16's exposure meter is, there will be occasions where you may need to step in and override its settings: the exposure compensation dial allows you to do just that. The exposure can be adjusted by ±3 stops in $1/3$-stop increments. No exposure compensation has been applied when 0 on the exposure compensation dial is aligned with the white mark to the right of the dial.

Setting exposure compensation

1) Compose your shot using the LCD screen and press the shutter-release button down halfway to activate the exposure meter.

2) Using the histogram overlay is the most objective way of assessing the exposure, so press ▼ / **DISP**. repeatedly until the histogram is displayed.

2) If exposure compensation needs to be applied, turn the compensation dial to a positive amount to increase the exposure or to a minus amount to decrease it. The amount of adjustment will also be shown on the LCD.

3) Press the shutter-release button down fully to take the shot.

4) Review the image, using the playback histogram to check the exposure. If the exposure is still incorrect re-take the shot, altering the compensation amount further.

5) When you're happy with the final image reset the exposure compensation dial to 0.

› AE lock

To lock the exposure, which will allow you to recompose a shot without the exposure changing, press ✱ after pressing the shutter-release button halfway. ✱ will be displayed on the LCD. Once the image has been shot AE lock will be cancelled.

> **Note:**
> In **Av** mode the shutter speed will be adjusted when you apply exposure compensation; in **Tv** mode, the aperture will change.

2 » ISO

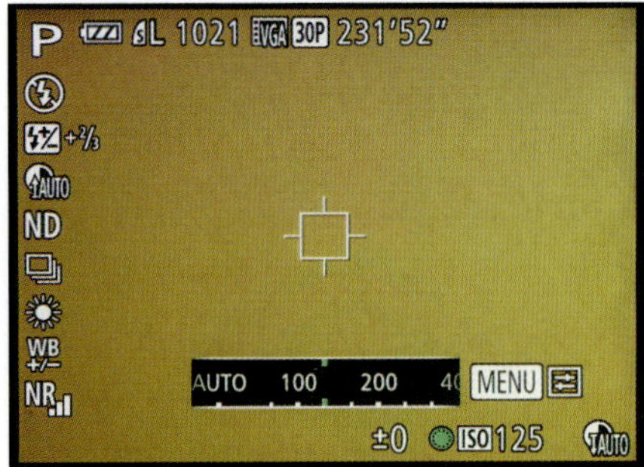

Setting the ISO is another way to control exposure. ISO sets the sensitivity to light of the digital sensor inside the camera: the lower the ISO value, the less sensitive it is; the higher the value, the more sensitive it is. The ISO setting you use will determine the shutter speed and aperture needed to make a correct exposure.

ISO can either be set manually or it can be adjusted automatically (ISO AUTO) according the light levels you're shooting in. The range of ISO values you can set on the G16 varies according to the shooting mode. The full ISO range of 80–12,800 (including ISO AUTO) is only available when the camera is set to **P**, **Tv**, or **Av**. The full ISO range (except ISO AUTO) is available in **M**. In all other modes ISO AUTO is used.

Using a high ISO value will enable you to use faster shutter speeds to avoid camera shake in low light, or a smaller aperture for increased depth of field.

Unfortunately this flexibility comes at a price, and the higher the ISO used, the more "noise" will be visible in the resulting images. Noise is seen as random specks and spots of color that breaks up fine detail. The ISO you choose is therefore often a compromise between camera usability and image quality.

Setting ISO

1) With the camera in Shooting mode press **ISO**.

2) Turn ⬤ until the required ISO value is between the green markers or press **MENU** to alter the ISO Auto Settings.

3) Press (FUNC SET) to save the new ISO setting and return to Shooting mode. The selected ISO will be displayed in the bottom right corner of the LCD (the ISO AUTO ISO value can be viewed by pressing the shutter-release button down halfway).

> **Note:**
> ISO 80 will give you the best image quality. If you're using a tripod and don't need to worry about shutter speeds, this is the optimum choice.

» FUNC. MENU OPTIONS

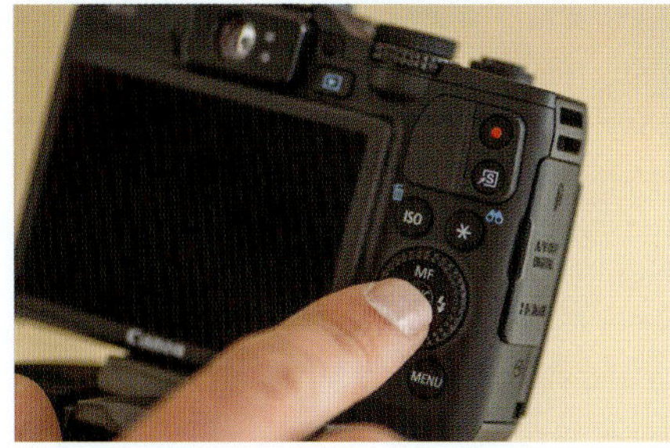

The FUNC. menu lets you quickly customize a range of useful shooting functions. These functions include aspects such as color saturation, how contrast is handled, and the file format used when the image is saved to the memory card.

Which functions are available depends on the shooting mode that the G16 is set to—as a rule, the more automated the shooting mode, the fewer functions will be available. The functions you can alter are shown as icons running down a strip at the left side of the LCD. The various options for the highlighted function are then displayed along the bottom of the LCD.

Setting FUNC. menu options

1) In Shooting mode press (FUNC. SET).

2) Use ▲ / ▼ to move the highlight bar to the required function.

3) Use ◀ / ▶ or turn ● to highlight one of the options for that selected function; an option that displays either a **MENU**, ▗▄▖, or **ISO** icon on the LCD can be adjusted further by pressing the button displayed to view a sub-screen for that option. Press (FUNC. SET) once you've set the required option on the sub-screen.

4) Press (FUNC. SET) to set the highlighted option and return to Shooting mode.

› DR Correction / Shadow Correct

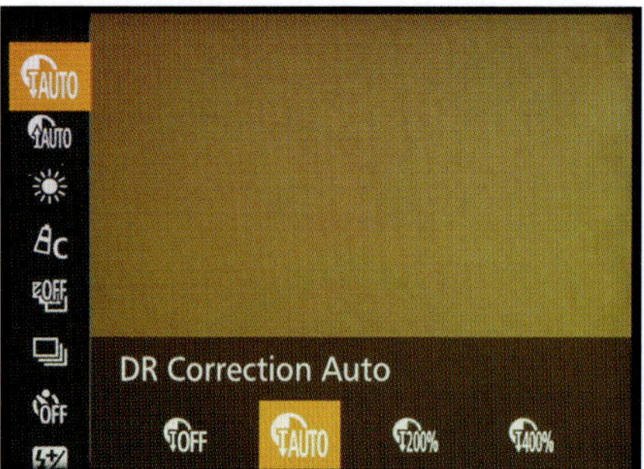

When DR Correction is used, the G16 will attempt to recover highlight detail automatically, toning down the brightest areas of the resulting image.

Shadow Correct lightens shadows, revealing details that would otherwise be hidden. However, neither option can work miracles, so you may find that your images appear grainier than anticipated, especially when Shadow Correct is used.

Contrast is often a problem in photography. If a scene has bright highlights and dark shadows it's often difficult to expose an image that retains detail in both. If you're shooting JPEG, applying either DR Correction/Shadow Correct (or both) is one solution to this problem.

> **Note:**
> Neither DR Correction nor Shadow Correct is available when you're shooting Raw.

Symbol	Notes	Available ISO range
OFF	DR Correction switched off	–
AUTO	G16 makes highlight alterations automatically.	Auto/80–12,800
200%	Highlight brightness is reduced by 200% compared to OFF.	Auto/160–3200
400%	Highlight brightness is reduced by 400% compared to OFF.	Auto/320–3200
OFF	Shadow Correct switched off.	Auto/80–12,800
AUTO	Shadow Correct adjusts shadows automatically.	Auto/80–12,800

› White balance

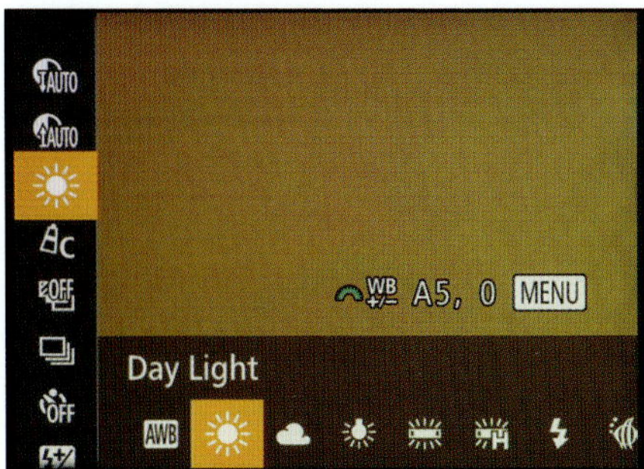

What may seem to be a neutral white light is often anything but, as all light sources have a color temperature that is measured using the Kelvin scale (K). A light source with a color temperature of 5500K is considered to be "neutral," as neither red nor blue predominate (flash and daylight at noon during summer have a color temperature of roughly 5500K). A light source with a color temperature below 5500K is biased toward red; above 5500K the light source is biased toward blue. These color biases make an image appear warmer or cooler respectively and this is particularly noticeable when there are white surfaces in an image, as the white will no longer look neutral.

White balance is the process used by a camera to compensate for the color temperature of the light source, so that the whites in a scene appear white.

Auto white balance is the default setting, but you can choose from a number of presets for different light sources or set your own white balance. You can also set two custom white balance settings for specific lighting situations.

White balance setting		Description	Color temp.
AWB	Auto	White balance set automatically	N/A
	Daylight	Outdoors in sunny conditions	5500K
	Cloudy	Overcast, shaded, and twilight scenes	6500K
	Tungsten	Domestic lighting	2800K
	Fluorescent	Warm-white fluorescent lighting	3500K
	Fluorescent H	Daylight-balanced fluorescent lighting	5000K
	Flash	Flash light (built-in and external units)	5500K
	Underwater	Deep blue underwater scenes	Variable
	Custom 1	Custom white balance 1	User-defined
	Custom 2	Custom white balance 2	User-defined

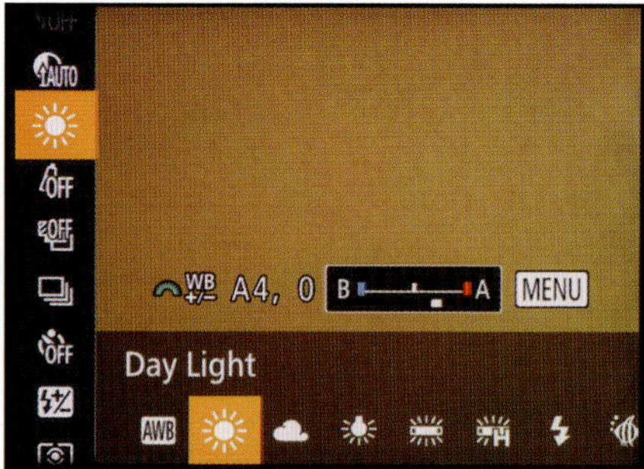

Setting white balance
1) Highlight **AWB.**

2) Highlight the required white balance (WB) setting.

3) If the selected WB setting looks too cool or too warm, turn to refine it. Turning to the left will add blue, making an image appear cooler, while turning to the right adds amber, making it warmer.

4) Press **MENU** to further refine WB. As above, pushing to the left or right adds (B)lue or (A)mber respectively, but turning to the left or right now adds more (M)agenta or (G)reen respectively to the image. These two adjustments are particularly useful when shooting under fluorescent lighting, which often has a slight green color cast (which can be removed by adding magenta). Press **ISO** to reset to the default setting, or **MENU**

to save your modified setting and return to the main WB screen. When WB has been refined (either in step 3 or 4), WB +/- is shown on the LCD.

5) Press (FUNC SET) to return to shooting mode. The selected WB setting will be displayed on the LCD.

Setting a custom white balance
1) Highlight either or (you can save two custom white balance settings at any one time).

2) Hold a piece of white paper or card in front of the camera lens so that it fills the LCD (ensuring that the paper or card is lit by the same light source as your scene).

3) Press **ISO** to record the custom white balance setting.

4) You can refine the new setting further by following steps 3 and 4 in Setting white balance (above).

5) Press (FUNC SET) to return to Shooting mode. The selected Custom WB symbol will be displayed on the LCD.

› My Colors

An image captured by a camera (digital or film) isn't an entirely accurate record of reality. When an image is captured, a

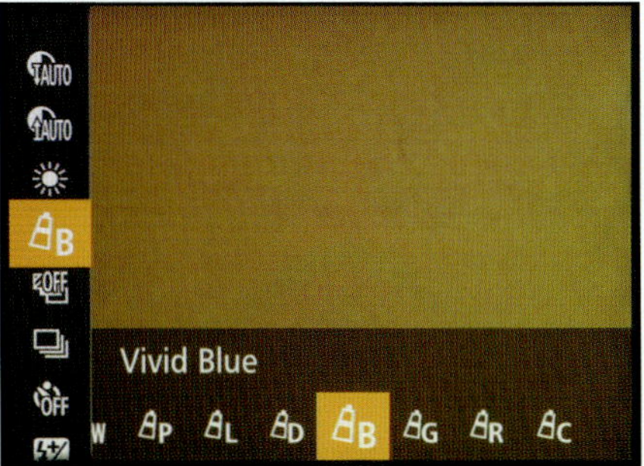

JPEG. This allows you to alter the look of an image either subtly or dramatically, depending on the emotion or reaction you are trying to convey. My Colors is not available in Raw mode, although it is possible to mimic the effects when converting the images, using a Raw converter or image-editing software.

choice can be made about how colors and contrast in the image are rendered: colors can be made more or less vivid, while contrast can be lowered or raised. That choice is either made in postproduction when shooting Raw, or when the camera processes a JPEG image.

My Colors allows you to tweak the color palette the G16 uses when processing a

Setting Custom Color

1) Highlight $\mathcal{A}$C and press ⊟. Use ▲ / ▼ to skip between the different $\mathcal{A}$C options: Contrast, Sharpness, Saturation, Red, Green, Blue, and Skin tone. Use ◄ to decrease the effect of each option, or ► to increase it.

2) Press ⊟ to save your settings, followed by (FUNC. SET) to return to Shooting mode.

My Colors Options		
$\mathcal{A}$OFF Off	My Colors not applied	
$\mathcal{A}$V Vivid	Color saturation and image contrast are increased	
$\mathcal{A}$N Neutral	Color saturation and image contrast are decreased	
$\mathcal{A}$Se Sepia	Overall light-brown tone applied to image	
$\mathcal{A}$BW BW	Black & white: all color removed	
$\mathcal{A}$P Positive Film	Mimics the highly saturated look of slide film	
$\mathcal{A}$L Lighter Skin Tone	Skin tones are lightened	
$\mathcal{A}$D Darker Skin Tone	Skin tones are darkened	
$\mathcal{A}$B Vivid Blue	Blue tones in the image are emphasized	
$\mathcal{A}$G Vivid Green	Green tones in the image are emphasized	
$\mathcal{A}$R Vivid Red	Red tones in the image are emphasized	
$\mathcal{A}$C Custom Color	User-adjustable color, contrast, and sharpness controls	

Setting white balance is easy if you have a single light source (or multiple light sources with the same color temperature), but problems can quickly arise when you mix different light sources: which do you set the white balance for? Generally, you'd use a white balance that is most aesthetically pleasing. In this example, the room was lit by daylight and a tungsten bulb. I decided to use ☀ to avoid the right side of the image appearing overly blue: the warm light on the bust is actually quite pleasing.

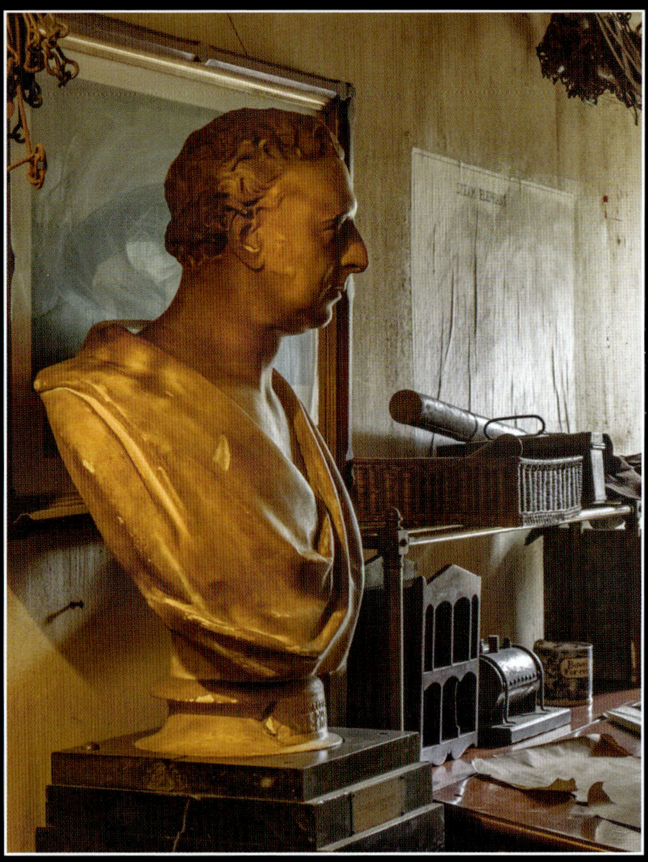

Settings

> Focal length: 18.1mm
> Exposure: 0.3 sec. at f/4
> ISO: 200

» VIVID

produces images that have highly saturated colors (resembling the color intensity of slide film). Although it's not subtle, can create images with impact, particularly when shooting scenes that are richly colored such as sunrises or sunsets.

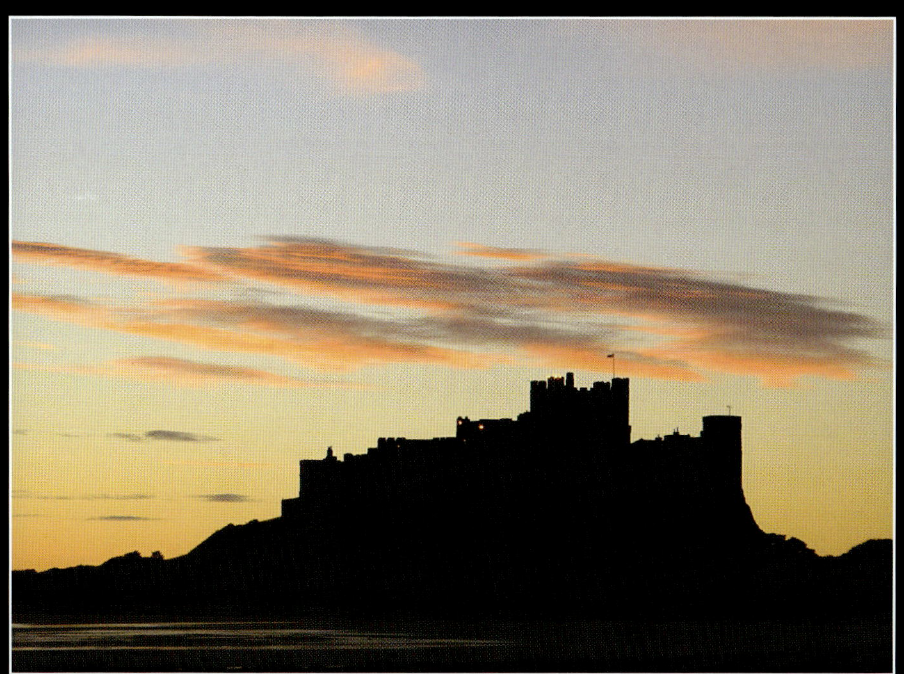

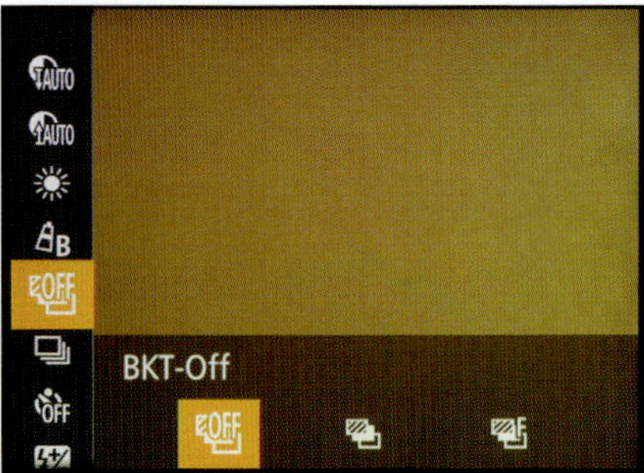

Bracketing is a photographic technique in which a sequence of shots is taken, each at a different camera setting. The most common use of bracketing is automatic exposure bracketing (AEB), in which the exposure is varied between frames. The G16 allows you to set AEB to fire three shots in which the exposure can be varied up to ±2 in $1/3$-stop increments relative to the set exposure (if you've applied exposure compensation, AEB will be based on the compensated exposure value). AEB is invaluable if you plan to create HDR images in postproduction.

When the G16 is set to ⊞ you can also bracket the distance at which the lens is focused. Bracketing is useful if you're not confident that the chosen exposure or focusing settings are correct and you want a variation of those settings as a safety net.

Setting AEB

1) Highlight ⊞ and then use ◄ / ► to highlight ⊞.

2) Press the ⊟ button followed by ◄ / ► or ◉ to select the AEB range. The further apart the outer orange markers are, the greater the difference in exposure between the frames. Press ⊟ once more followed by (FUNC SET) to return to Shooting mode.

3) Press the shutter-release button down fully to shoot the bracketed sequence.

Setting Focus-BKT

1) Press (FUNC SET), highlight ⊞, and then use ◄ / ► to highlight ⊞.

2) Press ⊟, followed by ◄ / ► or ◉ to select the Focus-BKT range. The further apart the outer orange markers are, the greater the difference in focus between the three frames. Press ⊟ once more, then (FUNC SET) to return to Shooting mode.

3) Press the shutter-release button down fully to shoot your bracketed sequence.

› Drive mode

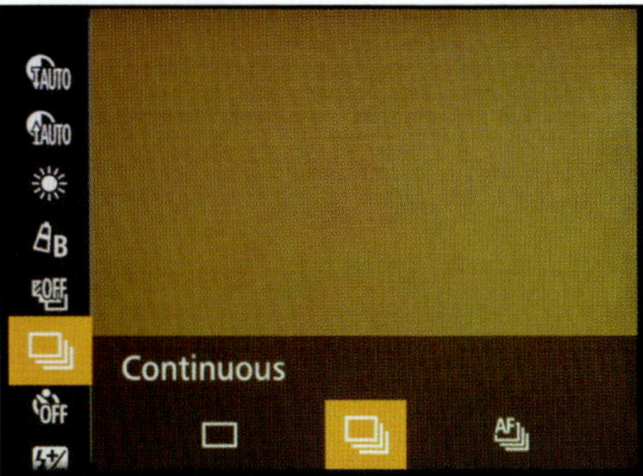

The G16 has four different still image drive modes that can be set via the FUNC. menu. Set to ▣ᴊ Continuous Advance the G16 can shoot at a maximum of 12.2fps (frames per second). However, this figure is heavily dependant on the shooting conditions and the type of file you are using. If the flash is switched on, the flash will need to recharge between shots and this will also slow down the maximum frame rate.

Drive mode	Frames per sec.	Notes
▢ Single-shot	N/A	Shutter-release button must be released and then re-pressed to continue shooting.
▣ᴊ Continuous	12.2 (reduced to 9.3fps after the eighth shot)	Images are shot continuously until the shutter-release button is released (or the memory card is filled). Exposure and focus are set on the first image when the shutter-release button is initially pressed halfway down. Images are grouped together during playback.
ᴬᶠᴊ Continuous Drive AF	5.7	Images are shot continuously until the shutter-release button is released (or the memory card is filled). Focusing is continuously adjusted between shots, with the AF frame set to **Center**.
ᴸⱽᴊ Continuous Drive LV	5.9	Only available in **MF** and ✳ modes, and when AF is locked. Images are shot continuously until the shutter-release button is released (or the memory card is filled).

› Self-Timer

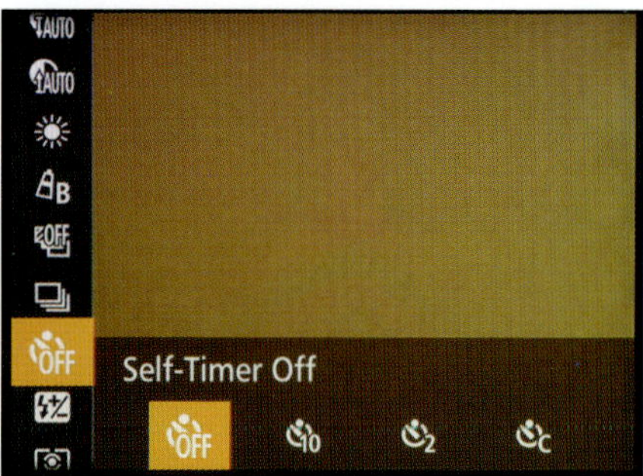

The G16's Self-Timer mode allows you to set the shutter to fire a specific number of shots automatically after a set period of time. Self-Timer is particularly useful when your G16 is mounted on a tripod and you don't have a Remote Switch RS60-E3, as it enables you to trigger the shutter without touching the camera (and potentially causing camera shake).

Setting Self-Timer

1) Highlight ⟲OFF and then press ◄ / ► or turn ◉ to select a Self-Timer option. Press (FUNC SET) to return to Shooting mode. The selected Self-Timer option will be displayed on the LCD.

2) If you've highlighted ⟲c, press the ▦ button to select further options. Turn 🜊 to set the timer delay to **1-15 sec**, **20**, **25**, or **30 sec**. Press ◄ / ► or turn ◉ to set the number of shots that will be taken

when the shutter fires. Press (FUNC SET) to return to Shooting mode.

3) Press the shutter-release button halfway down until the camera has successfully focused, and then down fully to start the Self-Timer countdown. The front lamp will blink and the Self-Timer noise will sound (if set). The Self-Timer noise will increase in rapidity just before the shutter fires. Press **MENU** during the countdown to cancel Self-Timer.

› Flash exposure compensation / Flash output settings

When raised, the G16 flash should expose your images correctly, but it is not infallible and there may be times when you need to step in and alter the flash exposure yourself. When flash exposure compensation is applied, 🜻 will be displayed on the LCD. See chapter 5 for more information about using flash.

> **Note:**
> The Self-Timer will remain active after an exposure has been made. To cancel Self-Timer repeat step 1, this time highlighting ⟲OFF.

› ND Filter

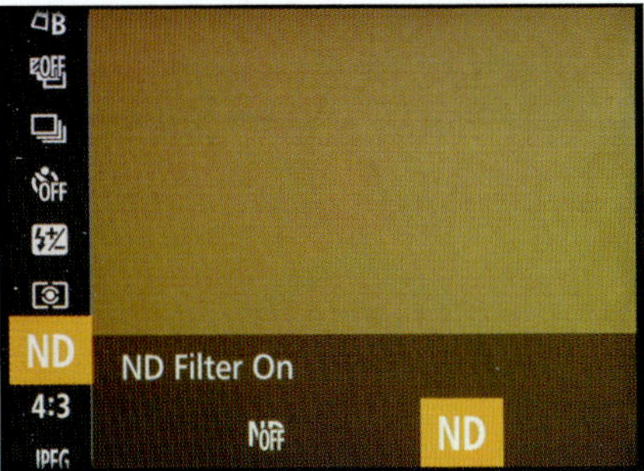

Activating ND Filter

1) Highlight **ND** on the vertical strip and then highlight **ND** on the horizontal. Press **(FUNC SET)** to return to Shooting mode. **ND** will be displayed on the LCD when the built-in ND filter is activated.

2) To switch off the ND filter repeat step 1, this time selecting **ND**.

Your G16 needs a certain amount of light to reach the sensor to create the correct exposure. The amount of light reaching the sensor is controlled by the shutter speed and aperture, but in bright conditions the G16's minimum aperture of f/8 may not be small enough to allow you to use a slow shutter speed, which is often desirable for aesthetic reasons.

One solution is to use what's known as an ND (neutral density) filter. An ND filter is a semi-opaque optical filter that reduces the amount of light reaching the sensor without affecting the color. ND filters are usually fitted to the front of a camera lens, but the G16 has a 3-stop ND filter built-in, so you don't need to buy one (although you could use one in combination with the G16's built-in filter to further extend the shutter speed).

WATER ⌄

The G16's ND filter was used in this image to extend the shutter speed to 1/2 sec. and blur the water in the waterfall.

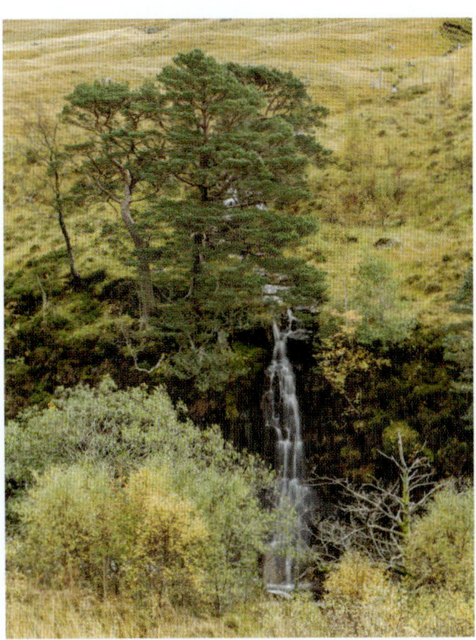

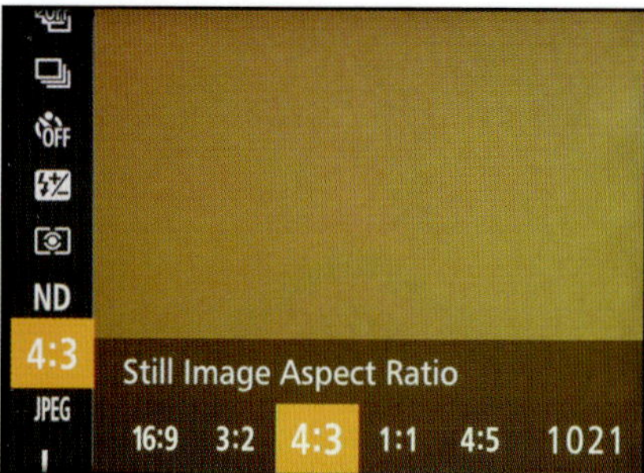

The aspect ratio of an image is the ratio of its width to its height. By default, the G16 shoots images with a 4:3 aspect ratio (the aspect ratio of the G16's sensor, LCD screen, and standard analog TVs).

However, you don't need to stick to this shape. You can also set the G16 to shoot using an aspect ratio of 16:9 (the aspect ratio of HDTV); 3:2 (the aspect ratio of most DSLRs); 1:1 (square); or 4:5 (the aspect ratio of 4x5-inch sheet film).

When you use an aspect ratio other than 4:3, the display on the LCD is altered by the addition of a black border. The area of the scene inside the border is the area that will be captured when an image is made. Images that use an aspect ratio other than 4:3 are cropped in-camera so don't use the full resolution of the sensor.

This loss is particularly noticeable if an image is created using a 4:5 aspect ratio: the resulting image will have roughly 40% fewer pixels than an image created at an

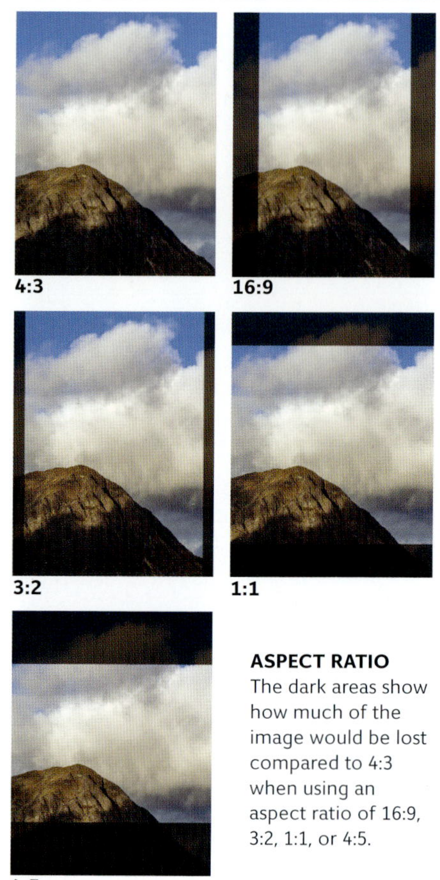

ASPECT RATIO
The dark areas show how much of the image would be lost compared to 4:3 when using an aspect ratio of 16:9, 3:2, 1:1, or 4:5.

aspect ratio of 4:3. If you're in doubt about which aspect ratio to use, bear in mind that a "full resolution" 4:3 image can be cropped on your computer using photo-editing software to achieve the same effect.

› File formats

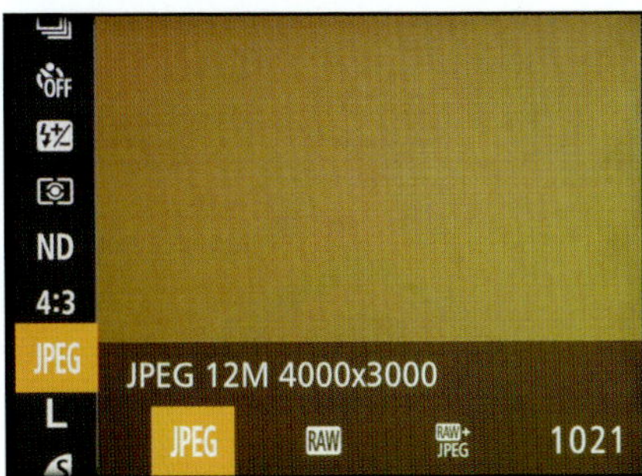

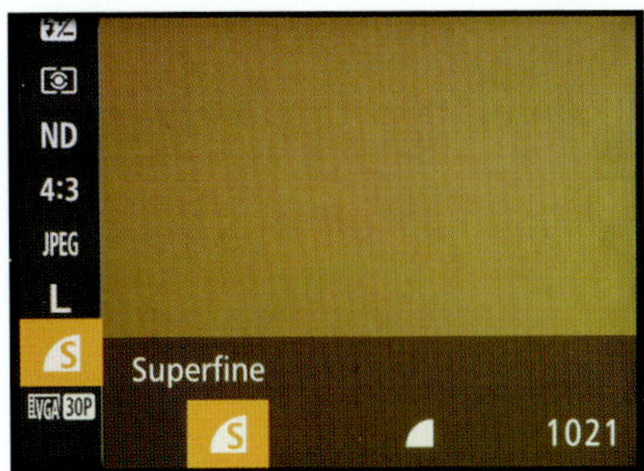

You can set your G16 to shoot in either JPEG or Raw, or both at the same time. The file format you choose will determine how immediately usable your images are, how much space they take up on the memory card, and what shooting functions can be applied to your photograph.

JPEG

JPEG is the image format to use if you need to use your images immediately after capture. They are "finished" images that theoretically won't need any adjustment in postproduction. This is because a JPEG has the style of the image (such as the level of contrast and sharpness) "baked" into it. Although you can alter the image later using software such as Photoshop, you'll find that image quality degrades quickly, even with relatively little adjustment.

However, JPEGs are compatible with virtually all software that can import an image, which includes word processors, web browsers, and photo-editing tools. JPEG files are identified by the extension .JPG (or occasionally .JPEG).

A JPEG file will take up far less room on a memory card than an equivalent Raw file, because the data in a JPEG is compressed. There is a penalty, though: the compression is achieved by a reduction in the fine detail in an image, and the greater the compression factor, the greater the loss of detail (a highly compressed JPEG will be a mess of colored blocks and strange image artifacts).

Fortunately, the G16 doesn't compress JPEG files to such a destructive degree. Instead, there are just two levels of compression available: **S** Super Fine and ◢ Fine. **S** produces higher quality files than ◢, although fewer images can be fitted onto a memory card.

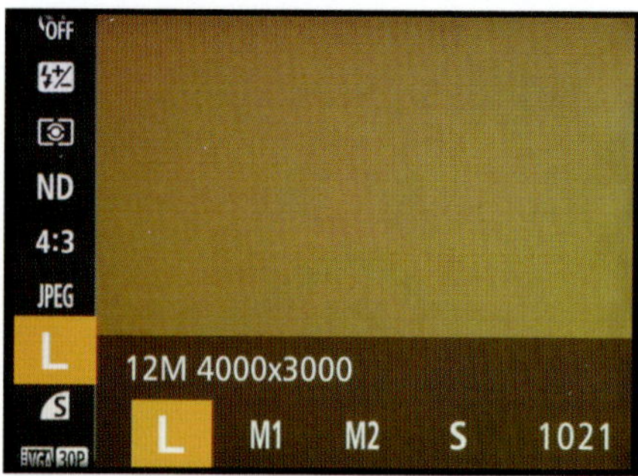

You can also choose to record your JPEGs at one of four different resolution settings: **L** (Large), **M1** (Medium 1), **M2** (Medium 2), or **S** (Small). The lower the resolution, the less space the file will occupy on the memory card, but the smaller the potential print size.

It is also worth noting that once the JPEG has been saved, the compression and resolution is set—any lost detail will never be recovered. However, if memory card space is tight it is better to have a lower quality image than no image at all.

Raw

A Raw file is essentially a "package" that contains all the image data captured by the camera at the moment of exposure. This means that no in-camera processing (such as contrast adjustments, saturation, or sharpening) is applied to the data before it is saved.

Instead, a Raw file is processed by the photographer using Raw conversion

software such as Canon's Digital Photo Professional or third-party software such as Adobe Lightroom. Canon uses the extension .CR2 for its Raw format files.

Shooting Raw files means spending time in postproduction polishing and preparing your images before you save them in a more usable format such as JPEG or TIFF. This makes Raw images less immediately useful than JPEG, but it also means that it's possible to have a more personal approach to image creation. You can create an almost infinite number of interpretations of the same Raw image, achieved with no loss of image quality, as the original image data of the Raw file is never overwritten.

As with JPEGs, Canon's Raw files are compressed, but they use a compression system that doesn't lose detail in the image. As a result, a Raw file takes up far more room on a memory card than an equivalent JPEG. Shooting Raw therefore requires the use of higher capacity memory cards or you will need to empty your memory card more frequently.

> **Note:**
> As the name suggests, **S** (Small) is the lowest JPEG resolution setting. It should only be used if you need to create images for email or web use.

» THE MODE DIAL

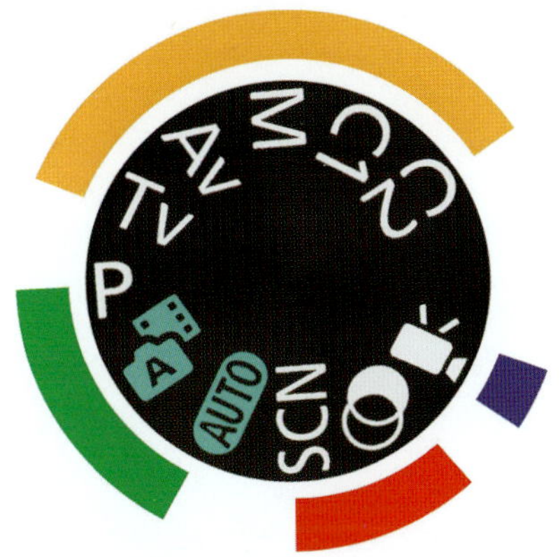

The mode dial on the top of the G16 is used to select the different shooting modes for both still images and movies. Although there are a number of different options, it's easier to think of the mode dial as being split into four segments, each allowing you to shoot in a specific way.

The first segment (colored orange on the diagram above) gives you the most control over how your G16 shoots still images. In this segment are **M** (Manual exposure), **Av** (Aperture Priority), and **Tv** (Shutter Priority). The segment also includes two custom modes (C1 and C2) that can be configured by you.

In the next segment (green) are three largely automatic shooting modes: **P** (Program), **AUTO**, and (Hybrid Auto) mode. **P** and **AUTO** allow you to quickly pick up and use your G16 without worrying about exposure or focusing, with **P** offering a little more control than **AUTO**. mode shoots both a still image and a short movie clip.

The third segment (red) contains **SCN** Specific Scene and Image Effects modes. Although these modes lock you out of certain aspects of how your G16 operates, they are useful when shooting in specific situations, or when you want to apply a distinctive look to your images.

The final segment (blue) contains the Movie modes. These are covered in more detail in the next chapter.

Selecting a shooting mode

1) Turn the Mode Dial to the required setting, aligning the mode icon to the white marker on the camera body.

2) If the LCD is turned on, the selected mode will be confirmed with a brief description of functions.

3) If you've selected **SCN** or ◓, press (FUNC SET) to select the required mode. Use ▲ / ▼ to highlight the currently selected mode (if it is not already highlighted). Press ◀ / ▶ or ⬤ to highlight the mode you want to use. Press (FUNC SET) to continue.

Mode dial options

Custom 2	**C2**
Custom 1	**C1**
Manual	**M**
Av (Aperture Priority)	**Av**
Tv (Shutter Priority)	**Tv**
Program	**P**
Smart Auto	**AUTO**
Hybrid Auto	
Specific Scene	**SCN**
Image Effects	
Movie	

Specific Scene modes

Portrait	
Smart Shutter	
Starry Skies	
Handheld Night Scene	
Underwater	

Snow	
Fireworks	

Image Effects

HDR	**HDR**
Nostalgic	
Fish-eye	
Miniature	
Toy Camera	
Background Defocus	
Soft Focus	
Monochrome	
Super Vivid	
Poster	

Movie

Standard movie shooting	
Super Slow Motion	

Function		P	Tv	Av	M	**AUTO**
Image type	RAW, RAW+JPEG	Y	Y	Y	Y	–
	L	Y	Y	Y	Y	Y
	M1, M2, S, ◣	Y	Y	Y	Y	Y
	S	Y	Y	Y	Y	Y
Change aspect ratio [1]		Y	Y	Y	Y	Y
Self-timer		Y	Y	Y	Y	Y
Drive mode	☐	Y	Y	Y	Y	Y
	A⊡	–	–	–	–	Y
	⊡, AF⊡	Y	Y	Y	Y	–
Exposure compensation		Y	Y	Y	–	–
ISO	ISO AUTO	Y	Y	Y	–	Y
	ISO 100 – ISO 12800	Y	Y	Y	Y	–
White balance	AWB	Y	Y	Y	Y	Y
	☀ – ◑	Y	Y	Y	Y	–
	■1 ■2	Y	Y	Y	Y	–
WB correction		Y	Y	Y	Y	–
Flash	⚡A	Y	–	–	–	Y
	⚡	Y	Y	Y	Y	–
	⚡★	Y	–	Y	–	[3]
	⚡⊘	Y	Y	Y	Y	Y
Metering	▣	Y	Y	Y	Y	Y
	▢ ▣	Y	Y	Y	Y	–
Focusing	▲	Y	Y	Y	Y	Y
	❀ MF/AF lock	Y	Y	Y	Y	–
	🌼 ≡📷	–	–	–	–	–
Alter AF frame position		Y	Y	Y	Y	–
Alter AF frame size		Y	Y	Y	Y	–
Face select		Y	Y	Y	Y	Y
Tracking AF		Y	Y	Y	Y	Y
Bracketing	OFF	Y	Y	Y	Y	Y
	▧	Y	Y	Y	–	–
	▧F	Y	Y	Y	Y	–
DR Correction	↑OFF	Y	Y	Y	Y	–
	↓AUTO	Y	Y	Y	–	Y
	↓200% ↓400%	Y	Y	Y	Y	–
Shadow Correct	◖OFF	Y	Y	Y	Y	–
	↑AUTO	Y	Y	Y	Y	Y

1. Not available when shooting Raw   **2.** ⊡ is set with MF, AF lock, or ✳
3. Not available, but will use ⚡★ automatically as required

› Smart Auto AUTO

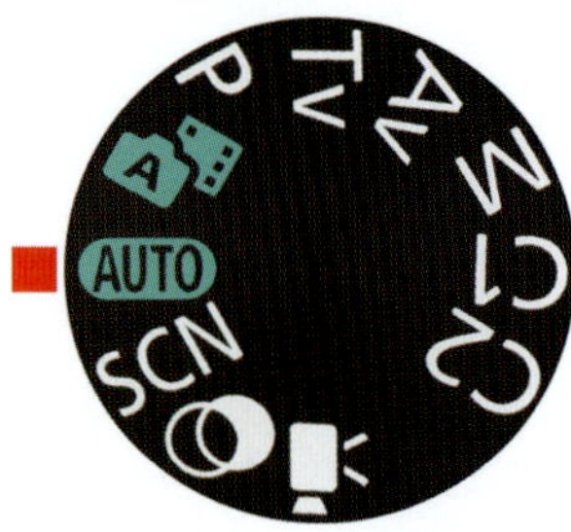

AUTO (Smart Auto) leaves the control of functions such as exposure and focus entirely with the G16. This means that all you have to do is frame your shot and press the shutter-release button—the camera will take care of the rest. AUTO is perfect when you're at an event and don't have time to think about the technical side of photography, but your creative options are obviously very limited. If you need greater creative control you may find that **P** Program mode is a better choice.

As you shoot using AUTO, your G16 analyzes the scene and tries to make intelligent choices about which functions to use. The decisions the camera makes are shown as a Scene icon at the top right corner of the LCD. AUTO will also set the G16's IS system to maximize sharpness, depending on the scene in question. The chosen IS mode will be shown next to the Scene icon.

In AUTO mode, the AF frame will change depending on the subject the G16 thinks you are trying to shoot. A white frame is initially displayed, centered on the subject. If there are several faces in the scene the main face will be surrounded by a white frame and the other faces by a gray frame. If the main subject begins to move, the white frame will turn blue and the AF will begin to track the movement.

Under certain conditions your G16 will also shoot continuously as you hold down the shutter-release button. This occurs when the icons in the grid below are displayed on the LCD.

Continuous shooting

Icon	Condition
	Smiling (including babies). If your subject smiles, multiple images are shot so you can choose which best captures the moment.
	Sleeping (including babies). Multiple shots are combined to reduce camera shake and noise. Allows you to capture the facial expressions of sleeping subjects. The AF Assist light is turned off, the flash will not fire, and the shutter sound is muted.
	Children. Three shots are fired every time you press the shutter-release button so that you don't miss an important moment.

» OBSERVATION

The beauty of the G16's **AUTO** mode is that it allows you to shoot without worrying too much about the technical details. This allows you more freedom to develop your photographic eye as you look at the world around you.

Settings
> Focal length: 21.5mm
> Exposure: 1/500 sec. at f/5
> ISO: 80

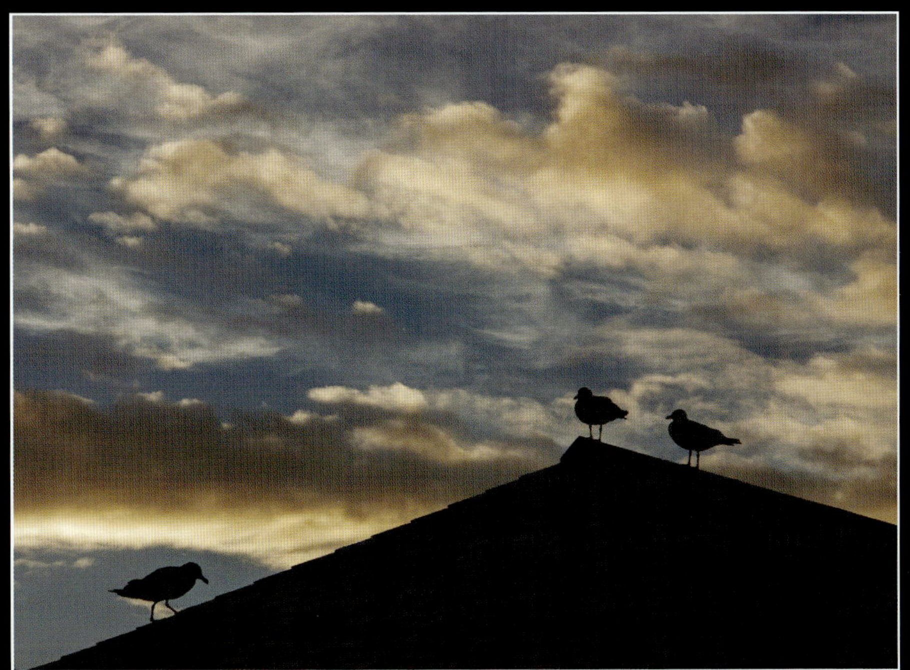

Using **AUTO** mode

1) Turn the mode dial to **AUTO**.

2) Compose your image.

3) Lightly press the shutter-release button to focus. In low-light conditions the words **Raise the Flash** will be shown on the LCD if flash is required. Push the ▶ꜛ button to raise the flash.

4) Depress the shutter-release button fully to take the photograph.

5) The photograph will be displayed on the LCD by default for 2 seconds, unless the review time has been adjusted.

Notes:
The G16 will automatically detect when you are trying to shoot a close-up and will adjust the focus and IS setting accordingly.

Press ▲ to toggle between Tracking AF **On** and **Off**. When Tracking AF is activated and the ⊡ focus point appears on the LCD, move the camera so that ⊡ covers the subject you want to focus on. Hold down the shutter-release button halfway and a blue frame should now surround your point of focus. If you move the camera, the G16 will try to maintain focus on this point using Servo AF.

IS mode

(ꞌꙮꞌ)	Standard IS for still images	(ꞌꙮꞌD)	Dynamic IS for movie shooting when walking.
(→)	IS for still images when camera is panned.	(ꞌꙮꞌP)	Subtle IS for movie shooting with little camera movement or when the lens is set to ⟦🌢⟧.
(ꞌꙮꞌ)	Hybrid IS—useful when shooting macro and close-up shots.	(ꞌꙮꞌ)	No image stabilization. Use when the camera is stationary such as when fitted to a tripod.

Subject	Background				
	Normal	**Backlit**	**Dark**	**Sunsets**	**Spotlights**
People	(2)	(1)		—	
People: In motion	(1)	(1)	—	—	—
People: Shadows on face	(2)	—	—	—	—
People: Smiling	(1)	(1)	—	—	—
People: Sleeping	(2)	(1)	—	—	—
Babies	(1)	(1)	—	—	—
Babies: Smiling	(1)	(1)	—	—	—
Babies: Sleeping	(2)	(1)	—	—	—
Children: In motion	(1)	(1)	—	—	—
Other	(2)	(1)			
Other: In motion	(2)	(1)	—	—	—
Other: At close range	(2)	(1)	—	—	

(1) Icon background is light blue (pictured) when the image background is blue sky, otherwise the icon background will be gray.

(2) Icon background is light blue (pictured) when the image background is blue sky, and dark blue when the image background is dark. Otherwise icon background will be gray.

› Program P

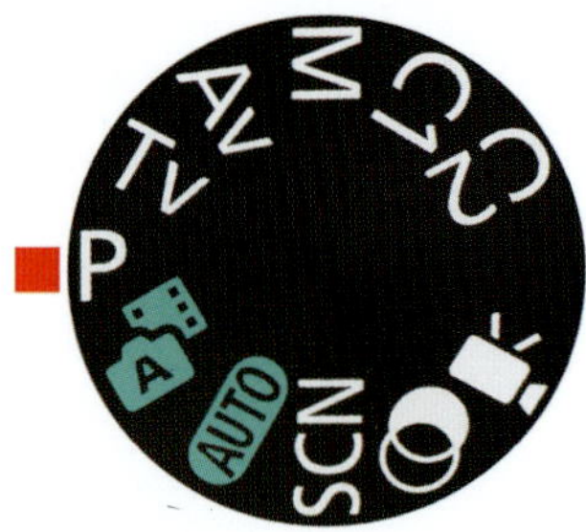

Using P mode

1) Turn the mode dial to **P**.

2) Compose your image.

3) Use the exposure compensation dial to fine-tune the exposure if necessary. Alternatively, press ✳ to lock the exposure and then turn ⬤ to apply Program Shift.

4) Lightly press halfway down on the shutter-release button to focus.

5) Press the shutter-release button fully to take the photograph.

6) The photograph will be displayed on the LCD by default for 2 seconds, unless the review time has been adjusted.

As with **AUTO**, Program is an automatic shooting mode. However, you're not entirely locked out of the creative process: you can change settings such as WB and drive mode, for example.

In **P**, both the shutter speed and aperture are determined automatically by the G16, but you can choose to ignore the exposure set by the camera. You can do this either by adjusting the exposure compensation dial to deliberately over- or underexpose, or you can adjust the aperture and shutter speed combination while still maintaining the same overall exposure level (known as Program Shift).

Because you still have a reasonable level of control over the camera, **P** is a good mode to use if you want automated shooting, but with the option of stepping in and overriding the settings if you feel the need.

› Shutter Priority **Tv**

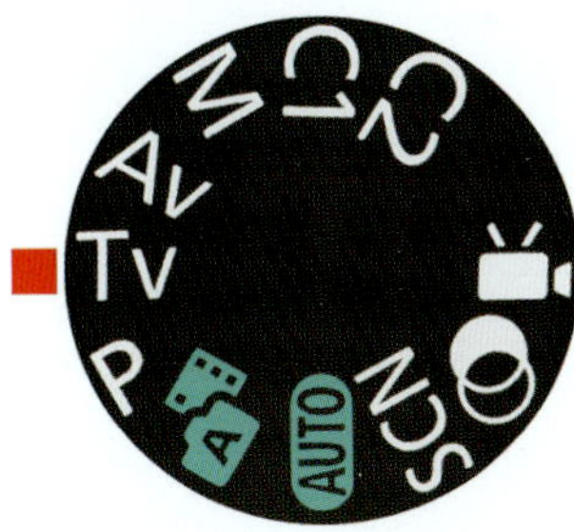

Tv and **Av** are semi-automatic exposure modes: you change one exposure control and the G16 automatically alters the other. **Tv** mode puts you in control of the shutter speed, while the camera sets the correct aperture value. The shutter speed controls the way that movement in a scene is recorded, which includes whether your images are affected by camera shake.

Camera shake is caused when the camera is unsteady during an exposure, typically when a camera is handheld: the longer the shutter speed, the greater the risk. The G16's image stabilization helps, but only to a certain degree. There's no single shutter speed that causes camera shake, as it varies from person to person (some people are steadier than others) so it's worth experimenting to see what your own tolerances are. Camera shake is more likely when the lens is set to ⬛, rather than ⬛.

Using Tv mode

1) Turn the mode dial to **Tv**.

2) Frame your shot and turn ⚙ to change the shutter speed. The camera will set the aperture value automatically.

3) Lightly press the shutter-release button to focus. If the displayed aperture value turns orange, you have exceeded the range of possible aperture settings and the image will be either under- or overexposed. Adjust the shutter speed until the aperture value turns white, or use the exposure compensation dial to fine-tune the exposure.

4) Press the shutter-release button fully to take the photograph.

5) The captured photograph will be displayed on the LCD for 2 seconds unless the review time has been adjusted.

It was slightly optimistic to hope I could handhold the G16 when using a shutter speed of 13 seconds, even though the camera was pressed against a glass display case. In retrospect, I should have set a higher ISO and a larger aperture (focusing carefully on the statue) to allow the use of a faster shutter speed. Next time...

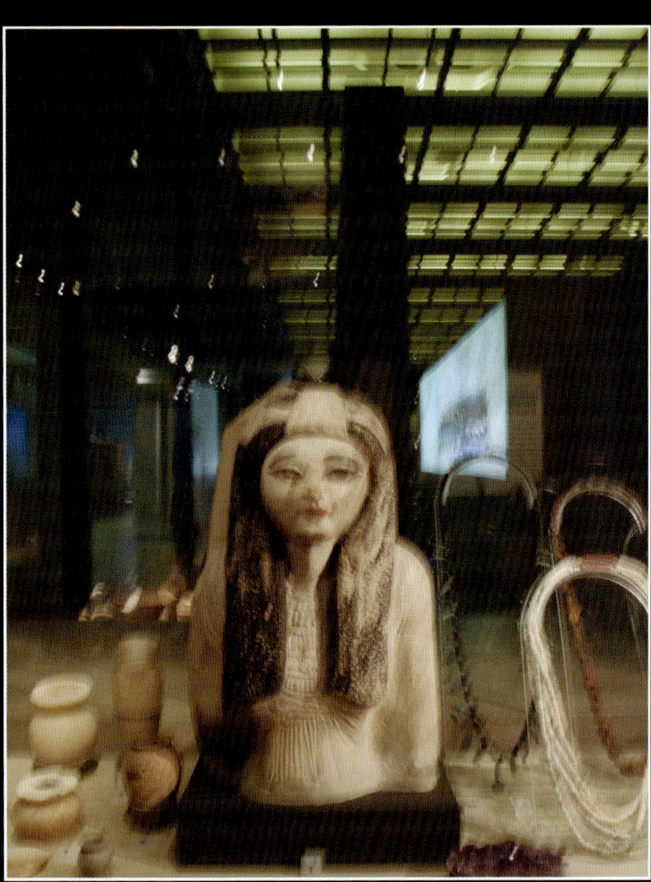

Settings

> Focal length: 6.1mm
> Exposure: 13 sec. at f/4.5
> ISO: 80

› Aperture Priority **Av**

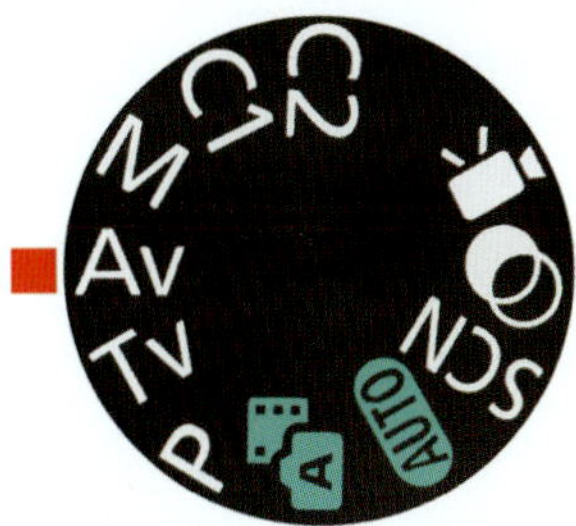

When you choose **Av** on the mode dial, you control the aperture and the G16 will set the shutter speed. The aperture also controls the amount of an image that is acceptably sharp (known as depth of field). The sharpest part of an image is always at the point of focus, but as the aperture is made smaller, the depth of field extends out from the focus point. Depth of field extends twice as far back from the focus point than it does in front, so a very rough-and-ready rule is to focus approximately one third of the way into the scene and not necessarily on the subject itself. However, it's worth experimenting with your G16 to see how different apertures affect depth of field.

As well as the aperture, there are two other factors that determine the extent of the depth of field. The first of these is the focal length of the lens. Depth of field is always greater at any given aperture when the lens is set to ⓦ, rather than ⓤ. The second factor is the camera-to-subject

distance. The closer your subject is to the camera lens, the less depth of field you will be able to achieve, even with the aperture set to the lens' minimum. This can be a particular problem when shooting using ❀ focusing.

Using Av mode

1) Turn the mode dial to **Av**.

2) Compose your image and use to change the aperture. The G16 will alter the shutter speed automatically.

3) Lightly press the shutter-release button to focus. If the displayed shutter speed turns orange, this means you have exceeded the range of possible shutter speeds and the image will be either under- or overexposed. Adjust the aperture until the shutter speed value turns white or use exposure compensation.

4) Press the shutter-release button fully to take the photograph.

5) The captured photograph will be displayed on the LCD screen for 2 seconds, unless the review time has been adjusted.

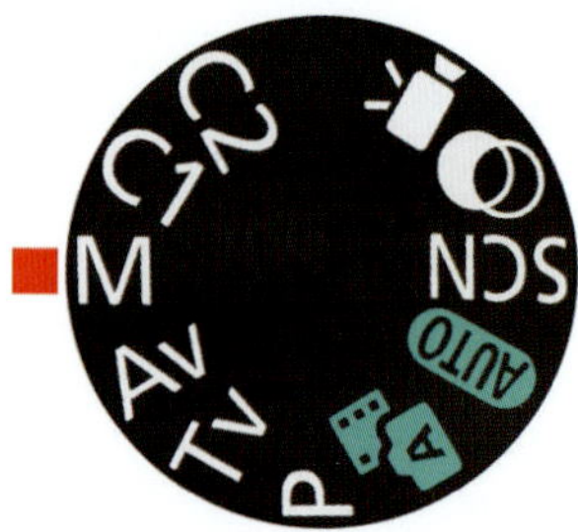

You're entirely responsible for setting the required exposure for your images when using **M**. This means setting the shutter speed, aperture, and ISO manually (hence the name). You can either use a handheld meter to determine exposure or use the G16's built-in meter as a guide: an exposure level indicator on the LCD shows you whether the exposure settings you are using are correct, or whether they will result in under- or overexposure.

The drawbacks to using **M** mode are that time must be spent refining the exposure and it's easy to make exposure errors. If you're in a hurry, one of the semi-automatic exposure modes described previously may be a better bet. However, the time refining an exposure in **M** mode will be time well spent if it helps you achieve the goal you have for an image.

Using M mode

1) Turn the mode dial to **M**.

2) Compose your image. Use the dial to change the shutter speed and/or to change the aperture.

3) As you change the shutter speed and aperture settings the resulting exposure is compared to the standard exposure determined by the G16. The settings you choose are "correct" when the set exposure bar (1) below the exposure level indicator is aligned with the standard exposure bar (2). If the set exposure exceeds the standard exposure by ±2 stops the set exposure bar turns orange.

4) Depress the shutter-release button fully to take the photograph.

5) The captured photograph will be displayed on the LCD for 2 seconds, unless the review time has been adjusted.

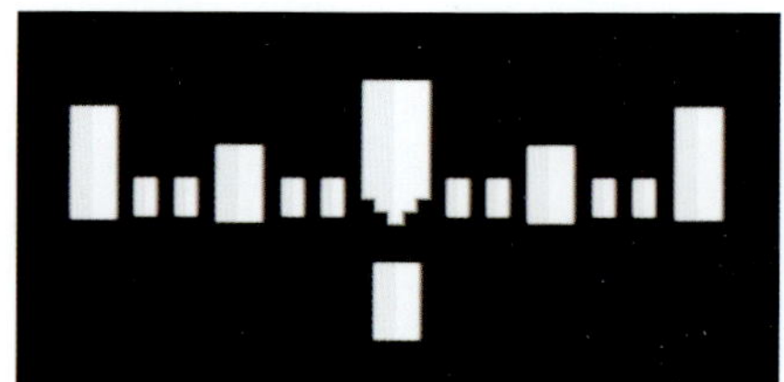

› Hybrid Auto

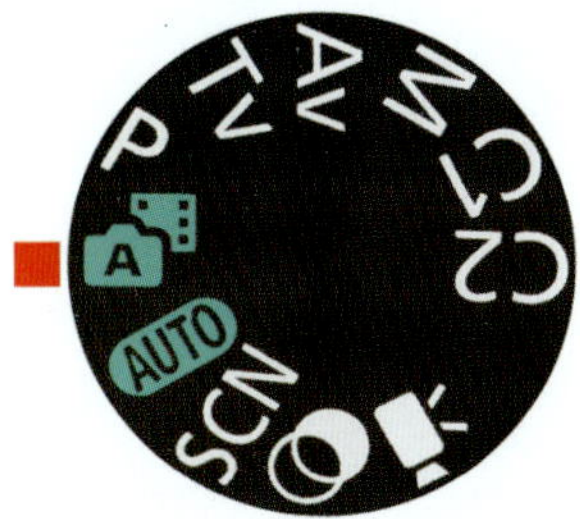

mode shoots a short movie clip of approximately 2–4 seconds, plus a still image, every time the shutter is fired. Clips from the same date are joined together to create one complete movie. These movies can then be viewed by selecting List/Play Digest Movies on the ▶ menu or by pressing ▶ and navigating to the required movie. Movies created using can be trimmed in the same way as "standard" movies (see chapter four).

allows you to build up a video log of your day quickly and simply, without needing to press the movie record button.

Using mode

1) Turn the mode dial to .

2) Compose your image. Press down on the shutter-release button halfway to focus and then all the way down to start recording the movie clip. After a few seconds (once the movie clip has been saved to the memory card) the camera will return to Shooting mode.

> **Notes:**
> You may find your G16's battery charge doesn't last as long when using as it does when using **AUTO**.
>
> The clips are viewed as one movie unless the file size exceeds 4GB or is longer than one hour in length.
>
> Movie quality is fixed at HD 30P.

› Specific Scene modes **SCN**

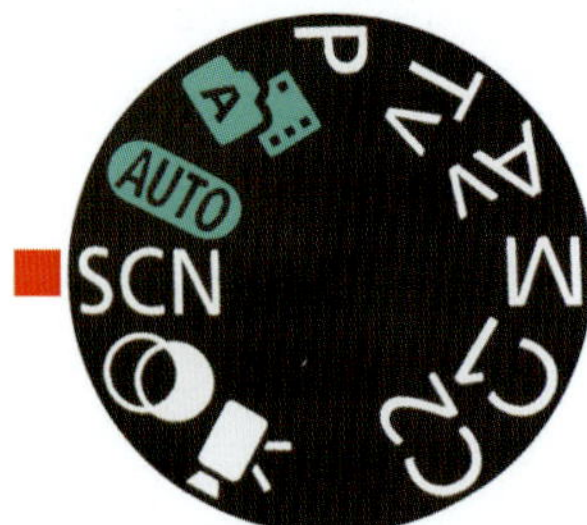

There are seven **SCN** modes, each of which is designed to help you shoot quickly and effectively in specific shooting situations. Each of the seven modes configures the G16 to the optimal settings for that situation, leaving you free to shoot without worry.

However, there's a downside to such a high level of automation: except for choosing the moment that the shutter is fired, the camera is effectively in control and you are locked out of many of the settings that make photography so creative and so much fun. The grid on page 76–77 shows what can, or cannot, be set in each **SCN** mode.

Setting a SCN mode

1) Turn the mode dial to **SCN**.

2) Press (FUNC. SET) and highlight 👤 (👤 is shown by default—once you've chosen another **SCN** mode the icon for that mode will be displayed subsequently).

3) Use ◀ / ▶ or ⬤ to highlight the required **SCN** mode and then press (FUNC. SET) to return to Shooting mode.

4) If there are any options for the Specific Scene they will be displayed on screen (and are noted in the pages that follow).

5) Lightly press halfway down on the shutter to focus, and then fully to take the photograph.

6) Your photograph will be displayed on the rear LCD for 2 seconds, unless the review time has been adjusted.

> *Note:*
> **SCN** limits you to using JPEG only.

» AQUARIUM

With a little bit of imagination it's possible to use the **SCN** modes in a way that wasn't intended by Canon. is supposed to be used when your G16 is underwater in a WP-DC52 Waterproof Case, but you can also use it on dry land in an aquarium!

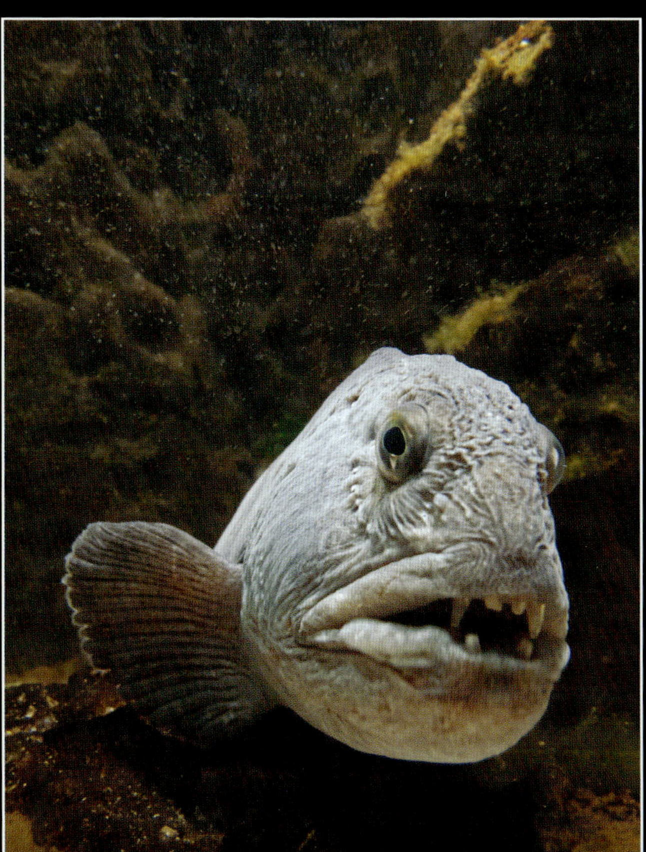

Settings
> Focal length: 6.1mm
> Exposure: 1/15 sec. at f/2.8
> ISO: 400

Function		👤	😊	😴
JPEG settings	L	Y	Y	Y
	M1, M2, S	Y	Y	Y
	🅂 (RAW)	–	–	–
	(RAW)	Y	Y	Y
Change aspect ratio		Y	Y	Y
Self-Timer		Y	–	–
Drive mode	▢	Y	Y	Y
	A-cont	–	–	–
	cont	Y	–	–
	AF-cont	–	–	–
Exposure compensation		Y	Y	Y
ISO	ISO AUTO	Y	Y	Y
	ISO 100 – ISO 12800	–	–	–
White balance	AWB	Y	Y	Y
	☀ – ¤	–	Y	Y
	Custom 1 / Custom 2	–	Y	Y
WB correction		–	–	–
Flash	⚡A	Y	Y	Y
	⚡	Y	Y	Y
	⚡★	–	–	–
	🚫	Y	Y	Y
Metering	◉	Y	Y	Y
	▢ ▢	–	–	–
Focusing	▲	Y	Y	Y
	❀	Y	–	–
	macro/manual	–	–	–
	MF / AF lock	Y	–	–
Alter AF frame position		–	–	–
Alter AF frame size		Y	–	–
Face select		Y	Y	Y
Tracking AF		Y	–	–
Bracketing	OFF	Y	Y	Y
	bracket	–	–	–
	bracket F	–	–	–
DR Correction	OFF	Y	Y	Y
	AUTO	–	–	–
	200% 400%	–	–	–
Shadow Correct	OFF	Y	Y	Y
	AUTO	–	–	–

[icon]	[icon]	[icon]	[icon]	[icon]	[icon]
Y	Y	Y	Y	Y	Y
Y	–	–	Y	Y	Y
–	–	–	–	–	–
Y	Y	Y	Y	Y	Y
Y	–	–	Y	Y	Y
–	Y	Y	Y	Y	Y
Y	Y	Y	Y	Y	Y
–	–	–	–	–	–
–	–	–	Y	Y	Y
–	–	–	Y	Y	Y
Y	Y	Y	Y	Y	Y
Y	Y	Y	Y	Y	Y
–	–	–	–	–	–
Y	Y	Y	Y	Y	Y
Y	–	–	–	–	–
Y	–	–	Y	–	–
–	–	–	–	–	–
Y	–	Y	Y	Y	–
Y	–	Y	Y	Y	–
–	–	–	–	–	–
Y	Y	Y	Y	Y	Y
Y	Y	Y	Y	Y	Y
–	–	–	–	–	–
Y	Y	Y	Y	Y	Y
–	–	Y	–	Y	–
–	–	–	Y	–	–
–	Y	Y	Y	Y	–
–	–	–	–	–	–
–	–	–	Y	Y	–
Y	–	–	–	Y	–
–	–	–	Y	Y	–
Y	Y	Y	Y	Y	Y
–	–	–	–	–	–
–	–	–	–	–	–
Y	Y	Y	–	Y	Y
–	–	–	Y	–	–
–	–	–	–	–	–
Y	Y	Y	Y	Y	Y
–	–	–	–	–	–

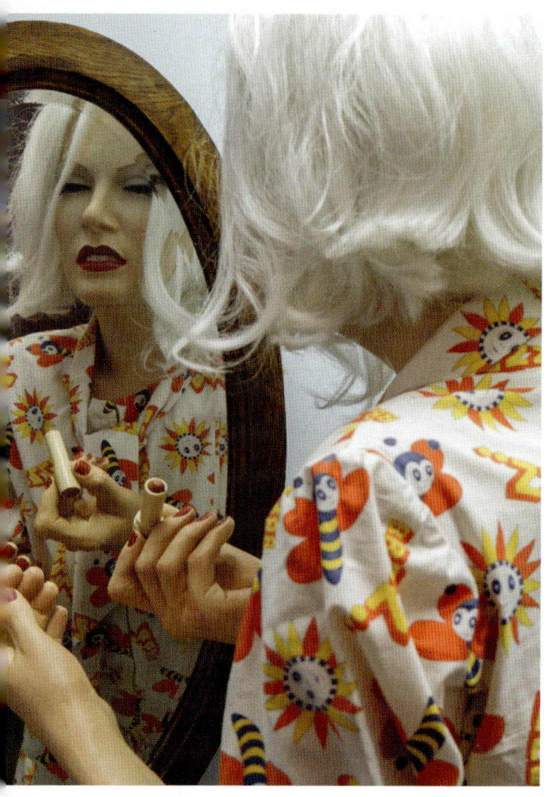

UNUSUAL
Look for interesting ways to shoot your subject, rather than straightforward head-and-shoulder shots.

Portrait mode on the G16 will help you achieve a well-exposed and correctly focused image of a person or group of people. However, there's more to portraiture than creating a technically correct image—a successful portrait involves developing a rapport with your subject so that something of their personality comes through.

Part of this process involves putting the subject at their ease (this is more difficult to achieve with a group, although groups tend to be more relaxed anyway—there is safety in numbers). If your subject is nervous, reassure them and, if possible, make them laugh by using gentle good humor. Mounting your camera on a tripod and using a remote release will mean that you can look directly at the subject once you've set up the basic composition. Images shot using 🂠 mode don't have as much sharpening applied in-camera as other **SCN** modes.

» RAPPORT

Creating a successful and pleasing portrait means having a friendly relationship with your subject. This is easy when you know the person, less so if you don't. Politeness goes a long way when asking strangers if you can take their photo. Make eye contact, smile, and ask in a straightforward manner. Thank them once you're finished and offer to show them the results on your G16's LCD screen.

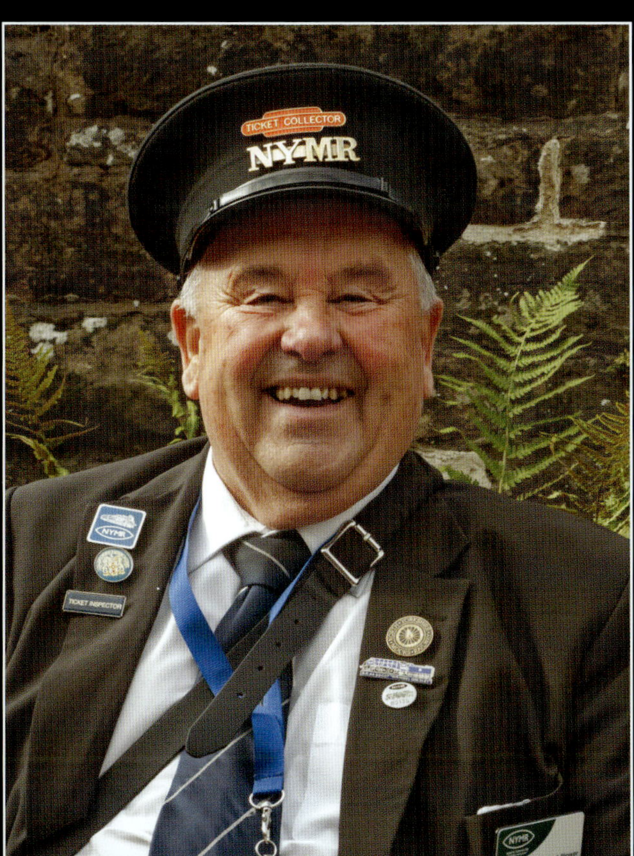

Settings
> Focal length: 21.5mm
> Exposure: 1/125 sec. at f/6.3
> ISO: 200

› Smart Shutter 📷

Smart Shutter is the ultimate portrait-shooting aid. People often don't smile when they're told to, and then smile when you're not ready—Smart Shutter helps you time your shots, so that an image is made when your subject is ready.

There are three Smart Shutter options: **Smile Detection** automatically fires the shutter when your subject smiles. **Wink Self-Timer** will only fire the shutter when your subject winks at the camera. Finally, **Face Self-Timer** will only fire the shutter when a new face enters the shot. If you're quick, this means that you can star in your own photos.

😊 Smile Detection

1) Select 📷 **Smart Shutter**.

2) Press **ISO** and either press ◀ / ▶ or turn ⚙ to highlight 😊. Press ▲ / ▼ to adjust the number of shots (from 1 to 10) you want to take with 📷.

3) Press **ISO** to return to Shooting mode.

4) Press ▼ to pause smile detection temporarily. Press ▼ again to unpause.

5) When your subject smiles—and the smile is detected by the G16—the front lamp will light and the camera will shoot the specified number of images. The shutter-release button can still be used to take shots in this mode.

😉 Wink Self-Timer

1) Highlight 😉 **Wink Self-Timer**.

2) Press ▲ or ▼ to adjust the number of shots (from 1 to 10) you want to take with 😉. Press **ISO** to return to Shooting mode.

3) Compose your shot and press the shutter-release button down halfway. A green frame should surround the face of your "winkee" on the G16's LCD. Recompose your shot if this does not happen. Press the shutter-release button down fully.

4) Wink to take Picture will be displayed on the LCD. The front lamp will blink and the Self-Timer sound will be played.

5) The shutter will fire approximately 2 seconds after a wink has been detected from your "winkee," with the camera shooting the number of images specified. Press **MENU** to cancel the 😉 countdown.

> **Tip**
>
> *When using 😊, the bigger the smile, the more likely the shutter will fire!*

⏱ Face Self-Timer

1) Highlight ⏱ **Face Self-Timer**.

2) Press ▲ or ▼ to adjust the number of shots (from 1 to 10) you want to take with ⏱. Press **ISO** to return to Shooting mode.

3) Compose your shot and press the shutter-release button down halfway. A green frame should surround the main face in your composition. A white frame will be displayed around other faces. Press the shutter-release button down fully.

4) Look straight at camera to start countdown will be displayed on the LCD. The front lamp will blink and the self-timer sound will be played.

5) When the camera detects a new face in the scene, the speed of the lamp blinking will increase: 2 seconds later the shutter will fire. Press **MENU** if you wish to cancel the ⏱ countdown.

> **Note:**
> The shutter will fire automatically if no new face is detected within 15 seconds of the shutter-release button being pressed down.

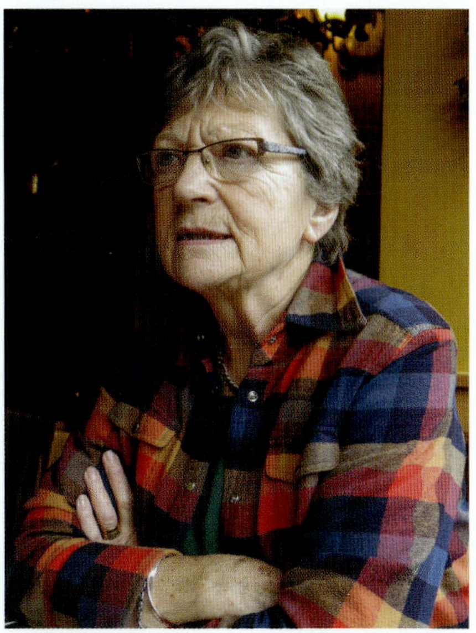

WINDOW LIGHT ⌃
Light from north-facing windows is an attractive, soft light that is ideal for portraiture.

⊞ is a mode that is making its debut on the G16. There are three ways to use ⊞.

The first, ⊞, allows you to shoot the night sky as a single exposure, lasting approximately 3 seconds.

The second, ⊞, enables you to shoot a number of shots (the shutter speed is determined by the G16) over an extended period of up to 2 hours to create a star trail image. The star trail image is created by the camera blending the individual shots.

The final mode, ⊞, is similar to ⊞, but rather than create a single blended image, the G16 creates a time-lapse movie using the images shot.

As there is so little light at night the various starry sky modes require your G16 to be mounted onto a tripod (⊞ and ⊞ particularly need a stable base). The use of a remote release is also recommended, and as the camera is shooting don't be tempted to move around—you may either bump into the camera or, if the tripod is on soft ground, cause one of the tripod legs to sink relative to the others.

Shoot on moonless nights and away from urban lighting. The darker the sky, the more stars will be recorded during the exposure(s). The lights from commercial aircraft will be recorded if they fly across the image space during exposure. These will be seen as straight lines of light rather than the circular pattern of the star trails.

Meteors will produce a similar effect, although these are less common except during meteor showers.

> **Notes:**
> In ⊞ the lens is set to 🔼 and can't be altered.
>
> Use a freshly charged battery before you begin shooting.
>
> There are several items on the 📷 menu that are applicable to ⊞: **Star Emphasis** (⊞ only), **Save ⊞ Stills** (⊞ only), and **Night Display**. See chapter 4 for details.
>
> If you turn your camera off, the memory card fills up, or the batteries deplete before ⊞ and ⊞ are finished, the images created before that point will still be saved to the memory card.

Using 🖼️

1) Mount your G16 on a stable tripod.

2) Select 🎆, press **ISO**, and then press ◄ / ► or turn ⚙️ to highlight 🖼️.

3) Press **ISO** to return to Shooting mode.

4) Turn 🕹️ to set the length of time the G16 will shoot. You can choose a value between 10 and 120 minutes.

5) Press the shutter-release button down fully to begin shooting. Either use self-timer or a remote release to reduce the risk of knocking the camera as it begins shooting.

6) When the G16 has finished shooting, **Busy** will be displayed on the LCD and the images will be processed and merged. You can't view the final image or shoot again until the processing is complete.

Using 🎞️

1) Follow steps 1–3 (left), this time selecting 🎞️ instead of 🖼️.

2) Turn 🕹️ to set the length of time the G16 will shoot: you can choose a value of between 60 and 120 minutes. A 60-minute movie will last approximately 4 seconds when viewed; a 120-minute movie will last approximately 8 seconds.

3) Press the shutter-release button down fully to shoot a test image. Adjust the exposure compensation dial if necessary.

4) Press the movie record button to begin shooting (and again to stop recording before the selected time has elapsed).

› Handheld Night Scene 🔲

After sunset (or before sunrise) light levels are generally very low. This usually requires the use of slow shutter speeds that are just too long to handhold successfully. One solution is to increase the ISO, but this increases the noise in the image, reducing image quality. Another solution is to use a tripod, which is fine if you have one.

🔲 Handheld Night Scene mode is Canon's solution to shooting in low light, avoiding the problems of image noise when a high ISO is used and the fact that you may not have a tripod.

The mode works by increasing the ISO (up to 6400) to maintain a reasonable shutter speed and then firing a rapid sequence of shots as you hold down the shutter-release button. To reduce noise, the G16 blends the sequence of shots together to produce the final image (this blending requires a few seconds after the exposure has been made, so using 🔲 isn't a rapid process).

Generally, this mode works well, allowing you to shoot handheld in low-light situations. However, it's not perfect. Like the G16's **HDR** mode, any movement during the sequence will be recorded as odd artifacts in the final image. If you don't mind that limitation (and if your subject is relatively still) you'll find that image noise is far lower in comparison to shooting in other modes with a high ISO.

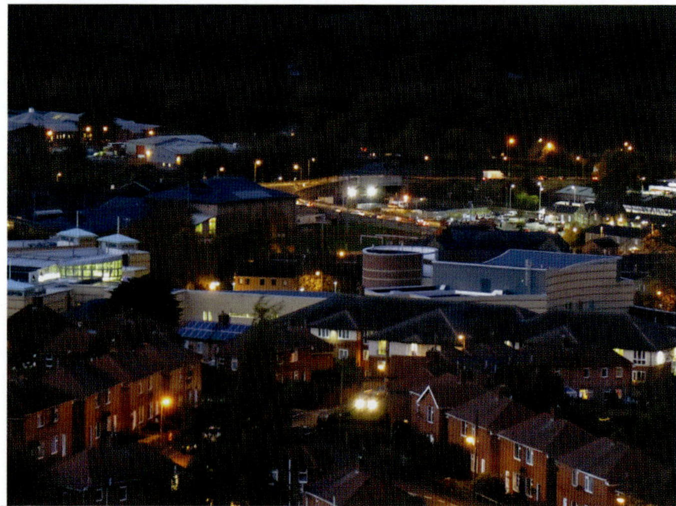

DUSK «
For best results using 🔲, shoot at dusk, approximately half an hour after sunset.

› Underwater 🐠

Your G16 can be taken underwater to a depth of 130ft (40m) if it is enclosed inside Canon's optional WP-DC52 Waterproof Case. 🐠 mode configures your G16 to shoot natural-looking images once you're underwater, altering the WB to compensate for the color shifts found in the inky depths.

Shooting successful underwater images means taking into account a different set of challenges. Water is far denser than air and light levels drop very rapidly the deeper you go. The color of light changes as well: the red end of the visible light spectrum is rapidly absorbed by water, so red objects can appear very muddy even when they are only a short distance from the camera. For these two reasons it's important to get as close to your subject as possible.

One solution to the lack of light at depth is to use a flash. However, the closer a flash is to the lens axis of a camera the greater the risk of backscatter. This is caused by particles in the water reflecting the light from the flash straight back toward the camera. The WP-DC52 Waterproof Case has a diffuser to reduce this effect with the G16's built-in flash, but if you have an external strobe you would get far better results using that, positioned away from the camera.

AQUARIUM ⊗

If you try shooting in an aquarium, clean the glass to remove any marks or fingerprints before you shoot.

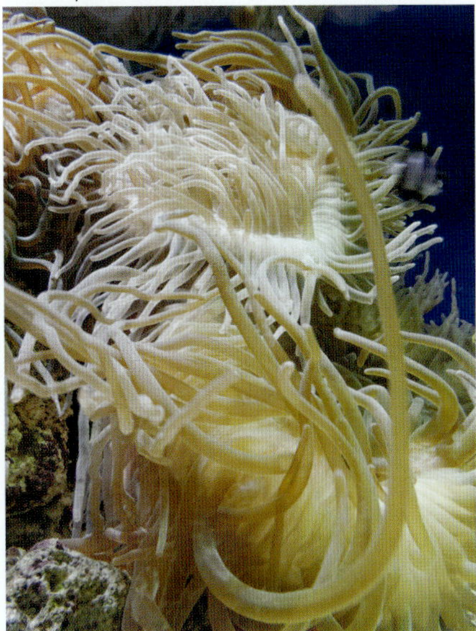

Notes:
If you don't like the idea of getting wet, use 🐠 mode at your local aquarium. Lots of modern aquariums have clear tunnels that allow you to walk "underwater." Don't use the flash, and keep the lens pressed against the glass to avoid reflections.

🐠 mode has two extra AF modes: 🐟 and ⇶📷. Use these modes for shooting macro and fast-moving subjects respectively.

There probably isn't a photographer working today who isn't excited by the prospect of snow. Snow turns a mundane landscape into a magical winter wonderland, but creating correctly exposed images of snow can prove problematical. As with sand on a beach, snow can cause problems with metering (typically causing your camera to underexpose). The G16's Snow scene mode takes care of these problems, leaving you to shoot without worry.

The best time to be out shooting a snow-covered landscape is just after the snow has fallen. This means that the snow will be undisturbed by footprints and won't look dirty. If snow has fallen overnight, you should be prepared to be out shooting at first light—once the sun has risen, the low raking light of morning will help emphasize the textural qualities of the snow.

Snow falls because it's cold, and this can prove detrimental to both you and your G16. If you plan to be outside for a long period of time, ensure that you wrap up warmly. This is particularly important when you're standing around for long periods of time. Carrying a chemical hand warmer is a good idea—it's difficult to use the G16's controls when wearing gloves so you'll need something to take the chill out of your fingers.

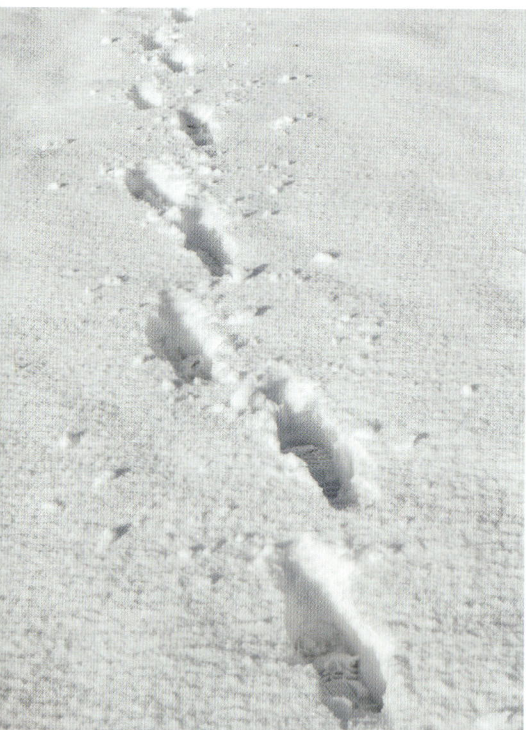

> **Tip**
>
> *Don't let falling snow settle on your camera: wipe it off before it has a chance to melt.*

SIMPLE «
One of the exciting things about snow is that it simplifies the landscape, allowing you to shoot simple, minimalist images.

› Fireworks ✦

Every country seems to have at least one day in the year when a firework display is part of the day's events. This regularity makes the job of preparation for the photographer far easier.

The first step in the preparation process is to find out where a display is to be held. Try to visit the location before nightfall, as this will allow you to find the best vantage point. Ideally, you need to be some distance from the area where the fireworks are to be launched, unless you want to be looking up all evening.

For obvious reasons, firework displays generally take place at night, and this means that light levels will be low, necessitating the use of a tripod to keep the camera steady. To make life easier it's worth investing in a remote release: using one will help you avoid knocking the camera as the shutter is fired.

Most organized firework displays have a certain rhythm, with larger, more impressive fireworks spaced out between smaller ones. Once you've worked out the rhythm it becomes surprisingly easy to work out when a big firework is about to explode. Displays also often build up to a dramatic climax, so knowing the planned length of the display is useful, as it means that you will be ready for the finale. Just be sure to leave space on your memory card!

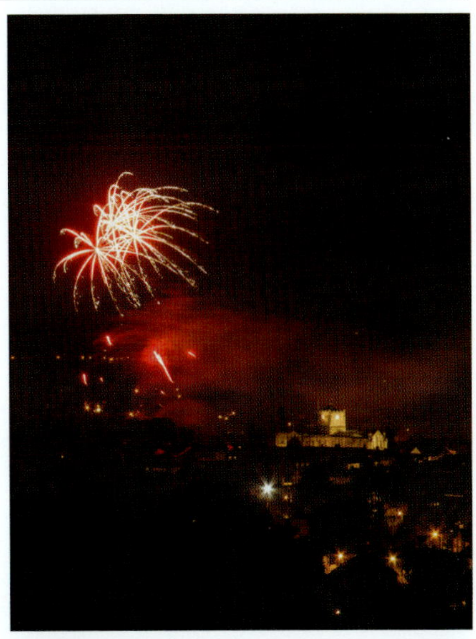

RHYTHM ⌃
Don't fill your memory card with images early in an organized firework display: most organized displays build up to a big finish.

> ### Tip
>
> *Keep a spare battery handy if it's a particularly cold night.*

Your G16 has 10 ⊖ Image Effect modes that allow you to produce images with an artistic twist. Several of these effects are based around the visual quirks of specific types of cameras or lenses. ⟦📷⟧ mode mimics the types of images created by film-based toy cameras, for example, while 🐟, 🔭, and 🌲 digitally recreate the look of images shot using particular types of lenses on a DSLR camera. Other effects are based on techniques that can be achieved using image-editing software.

As with **SCN**, ⊖ is highly automated—the grid on page 90–91 details what can (or cannot) be set in each ⊖ mode. It is also worth noting that once an image has been captured using ⊖ you can't undo the effect.

Setting an Image Effect mode

1) Turn the mode dial to ⊖.

2) Press (FUNC SET) and highlight **HDR** (shown by default; once you've chosen another ⊖ mode the icon for that mode will be displayed subsequently).

3) Use ◀ / ▶ or ⬤ to highlight the required ⊖ Image Effect mode and then press (FUNC SET) to return to shooting mode.

4) If there are any options for the selected ⊖ they will be displayed on screen (and are noted in the pages that follow).

5) Lightly press halfway down on the shutter-release button to focus, and then fully to take the photograph.

6) The captured photograph will be shown on the LCD for 2 seconds, unless the default review time has been adjusted.

> **Note:**
> You can only shoot JPEG when using ⊖.

» BOLD

The ⬭ modes generally benefit from fairly simple compositions. A lot of detail is often lost (particularly when using 🏬, the mode used for this image), so it doesn't pay to create fussy, over-detailed images.

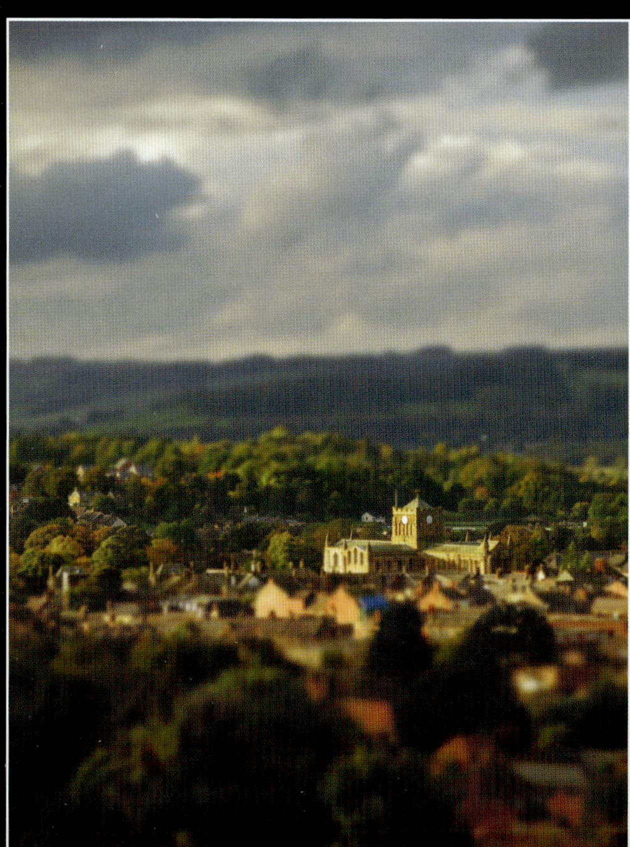

Function		HDR	⏲	🎆	🎇
JPEG settings	L	Y	Y	Y	Y
	M1, M2, S	–	–	–	–
	S (RAW)	–	–	–	–
	(RAW)	Y	Y	Y	Y
Change aspect ratio		–	–	–	Y
Self-timer		Y	Y	Y	Y
Drive mode	☐	Y	Y	Y	Y
	A⏵	–	–	–	–
	⏵⏵	–	Y	Y	Y
	AF⏵	–	Y	Y	Y
Exposure compensation		Y	Y	Y	Y
ISO	ISO AUTO	Y	Y	Y	Y
	ISO 100 – ISO 12800	–	–	–	–
White balance	AWB	Y	Y	Y	Y
	☀–p📷🔆	–	–	–	–
	◨¹ ◨²	–	–	–	–
WB correction		–	–	–	–
Flash	⚡A	–	Y	Y	Y
	⚡	–	Y	Y	Y
	⚡★	–	–	–	–
	🚫⚡	Y	Y	Y	Y
Metering	◉	Y	Y	Y	Y
	▯, ◉	–	–	–	–
Focusing	▲A	Y	Y	Y	Y
	🌷	Y	Y	Y	Y
	🌼, ≡📷	–	–	–	–
	MF / AF Lock	Y	Y	Y	Y
Alter AF frame position		–	–	–	–
Alter AF frame size		–	Y	–	–
Face select		Y	Y	–	–
Tracking AF		–	Y	–	–
Bracketing	OFF	Y	Y	Y	Y
	▱	–	–	–	–
	▱F	–	–	–	–
DR Correction	OFF	Y	Y	Y	Y
	AUTO	–	–	–	–
	200% 400%	–	–	–	–
Shadow Correct	OFF	Y	Y	Y	Y
	AUTO	–	–	–	–

📷	🏔	👤	◨	🏎	🎬
Y	Y	Y	Y	Y	Y
–	–	–	–	–	–
–	–	–	–	–	–
Y	–	Y	Y	Y	Y
–	–	–	Y	Y	Y
Y	Y	Y	Y	Y	Y
Y	Y	Y	Y	Y	Y
–	–	–	–	–	–
Y	–	Y	Y	Y	Y
Y	–	Y	Y	Y	Y
Y	Y	Y	Y	Y	–
Y	Y	Y	Y	Y	Y
–	–	–	–	–	–
Y	Y	Y	Y	Y	Y
–	–	–	–	–	–
–	–	–	–	–	–
–	–	–	–	–	–
Y	–	Y	Y	Y	Y
Y	–	Y	Y	Y	Y
–	–	–	–	–	–
Y	Y	Y	Y	Y	Y
Y	Y	Y	Y	Y	Y
–	–	–	–	–	–
Y	Y	Y	Y	Y	Y
Y	Y	Y	Y	Y	Y
–	–	–	–	–	–
Y	–	Y	Y	Y	Y
–	–	–	–	–	–
Y	–	Y	Y	Y	Y
Y	Y	Y	Y	Y	Y
–	–	–	Y	Y	Y
Y	Y	Y	Y	Y	Y
–	–	–	–	–	–
–	–	–	–	–	–
Y	Y	Y	Y	Y	Y
–	–	–	–	–	–
–	–	–	–	–	–
Y	Y	Y	Y	Y	Y
–	–	–	–	–	–

Cameras often struggle with high contrast scenes, but HDR (High Dynamic Range) imaging can help. HDR usually involves shooting several different images of a scene, bracketing the exposure between shots to capture a full range of tones. These images are then blended together using specialist HDR software.

However, the G16's **HDR** mode does away with the need for this postproduction step: when you press the shutter-release button, the G16 captures three images and blends them in-camera to produce a single HDR image. This image should preserve details in both the shadows and highlights, making it closer to how the human eye would see the scene.

The drawback of HDR is that you need to keep your G16 perfectly still until all three images have been exposed, which in a scene with low levels of light could take several seconds. This makes it almost impossible to achieve good results without a tripod and remote release (or Self-Timer).

HDR options

Press **ISO** to change how the image sequence is blended.

ART BOLD
With the exception of Natural, the G16's HDR effects aren't subtle.

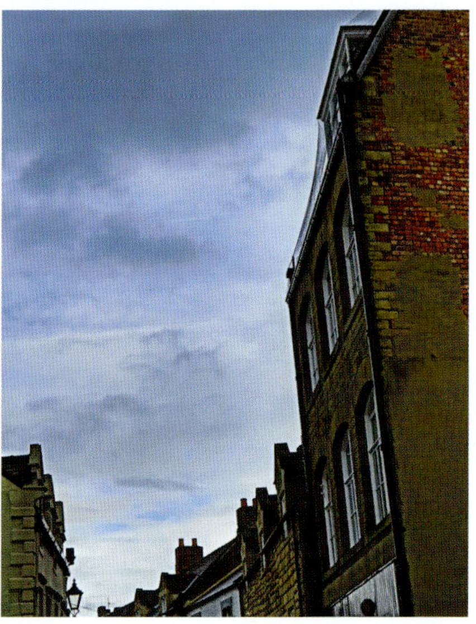

Effect Result	
Natural	Creates natural-looking images.
Art Standard	Edge contrast increased and colors more saturated than Natural.
Art Vivid	Color saturation increased over Natural and Art Standard.
Art Bold	Creates saturated images with high contrast.
Art Embossed	Edge contrast at maximum resulting in halos appearing around high-contrast edges. Color less saturated than other Art modes.

› Nostalgic ⏱

⏱ is the mode to use if you want to give your images a more timeless quality. This is achieved by altering how much color is leached out of them and by adding film-like grain.

When shooting with ⏱ set to maximum, you need to be careful of contrast. If the lighting creates high contrast (particularly if your subject is highly reflective) you'll find that highlights and shadows will be lost more quickly than when shooting using other modes. Shooting in softer light will therefore help you retain a greater range of tones.

To make your photos appear more authentically nostalgic think about composition too. Photographs from the Victorian period and into the early 20th century were more formally composed than you'd see today (this is particularly true of portraiture). Our ancestors weren't that serious, it's just that the limitations of low sensitivity film meant they had to maintain a pose for seconds at a time. If you really want to emulate this style, think carefully about your subject and your way of shooting—taking photographs from unusual angles is a relatively recent development, so use the G16's electronic level to keep your camera straight and parallel to your subject.

Nostalgic options

Turn ⛭ to the left to decrease the amount of grain and color loss, or to the right to increase the grain and remove the color.

HALLOWEEN ⯆

A skeleton in a shop window framed by the reflections on the window. Because of the relative darkness of the shop interior you can't make out any details, other than the skeleton.

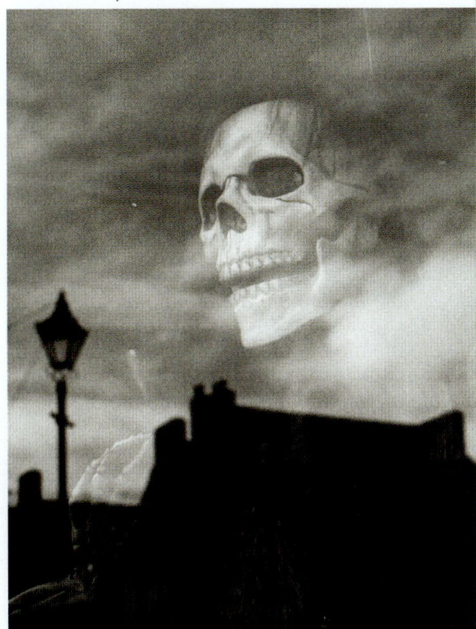

A fish-eye lens is a specific type of lens that has an extremely wide angle of view—often 180° or greater. This means that everything in front of the camera will be included in the final image, including the photographer's feet if care isn't taken!

The G16's Fish-eye mode cannot replicate this specific trait, but it can emulate the extreme distortion exhibited by this type of lens. In images shot using a fish-eye lens, lines that should be straight are bent into curves, so the image no longer appears natural. It's not a lens that would be used often, as the effect quickly looks gimmicky with repetition. It's also not a great portrait technique!

However, it can be very effective when shooting architectural subjects—especially modern architecture. The G16's Fish-eye mode distorts the image in-camera to produce a reasonable approximation of a fish-eye lens. The mode can be used with the lens set at any focal length, but looks more "true" when used at the widest end of the G16's zoom.

Fish-eye options
Turn to the left to decrease the strength of the fish-eye effect or to the right to increase it.

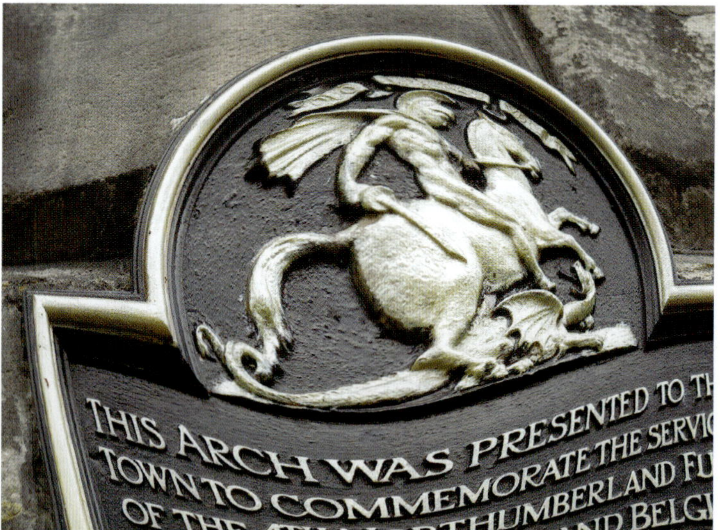

SQUARE «
works best with subjects that are very geometric, rather than soft and organic shapes.

› Miniature

Shooting macro with larger format cameras such as DSLRs often means creating images with a very small depth of field. This gives macro imagery a particular look, in which there is only a very small zone of sharpness with most of the image soft and out of focus. We've become so used to seeing this, that we're inclined to see images with a very limited depth of field as macro shots.

The G16's mode exploits this peculiarity of human perception by blurring out large areas of an image so that even large vistas look like model sets. The effect isn't achieved using maximum aperture (which would be ineffective on the G16), but by selectively blurring parts of the image as a processed effect. Simple compositions work best in mode, with your main subject placed precisely in the area of sharp focus.

Miniature options

The area of the image that is sharp and in focus is within a white frame. Press **ISO** to select the Miniature mode options. Use to move the frame up and down, or left and right across the screen. The zoom lever can be used to increase or decrease the size of the frame (increasing and decreasing the zone of sharpness respectively). To change the orientation of the frame use ▲ / ▼ when the frame is vertical or ◄ / ► when it is horizontal. Press **ISO** to return to the main Shooting screen. Movies can also be shot using mode (see page 107).

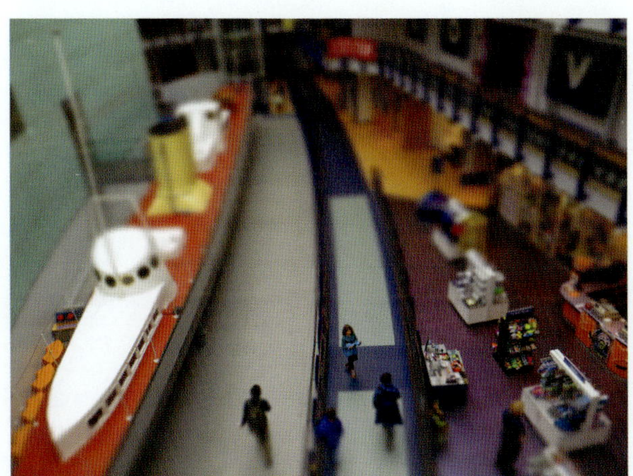

PEOPLE «
Including people in your shots can add another surreal layer to the image.

› Toy Camera 📷

A toy camera is a cheaply made film camera. Generally, every part of a toy camera is made of plastic, including the lens, and because of this the images shot with a toy camera have a particular aesthetic, often with unusual color casts and lens distortions. On some cameras, the image circle projected by the lens isn't large enough to expose the whole of the film frame correctly, which leads to vignetting, with the corners of the image noticeably darker than the center.

It may seem odd to deliberately use a camera that is so lacking in technical quality, but toy cameras are popular and have a cult following. Indeed, it's the shortcomings of toy cameras that makes them so appealing: they are the antithesis of digital perfection.

The G16's Toy Camera mode replicates the aesthetics of a toy camera, by darkening and softening the edges of the image. As the sharpest part of the image is the center, it's a good idea to keep your subject somewhere in the middle of the frame. This mode is also more suited to simpler compositions, so keep your shots uncluttered and use just one or two elements, rather than many.

Toy Camera options
Turn ⚙ to change the color tone of your image. Standard (the default) produces relatively normal colors, while Warm and Cool add more red and blue to the image respectively.

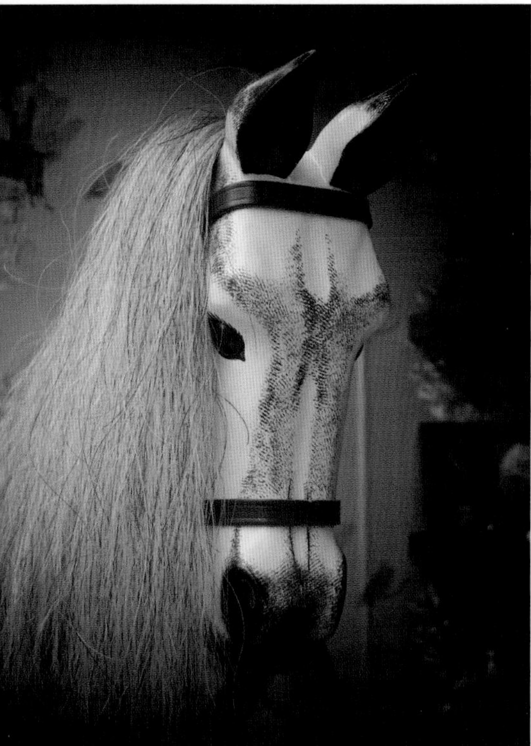

CENTRAL «
Keep you subject roughly in the middle of the composition so that it's less affected by the darkened edges of 📷.

› Background Defocus

Thanks to the small size of the G16's sensor and the resulting short focal length of the lens it's easy to achieve front-to-back sharpness. What's more difficult is creating a shallow depth of field so that only a narrow slice of the image is sharp.

is Canon's solution to the problem. It works by taking two shots in rapid succession and processing the results so that the background in the final image is more out of focus than would normally be possible. It works to a point, but it can't match the effect that's achievable when shooting with a larger sensor camera such as a DSLR.

As the camera is taking two shots, you need to keep it steadier than you would for modes such as . In low light, when the shutter speed will be relatively long, you'll also need to mount the camera on a tripod and make sure that your subject doesn't move during the two exposures. If the image cannot be processed, will be displayed on screen and you'll need to reshoot.

Background Defocus options

Turn to select the strength of the effect, choosing between **Low**, **Medium**, and **High**. **Auto** adjusts the strength of the effect automatically.

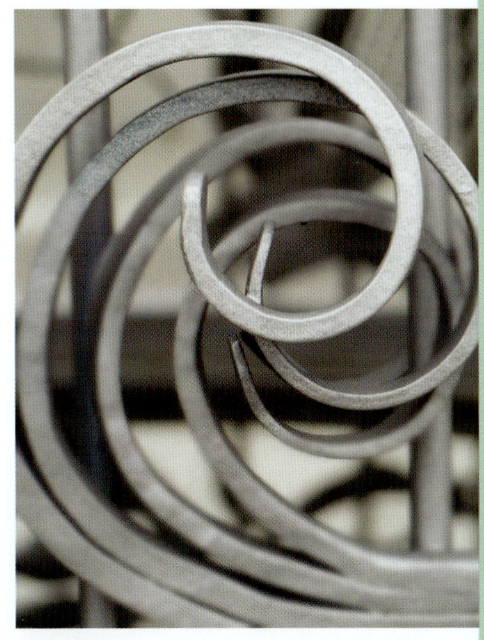

CLUTTER
can help cut down some of the visual clutter when a background is visually busy.

A traditional soft focus filter is usually used when shooting portraits. The filter softens details and makes skin blemishes less noticeable. The filter also helps to convey a romantic feel to an image as it slightly reduces contrast too.

 does away with the need to fit a filter as it creates the same effect electronically. Soft focus is arguably an effect that would suit a female subject better than a male, although that shouldn't stop you from experimenting. Try shooting your subject under soft lighting for maximum effect.

There's also no reason why you shouldn't use the effect on other subjects. Landscape photographers are generally more concerned with achieving maximum sharpness across an image, but the soft focus effect will allow you to take more romantic landscape images.

Soft Focus options
Turn to the right to increase the amount of softening and to the left to decrease it.

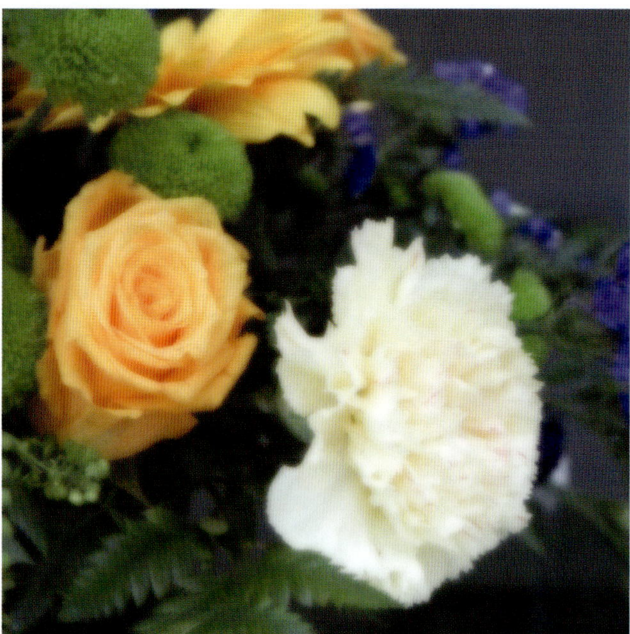

FLORAL «
Flowers benefit from the soft approach as this helps to hide any small blemishes on the blooms.

› Monochrome ◿

Monochrome produces images that are stripped of color. The lightness of a gray pixel in the image is determined by the intensity of light that is reflected back to the camera by an object in the scene: the less light an object reflects, the darker the pixel; the more light, the brighter the pixel.

However, some objects that are different colors have similar levels of reflectivity. This means they will share similar gray values when rendered in a monochrome image, making the image appear "flat."

The solution is to use colored filters. These filters block color that is on the opposite side of a standard color wheel to the filter, and increase the brightness of colors that are similar. For landscape photography, yellow, orange, and red filters are often used as these filters lighten greens slightly and darken blue. Portrait photographers would be more likely to use green filters to enhance skin tones.

The G16 doesn't have a facility to replicate these filters electronically, but traditional colored filters can be added in front of the lens using the optional FA-DC58B filter adapter.

Alternatively, shoot in color and convert your images to monochrome using your software if it features color filters.

Monochrome options

Turn ⚙ to change the color tint of your image. **B/W** (the default) produces neutral grays; **Sepia** and **Blue** add more red and blue to the image respectively.

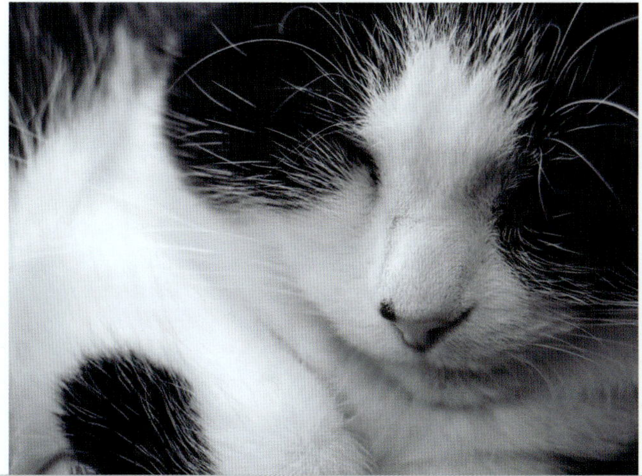

COOL «
Blue adds an appealing coolness to your black-and-white images.

mode increases the vividness (also known as the saturation) of the colors in your images. This makes the images punchier and far from realistic, and isn't the one to choose if you want subtlety. Some subjects—such as portraiture or landscapes—won't necessarily benefit from the colors being pushed in such a way (faces can look too florid and landscapes can appear garish), but subjects that are already bold in color may benefit from an extra push: modern architecture works well, as do events such as carnivals and fairgrounds. Discovering what works is part of the mode's fun, so experimentation is the key.

Be warned, though: can lead to disappointment when the resulting images are printed. Printers have a far smaller color gamut than a computer monitor, so they can't reproduce the same range of colors as a monitor can display. As a result, an image that looks good on screen may appear flat or muddy when printed. To get the best results you may need to desaturate the color slightly in your image-editing software before printing.

Poster Effect reduces the tonal range of your images, so that images become composed of areas of flat color. This effect is also known as *posterization*, and as with Super Vivid, the effect isn't subtle. It's best suited to simple subjects—subjects that are highly detailed are less effective when shot using . For inspiration try looking at the work of artists such as Andy Warhol, who often produced artwork that relied on a flat, poster-like style.

Super Vivid and Poster Effect

There are no options for these modes.

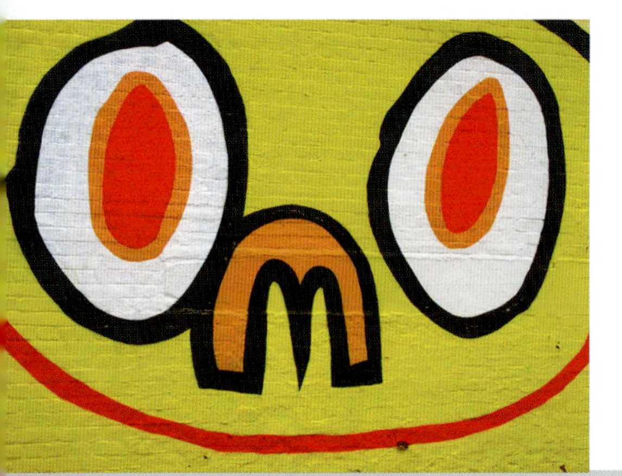

IMPACT «

For maximum impact look for subjects that are already boldly colored.

» LIGHT

Successful monochrome photography is arguably more dependent on the quality of light than color photography is. "Moody" lighting that creates contrast will add drama to a monochrome image. In this image there was no direct light on the foreground due to the stormy sky, but the streams of water picked up ambient light from above, which adds interest (and contrast) to the foreground.

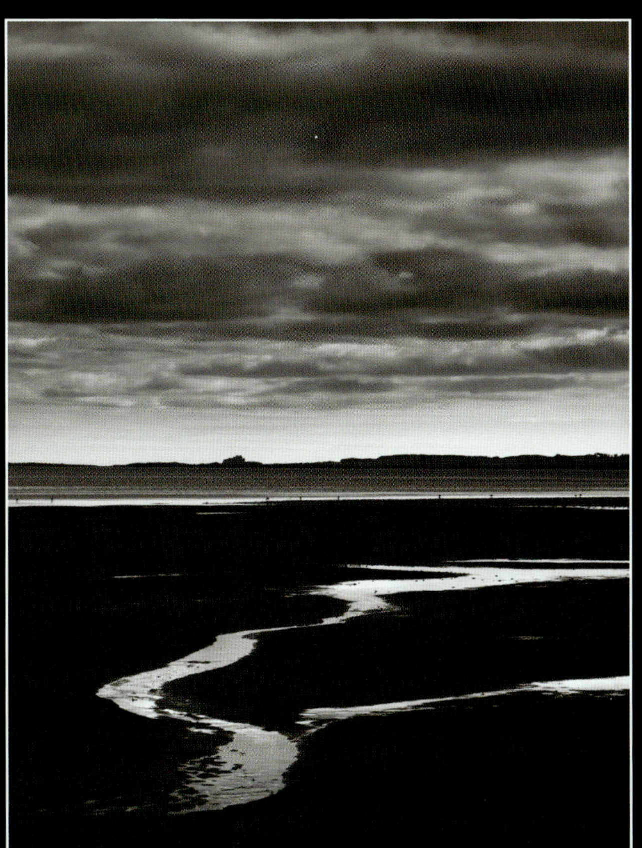

Settings
> Focal length: 25mm
> Exposure: 1/500 sec. at f/4.5
> ISO: 80

3 MOVIES

The PowerShot G16 is not just capable of shooting still images; it is also able to shoot movies. Unlike most compact cameras the G16 can shoot at Full HD resolution.

In some ways, shooting movies is similar to shooting stills, but in other ways it is quite different. When composing a movie sequence you have to be aware of changes that could occur as you shoot, for example. This is typically either because something moves in, out, or around the scene, or because the camera itself moves.

The latter is often the hardest to get right: if the camera doesn't move smoothly the sequence will be uncomfortable to watch. If the movement is too extreme it may even cause nausea in the viewer, so if you want to move the camera while shooting, do it slowly and smoothly. If you do move the camera rapidly, try to limit the length of time this footage is used for.

The G16 allows you to use image stabilization when shooting movies. This makes a handheld sequence less prone to random and disconcerting movement, but for better stability you should consider using a tripod. A tripod with a dedicated video head will give you the ultimate platform to shoot movies from, allowing you to make smooth movements as you tilt or pan with your camera.

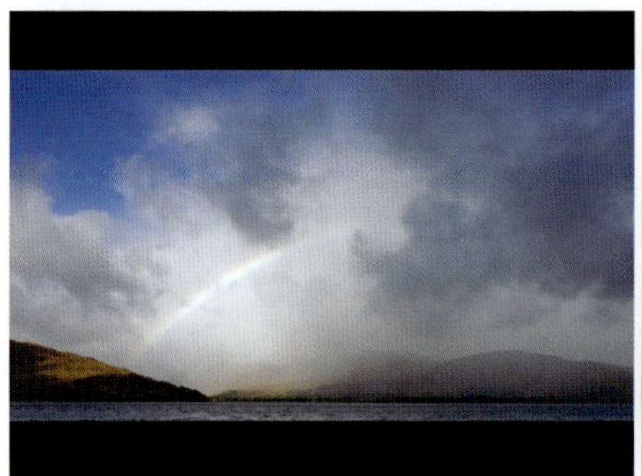

ZOOM ⌃
Although it's possible to zoom when shooting a movie, it is not recommended.

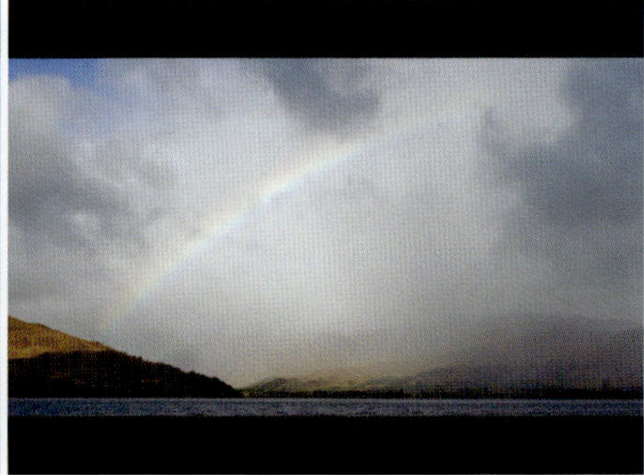

MOVEMENT »
A movie sequence is arguably better at capturing the effects of movement than a still image.

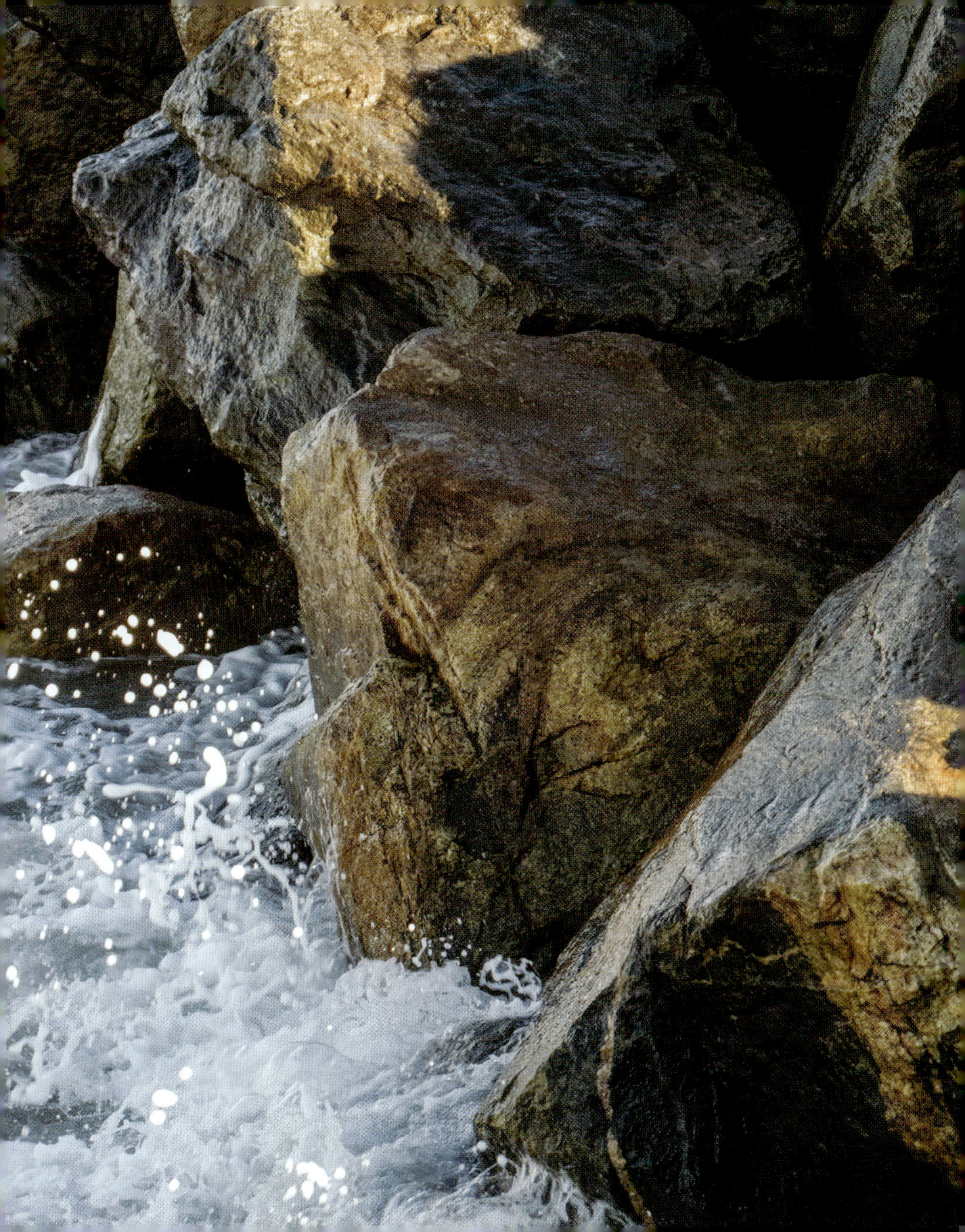

As you shoot a movie with your G16, the resulting data is compressed. Without this in-camera compression the space needed to store a movie on a memory card would be huge, but even compressed movie files can fill a small memory card quickly. If you plan to shoot movies on a regular basis it's definitely worth considering buying one or two high-capacity memory cards and keeping them solely for the purpose of recording movies.

The method that's used to compress video on the G16 is relatively simple in concept. Imagine a movie with just two frames and these two frames are identical. Instead of storing the full image data for the two frames, you could store the data for the first frame and then specify that the same information be used again for the second frame (or for however many frames you needed). The G16's compression is slightly subtler, but the principle is the same: as a movie is recorded, the G16 analyzes the differences between frames and only stores those areas that are different (essentially reusing data for areas that haven't changed between frames).

This is a very efficient way of reducing the file size of a movie to manageable proportions. However, the more visually "busy" the scene is—if there's lots of fast movement, for example, or if the camera moves during recording—the less well the compression works. Therefore, you will find that movies of equal duration may vary in the amount of space they take up on a memory card.

Notes:
The G16 can only shoot movies up to 4GB in size. Once a movie file reaches this size, shooting will stop automatically. A memory card larger than 4GB is therefore more useful for storing multiple movie clips, rather than one large movie.

Memory card space isn't the only issue when shooting movies. There's a lot of data being transferred from the camera to the memory card as a movie records, so it's advisable to use a memory card with a fast read/write time. The use of a memory card with a Class Rating of 6 or higher is recommended by Canon.

If you bought your G16 in the European Union, you will also be restricted to shooting movies that don't exceed 29 minutes and 59 seconds in duration.

› Movie files

The G16's movies are recorded using the MOV format. MOV is a "container" format that can generally be played back using a Windows PC or a Mac. However, not all MOV files are the same. The movie data in a MOV file can be compressed in a number of different ways, and in order to read the data, a computer needs a file known as a *codec*. A codec is used by the computer's movie player to decompress the movie data to a form that can be played back smoothly.

The G16 uses the common MP4/H.264 video compression standard, which is also used by Blu-ray players, YouTube, and many other platforms. Movie-editing software compatible with H.264 video encoding includes Final Cut Express for Mac OS X and Adobe Premiere Elements for both Windows and Mac.

However, one downside to MP4/H.264 is that the data needs to be decompressed by the software, which can make editing a laborious process if you are dealing with long or multiple movie clips. Many movie professionals will therefore convert their H.264 files to a less compressed format for the purposes of editing, even though the resulting movie file will require far more storage space.

Note:
H.264 is also known as MPEG 4 Part 10 and AVC (Advanced Video Coding).

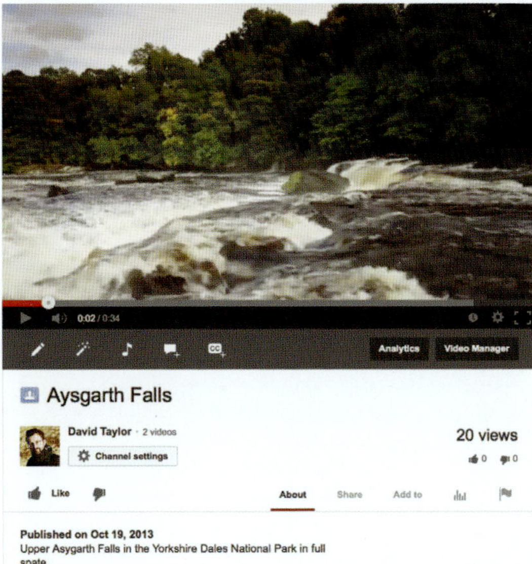

YOUTUBE «
Your G16 will allow you to shoot movies that can be uploaded to file sharing web sites, such as YouTube.

The G16 has a dedicated video record button. Although there is a setting on the mode dial, you can shoot video in any other mode simply by pressing the video record button on the back of the camera. However, you will have more control over your movie's settings when shooting with the Mode dial set to (although certain movie effects—such as —can only be used when shooting a movie with the mode dial set to a **SCN** or mode).

THE DEDICATED VIDEO RECORD BUTTON ⌄

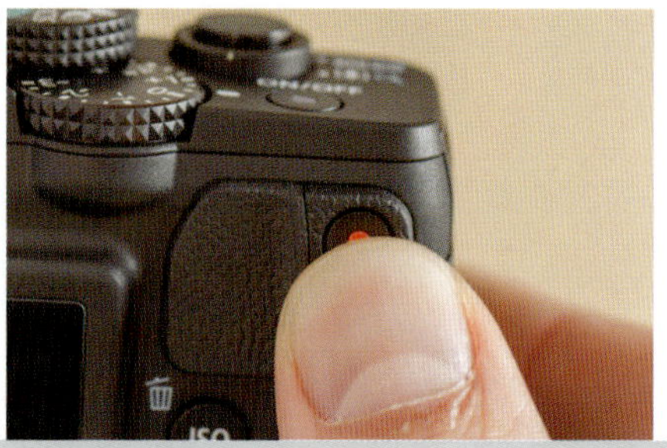

Shooting a movie

1) Turn the mode dial to .

2) Compose your shot using the zoom lever. Press (FUNC SET) to alter the movie settings as required.

3) Press the shutter-release button down halfway to focus (if **Mute** is set to **Off** the G16 will beep once to confirm focus lock).

4) Press the video record button on the back of the camera to start recording.

5) While recording, ●Rec will be displayed in orange at the right side of the LCD and the elapsed time will be displayed at the top of the screen.

6) Press the video record button again to stop recording.

> **Notes:**
> If you recompose your shot while you are shooting video footage, the exposure will alter if the lighting changes, and the focusing will also slowly adjust.
>
> You can still use the G16's zoom when shooting a movie, but the zoom action is slower than it is when shooting still images. The camera's microphones will pick up the noise of the lens motor.

› Exposure lock

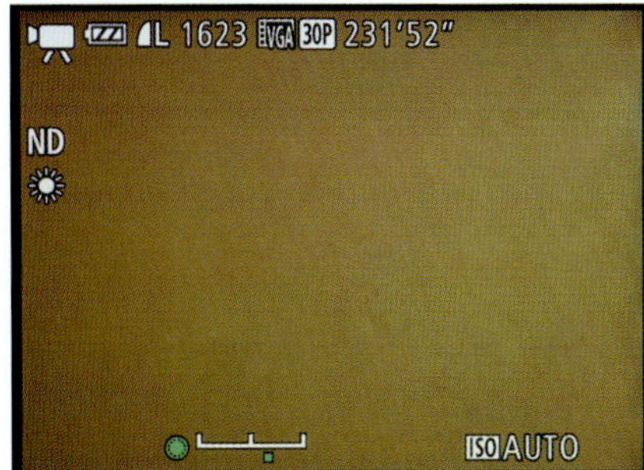

The G16 automatically controls the exposure of your movies, both before and during shooting. You can, however, override the exposure before you begin recording. The exposure can be adjusted up to ±3 stops in $^1/_3$-stop increments, and you can lock it at the level you prefer.

Setting exposure lock

1) Follow steps 1–3 for *Shooting a movie*.

2) Press the ✳ button. An exposure bar will be displayed at the bottom of the LCD. Turn ⚙ to the left to darken the exposure, or to the right to lighten it.

3) Press the video record button to begin recording your movie.

› Miniature mode

The effect of the mode is similar to that applied to still images when you choose the mode of the same name. To use the effect, set the Mode dial to and then choose . Press **ISO** and follow the instructions on page 95 to set the position of the sharp and blurred areas.

Miniature mode differs from the other movie modes in that you can't shoot at the standard frame rate. Instead, you must choose between 5x, 10x, or 20x speed. This will cause any motion in the movie to be sped up: a 1 minute clip will last just 3 seconds at 20x speed, for example. To alter the movie speed turn , and once you've made your choice press **ISO** to return to shooting mode. Press the video record button to start recording. Note that audio is not recorded in Miniature mode.

Note:
Movies shot using are restricted to an aspect ratio of 4:3 and a resolution of VGA, or 16:9 and a resolution of HD.

» FUNC. SET OPTIONS

As with still image shooting, pressing (FUNC. SET) in ►🎥 mode allows you to set the movie shooting functions. These settings will affect how your movies are recorded. Several of these functions have the same effect as they do with still images, and have been covered previously (white balance, My Colors, ND filter, and Self-Timer).

› Movie mode

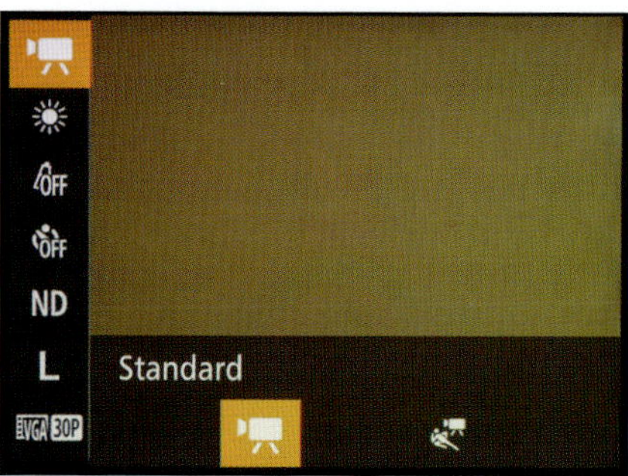

The G16 has two different movie modes: Standard ►🎥 and Super Slow Motion Movie 🎥. If you shoot using 🎥, the clip will be replayed in slow motion. This is particularly useful if you're shooting fast moving action, but the penalties for shooting using 🎥 are a reduced movie resolution (compared to ►🎥), no sound recording, and a maximum clip length of 30 seconds.

Using 🎥 mode

1) Turn the mode dial to ►🎥.

2) Press (FUNC. SET), highlight ►🎥, and then press ► to highlight 🎥.

3) Press ▼ to highlight QVGA 240P. Press ◄ / ► to highlight your preferred frame rate and then press (FUNC. SET).

4) Press the video record button to start recording.

> **Notes:**
> Touching the G16's microphones during movie capture may cause unwanted sound to be recorded.
>
> You can't zoom when shooting 🎥 movies.

Super Slow Motion Movie options		
Frame rate	**Resolution**	**Playback time (30 second clip)**
QVGA 240P	320 x 240 pixels	Approx. 4 minutes
VGA 120P	640 x 480 pixels	Approx. 2 minutes

› Movie resolution

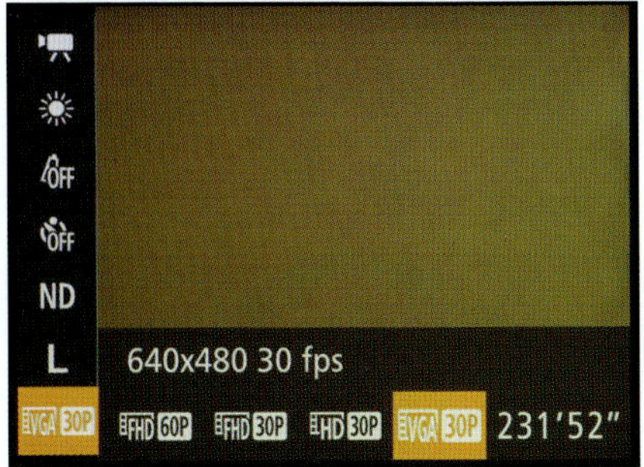

When shooting using movie mode you can choose between three resolution settings: FHD, HD, and VGA.

FHD is the highest resolution file and can be shot using one of two frame rates: 60P and 30P. The frame rate refers to the number of individual frames shot each second. 60P will produce smoother looking movies (particularly when you're shooting fast action), and it's also more suitable for

slowing footage down in postproduction. However, 30P is arguably the more "filmic" of the two, as it's closer to the standard 24fps rate of a film movie camera. It is also more effective in low light.

FHD will give you better image quality than HD or VGA, but it will also use up the space on your memory card more quickly. VGA will take up the least amount of space on your memory card (at the expense of image quality).

Note:
The F in FHD stands for Fine Detail Movie Processing. This is new technology that uses the G16's Digic 6 processor and sensor to capture more detail in a movie than was previously possible with a G-series camera.

Image quality	Notes
FHD 1920 x 1080 pixels 60P/30P	Suitable for 1080p HDTV or other high-resolution displays (16:9 aspect ratio).
HD 1280 x 720 pixels 30P	Suitable for 720p HDTV or other high-resolution displays (16:9 aspect ratio).
640 640 x 480 pixels 30P	Standard quality. Suitable for web site use or analog TV (4:3 aspect ratio).

» MOVIE CONTROL PANEL

Once you've shot a movie you can view and edit it using the G16's comprehensive movie control panel.

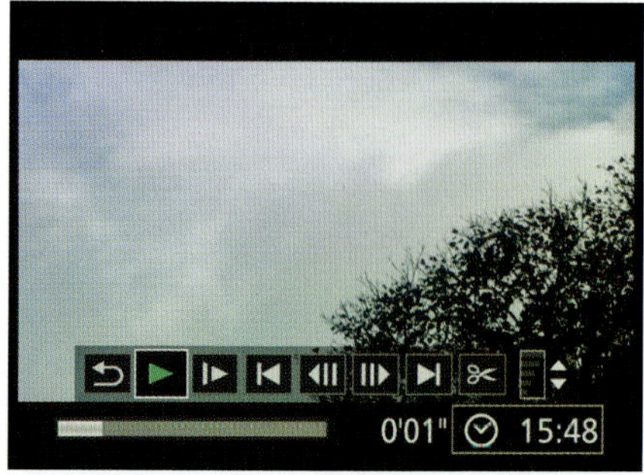

Using the movie control panel

1) Press ▶ and navigate to the movie you wish to view or edit. A movie is differentiated from a still image by a **SET** ▶ symbol displayed at the top left corner of the LCD.

2) Press (FUNC SET) to display the movie control panel on screen.

3) Press ◀ / ▶ or turn ⬤ to highlight an option on the control panel and then press (FUNC SET). Some options, such as ◀II, require you to hold down (FUNC SET).

4) Highlight ↶ and press (FUNC SET) to return to playback mode or lightly press down on the shutter-release button to go to shooting mode.

Playing a movie

1) Follow steps 1–2 in *Using the movie control panel*.

2) Highlight ▶ and press (FUNC SET) to begin playing the displayed movie. Press (FUNC SET) to pause the movie and return to the movie control panel. Press (FUNC SET) to continue playing the movie from the same point.

3) During movie playback press ▲ / ▼ to increase or decrease the movie volume respectively, or press ◀ / ▶ to skip quickly backward or forward through your movie.

4) When the movie has finished playing the first frame of the movie will be displayed on the LCD, with **SET** ▶ displayed at the top left corner once more.

Movie control panel

Symbol	Description
↺	Exit control panel
▶	Movie playback
I▶	Slow motion playback (press ◀ / ▶ or turn ⬤ to adjust playback speed)
◀I	Skip backward approximately 4 seconds (hold down (FUNC/SET) to skip backward continuously)
◀II	Jump back one frame (rewind with (FUNC/SET) held down)
II▶	Jump forward one frame (fast forward with (FUNC/SET) held down)
▶I	Skip forward approximately 4 seconds (hold down (FUNC/SET) to skip forward continuously)
✂	Edit movie
🗑	Delete clip
🖶	Displayed when a PictBridge printer is connected to G16

› Editing movies

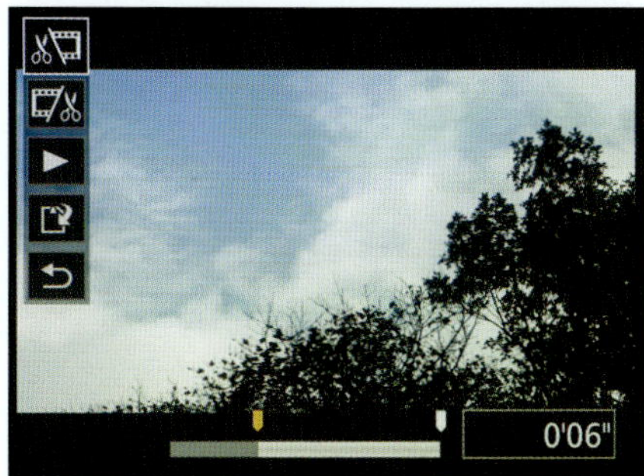

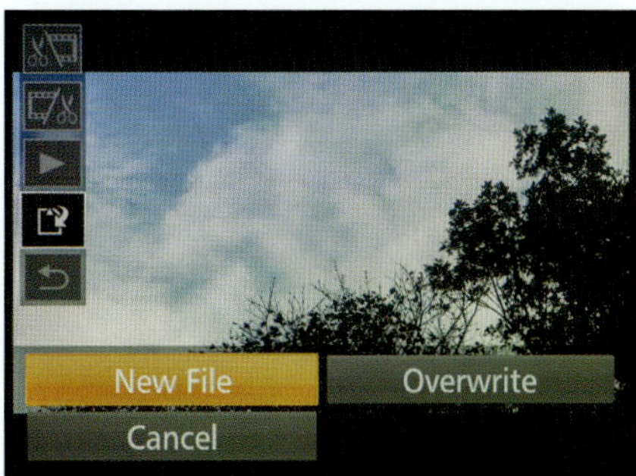

If your movies are too long you can edit (or trim) their length using the movie control panel. What you can't do is join separate movie clips together—that can only be done using third-party software in postproduction.

Trimming a movie

1) Follow steps 1–2 in *Using the movie control panel* on the page opposite.

2) Highlight ✂ and press (FUNC/SET) to display the movie editing screen.

3

3) Highlight ✂ to trim footage from the beginning of the selected movie, or ✂ to trim footage from the end.

4) Use ◀ / ▶ or ⚫ to move the orange ▼ edit point along the movie timeline. Movies can only be trimmed from points on the timeline where ✂ is displayed to the left of the movie timeline; when the edit point is moved and ✂ is not displayed, the movie will be trimmed to the nearest ✂ point. The lighter section between the two edit points on the timeline is the portion of the movie that will be kept after trimming.

5) Select ▶ to view the trimmed movie.

6) Select ⬆ to save the trimmed movie. Select **New File** to create a new movie; **Overwrite** to replace the original movie; or **Cancel** if you want to return to the movie editing screen without saving.

Notes:
At any point prior to step 6 you can highlight ↰ and press (FUNC SET) to return to the movie control panel. When asked to **Quit without saving**, highlight **Cancel** to return to the movie editing screen or highlight **OK** to return to the movie control panel. Press (FUNC SET) to confirm your choice.

If there is not sufficient space on the memory card you will only be able to **Overwrite** a movie at step 6.

JOINING TOGETHER ⌄
You can't join individual movies together on your G16. This has to be done using post-production software. When joining movies together think carefully about the sequence and how the individual movies relate to each other.

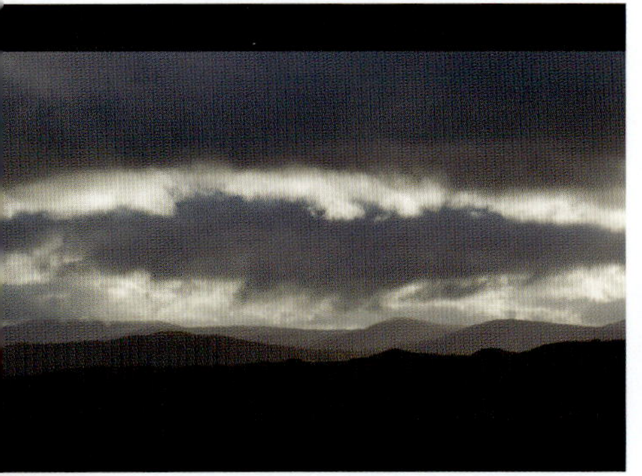

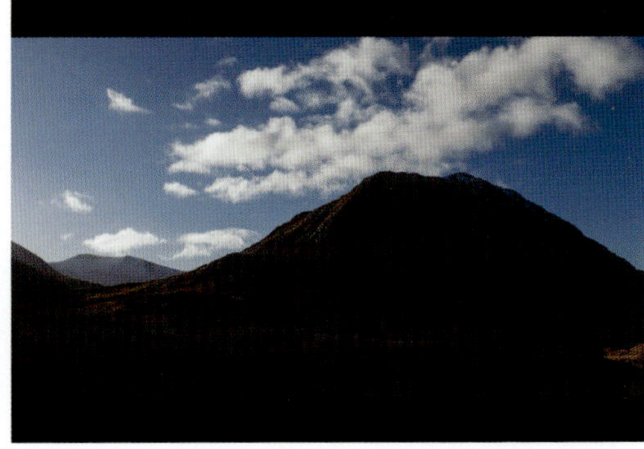

» SOUND

The G16 has two microphones, one on either side of the flash hotshoe. Built-in microphones such as these aren't ideal for recording sound, as they tend to pick up extraneous noise generated by the camera and they won't necessarily be close to your subject. However, as the G16 lacks a socket that would allow you to attach an external microphone, they are your only option.

Another problem with built-in microphones comes from wind noise. Professional microphones can be fitted with covers and baffles that are used to help reduce the noise of wind, but on the G16 you have to rely on the Wind Filter option on the ◘ Shooting menu. This removes any wind noise electronically, although in doing so it can also degrade the quality of the soundtrack.

If you're serious about shooting movies and want to make the best possible job, the answer is to record the soundtrack separately and combine it with the movie footage using video-editing software. This will require good organizational skills, particularly if dialog has to be recorded, as it will need to synchronize with the movement of your actors' lips.

Movies often benefit from music, which is generally added at the editing stage. Music usually has a rhythm and this can be used to decide when to cut from one shot to the next. If you intend to upload your video to a sharing website such as YouTube, or perhaps broadcast your video, don't use copyrighted music, or at least obtain the copyright owner's permission before you do so.

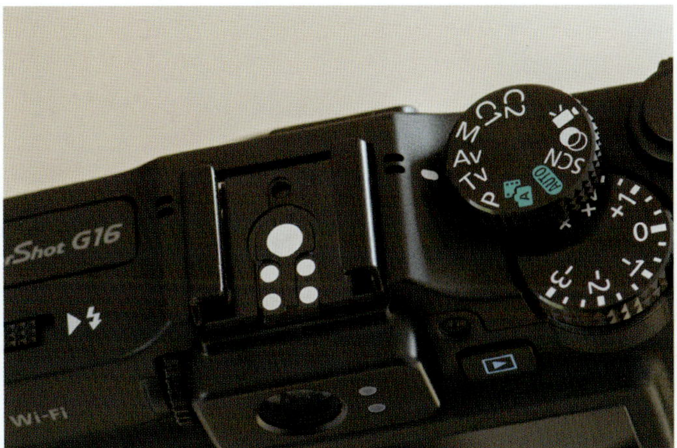

MICROPHONES »
The G16's stereo microphones are at either side of the hotshoe.

4 MENUS

If you want to master your G16 you'll need to delve into the menu system. Despite the number of options, the menus are laid out logically and are easy to navigate.

One of the keys to using a camera well is to understand exactly what it's doing as you use it. It's therefore a good idea to work your way through the various menu options, making sure you familiarize yourself with what they do and that they're set correctly for your needs.

Fortunately, there are a few ways to make using the menu system less painful. The first is to create your own custom menu using the ★ menu; this allows you to add five options that you regularly use, so they are easily accessible.

You can also view hints about the various menu options by setting **Hints and Tips** to **On** from the ↑T menu. These can be turned **Off** once you're familiar with the menu system.

And if you really make a mess of things and can't remember what's what, you can restore the factory default menu settings by selecting **Reset All...** from the ↑T menu.

> ### Tip
>
> *Press lightly down on the shutter-release button to cancel the menu screen and return the G16 directly to Shooting mode.*

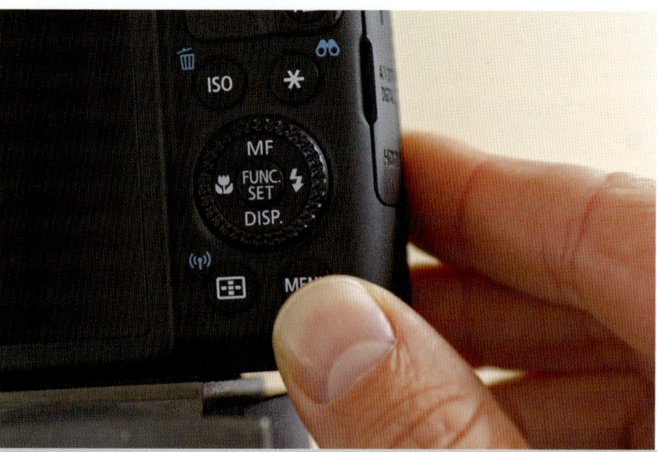

KNOWLEDGE »
Successful photography requires you to understand how your camera works and how the various camera functions affect the look of your images.

VIEWING THE MENU «

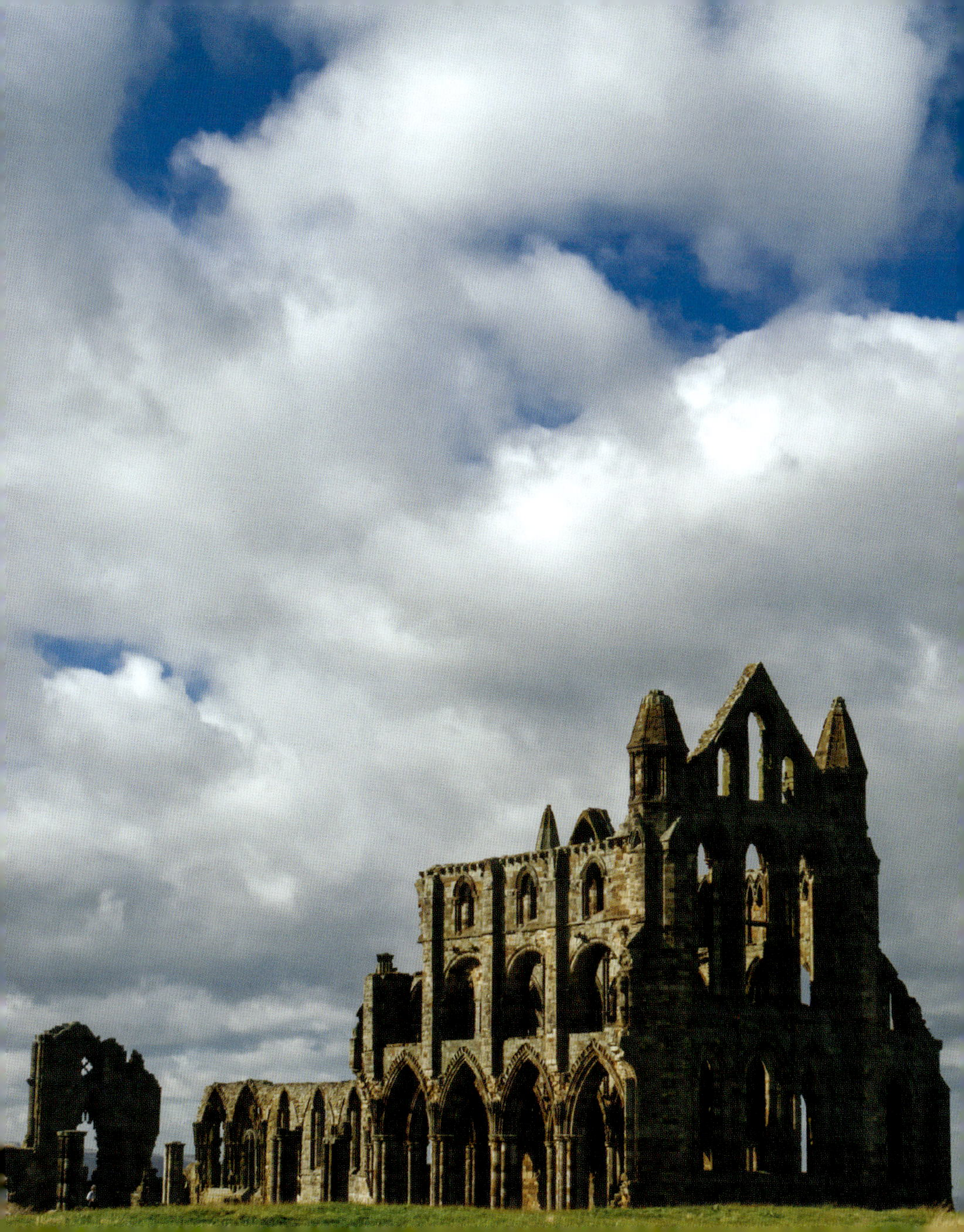

» MENU SUMMARY

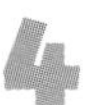 Shooting menu	Options
AF Frame	FlexiZone/Center; Face AiAF; Tracking AF
Digital Zoom	Standard; Off; Digital Tele-Converter (1.5x/2.0x)
AF-Point Zoom	On; Off
Servo AF	On; Off
Continuous AF	On; Off
AF-assist Beam	On; Off
MF-Point Zoom	On; Off
Safety MF	On; Off
MF Peaking settings	Peaking (On; Off); Level (High; Low); Color (Red; Blue; Yellow)
Flash Control	Flash mode (Auto; Manual); Flash Exp. Comp (±2 stops); Flash Output; Shutter Sync (1st-curtain; 2nd-curtain); Red-Eye Corr. (On; Off); Red-Eye Lamp (On; Off); Safety FE (On; Off)
ISO Auto Settings	Max ISO Speed (ISO 400–12,800); Rate of Change (Standard; Fast; Slow)
High ISO NR	Standard; High; Low
HG Lamp Corr.	On; Off
Spot AE Point	Center; AF Point
Safety Shift	On; Off
Wind Filter	Auto; Off
Review image after shooting	Display Time (Off; Quick; 2 sec.; 4 sec.; 8 sec.; Hold) Display Info (Off; Detailed)
Blink Detection	On; Off
Custom Display	Shooting Info; Grid Lines; Electronic Level; Histogram
Night Display	On; Off

▣ Shooting menu cont.	Options
FUNC. Menu Layout	Customize FUNC. menu
IS Settings	IS Mode (Continuous; Shoot Only; Off); Dynamic IS (1; 2)
Converter	Specifies the use of the (optional) TC-DC58E tele-converter
Date Stamp ▣	Off; Date; Date & Time
Digest Type	Include Stills; No Stills
Save ▣ Stills	On; Off
Star Emphasis	On; Off
Face ID Settings	Register and sort facial identification
Set ▣ ▣ Func.	Set functions assigned to ▣ and ▣
Set Shortcut button ▣	▣; ▣; ▣; WB; ▣¹; ▣²; ▣; ▣; ▣; AF; ▣; ND; ▣; ▣; SERVO; PEAK; AFL; ▣; ECO; ▣
Set ▣ button	As above
Save Settings	C1; C2

▣ Settings menu	Options
Mute	On; Off
Volume	Start-up; Operation; Self-Timer; Shutter
Sound Options	Start-up; Operation; Self-Timer; Shutter
Hints & Tips	On; Off
Date/Time	Date; Time; Date Format (dd/mm/yy; yy/mm/dd; mm/dd/yy); Daylight Saving (On; Off)
Time Zone	Home; World
Lens Retract	1 minute; 0 sec.
Eco mode	On; Off

⚙ **Settings menu cont.**	**Options**
Power Saving	Auto Power Down (On; Off); Display Off (10; 20; 30 sec.; 1; 2; 3 min.)
LCD Brightness	5 levels
Start-up Image	None; 2 pre-defined choices or user-defined image (set in Playback mode)
Format	Standard; Low Level
File Numbering	Continuous; Auto Reset
Create Folder	Monthly; Daily
Units	m/cm; ft/in
Electronic Level	Calibrate (Horizontal Roll Calibration; Vertical Pitch Calibration); Reset
Video System	NTSC; PAL
Ctrl via HDMI	Enable; Disable
Wi-Fi Settings	Set Wi-Fi options for image transfer
Copyright Info	Display Copyright Info; Enter Author's Name; Enter Copyright Details; Delete Copyright Info
Certification Logo Display	Shows the certification requirements of the G16
Language	English; German; French; Dutch; Danish; Italian; Ukrainian; Malay; Indonesian; Vietnamese; Finnish; Norwegian; Swedish; Spanish; Chinese (traditional); Russian; Portuguese; Greek; Polish; Czech; Hungarian; Turkish; Simplified Chinese; Korean; Thai; Arabic; Romanian; Farsi; Hindi; Japanese
Reset All	Restore settings to factory default

▶ **Playback menu**	**Options**
List/Play Digest Movies	View by date
Smart Shuffle	Shuffles images on memory card (50+ required)
Slideshow	Sets slideshow parameters
Erase	Select; Select Range; All Images
Protect	Select; Select Range; All Images

▶ **Playback menu cont.**	**Options**
Rotate	Rotates images
Favorites	Set; Unset images as favorites
Photobook Set-up	Select images for printing in a photobook
i-Contrast	Apply i-Contrast effect to images
Red-Eye Correction	Reduce red-eye effect in images of people and animals
Cropping	Crop images to different sizes
Resize	Resize and save images
My Colors	Alter colors in previously shot images
Face ID info	Edit face ID information
Transition Effect	Fade; Scroll; Slide; Off
Index Effect	On; Off
Scroll Display	On; Off
Group Images	On; Off
Auto Rotate	On; Off
Resume	Last seen; Last shot
Set Shortcut button	

🖶 **Print menu**	**Options**
Print	Displays printing screen (when G16 is connected to a printer)
Select Images & Qty.	Set images and quantity for printing
Select Range	Set start and end images for printing
Select All Images	Set all images for printing
Clear All Selections	Cancels all printing settings
Print Settings	Print type (Both; Standard; Index); Date (On; Off); File No. (On; Off); Clear DPOF data (On; Off)

★ **My Menu**	**Options**
My Menu Settings	Select items; Sort; Set default view (No; Yes)

» 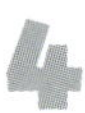 SHOOTING MENU

The Shooting menu allows you to set the still-image and movie shooting functions of your G16. The options you can alter depend on the shooting mode you were using when you pressed **MENU**. Any option that is not available will be ghosted out and will be skipped over as you move up and down the menu. The ▶ Playback menu replaces the Shooting menu when **MENU** is pressed in playback mode.

› AF Frame

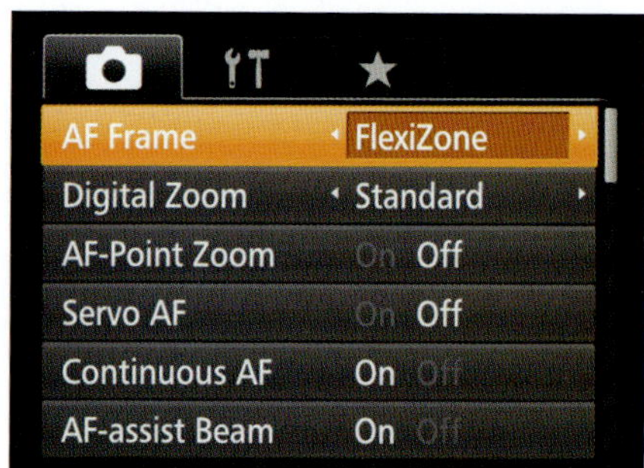

You can choose to use one of three **AF Frame** modes, each suited to different shooting situations: **Face AiAf**, **Tracking AF**, and **FlexiZone**.

    Face AiAF's neat trick is its ability to quickly focus on any faces in a scene, and then adjust exposure and WB as necessary (when 💽 and **AWB** are set).

    Tracking AF will track a moving subject once the focus point is set on the subject.

FlexiZone gives you the greatest control over where the G16 focuses. Only one AF frame is shown on screen, but it can be moved anywhere around the LCD. See chapter 2 for a full description of how to use the three different AF frames.

› Digital Zoom

For details see page 32.

› AF-Point Zoom

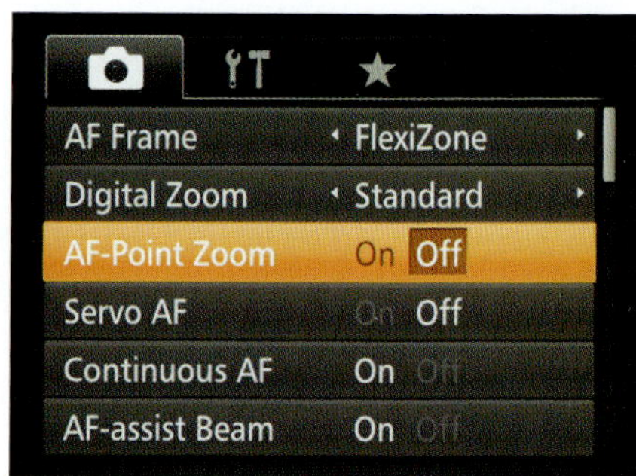

The G16's AF system is generally accurate, but **AF-Point Zoom** allows you to check visually how precise it actually is. When **AF-Point Zoom** is set to **On**, the current AF point will be magnified when you press the shutter-release button halfway down. This makes it easy to see if your subject is in focus or not.

> **Note:**
> **AF-Point Zoom** is not available when the G16 is set to **Digital Zoom**, **Tracking AF**, or 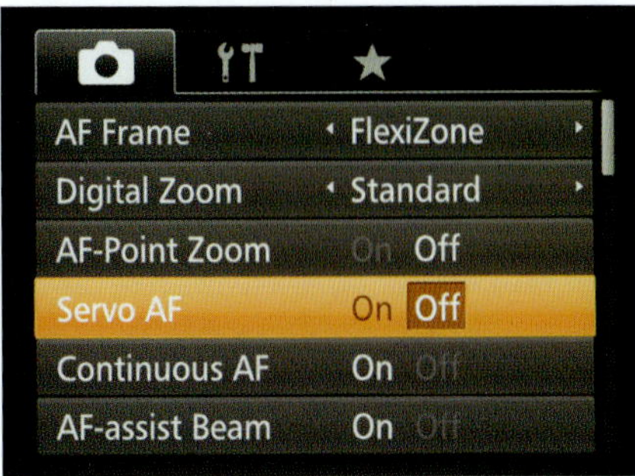.

Unfortunately, this makes the LCD more cluttered, and it can also obscure any changes that occur in the scene behind the magnified area. However, this may be a small price to pay for peace of mind. Switch **AF-Point Zoom** to **Off** if you don't want to use this facility.

When **AF Frame** is set to **Face AiAF**, the face detected as the main subject is magnified, unless the face is too big in relation to the LCD, or a face has not been detected. When **FlexiZone** is set, the area within the AF frame is magnified unless the G16 cannot lock focus.

› Servo AF

When **Servo AF** is set to **On**, the G16's AF system will track and maintain focus on a moving subject for as long as you keep the shutter-release button pressed halfway down. Final focus and exposure is only set when you press the shutter-release button down fully to take the photo.

Servo AF isn't perfect, though. If your subject is moving fast the focus may not keep up and its efficiency also drops when light levels are low. If focus cannot be achieved **Servo AF** is automatically deactivated and the current **AF Frame** setting is used instead.

If focus can't be achieved at all, the focus frame will turn yellow. If you mainly shoot static subjects, set **Servo AF** to **Off**.

> **Notes:**
> If the light levels are too low and a satisfactory exposure can't be set when **Servo AF** is set to **On**, the shutter speed and aperture values on the LCD will turn orange. Release the shutter-release button and try pressing down halfway again.
>
> AF lock will not operate in **Servo AF**.
>
> **Servo AF** is not available when the Self-Timer is activated.

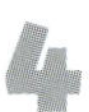

› Continuous AF

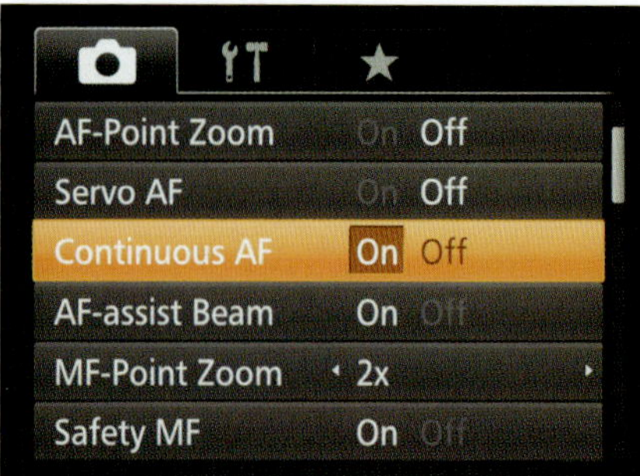

The G16's AF system uses a technology known as "contrast detection." This is generally precise, but it's far slower than the AF systems commonly found on DSLR cameras. When **Continuous AF** is set to **On**, your G16 will focus continuously until you press the shutter-release button down halfway, at which point focus and exposure are locked.

Using **Continuous AF** means that there is less or even no delay between pressing the shutter-release button down to take the shot and the AF system achieving focus. This should mean fewer missed opportunities. However, **Continuous AF** will deplete your camera's battery more quickly. If battery power could be an issue or if your subject is relatively static, set **Continuous AF** to **Off**.

› AF-assist Beam

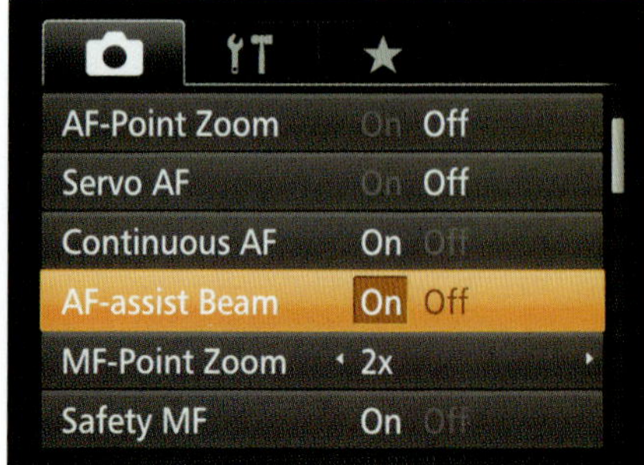

If the ambient light levels are low, the G16's AF system will start to struggle. When **AF-assist Beam** is set to **On**, the G16 will literally throw some light on the situation to help, using the lamp on front of the camera. However, this light is not discreet and may distract or startle your subject. Set **AF-Assist Beam** to **Off** if you think this may be the case.

› MF-Point Zoom

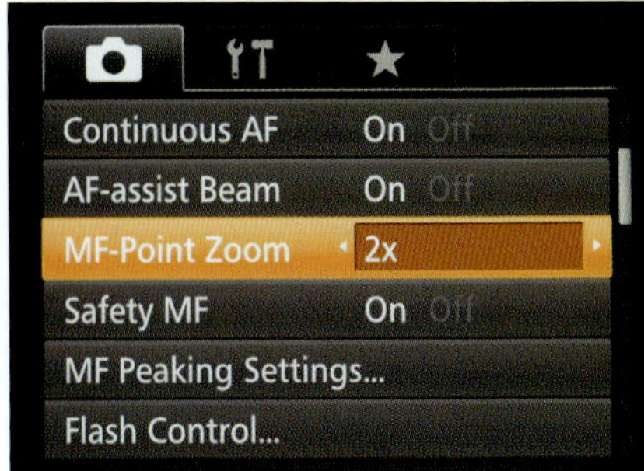

› Safety MF

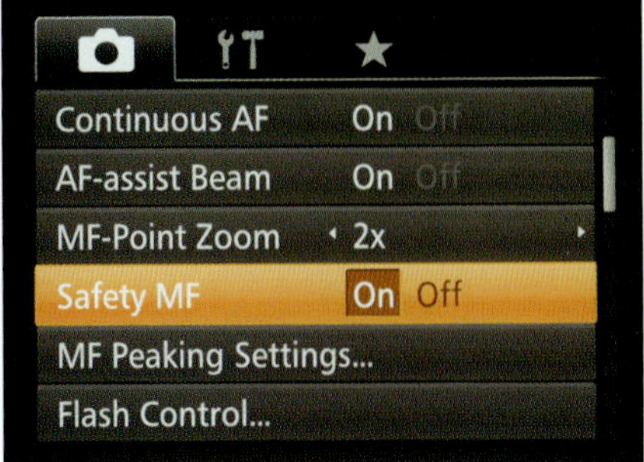

If you decide to focus manually, the G16 tries to help by displaying a magnified square (either **2x** or **4x** magnification) at the center of the LCD as a focusing aid. However, this obscures part of the image, making composition more difficult.

If this doesn't bother you, leave **MF-Point Zoom** set to **On** (you could compose your image first and then switch focusing to **MF**). Alternatively, set **MF-Point Zoom** to **Off** so that the center area of the LCD isn't magnified.

MF gives you complete control over focusing. However, because of the relatively low resolution of the LCD screen it can be difficult to see whether focus is set correctly or not (although **MF Peaking** may help). When using **MF** with **Safety MF** set to **On**, your G16 will automatically fine-tune focus for you when you press halfway down on the shutter-release button. If you're happy to set focus entirely unaided set **Safety MF** to **Off**.

Tip

When shooting a subject that is moving across your field of view, follow the movement smoothly in an arc and press the shutter-release button at the center point of the arc. Continue to follow the movement through after you've taken the shot.

4

› MF Peaking Settings

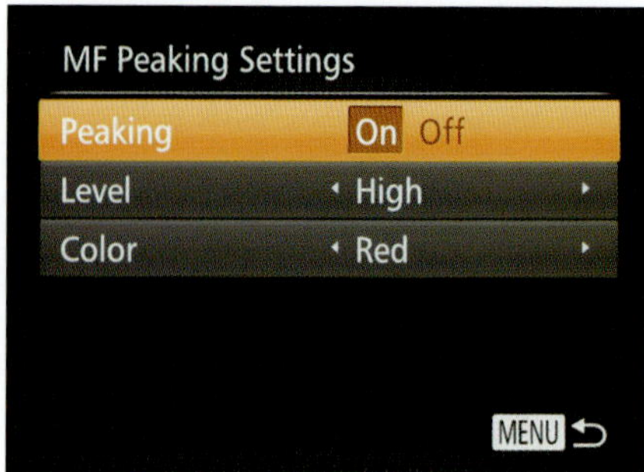

› ISO Auto Settings

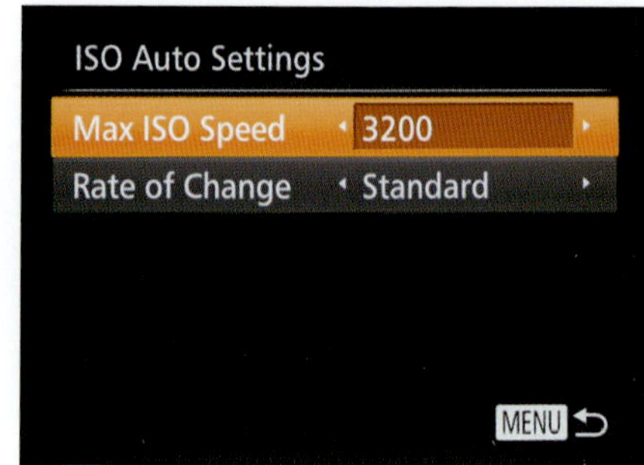

When using 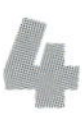, focus peaking is an incredibly useful tool to help you achieve accurate focus. The idea is derived from similar systems found on camcorders. With **Peaking** set to **On**, the G16 will turn the outline of the sharpest (in-focus) point of the image **Red** (or **Yellow** or **Blue**, if you change how **Color** is set). You can also set the sensitivity of the peaking **Level** to **High** or **Low**.

The drawback with using focus peaking is that it relies on edge contrast to detect sharpness. If you're shooting in a low contrast scene, such as a misty landscape, **Peaking** may be less effective or possibly not work at all, but at all other times it can prove invaluable.

In low-light conditions there's a risk that a slow shutter speed will cause camera shake. Using **ISO AUTO** can help to avoid this scenario, as the G16 will increase the ISO automatically when necessary to raise shutter speeds. However, this increases the likelihood that noise will affect image quality.

ISO Auto Settings allows you to decide where the best compromise lies. This is achieved by specifying the highest ISO that will be set by **ISO AUTO**. The G16 can be set to stop at ISO **400** or continue to increase the ISO as necessary up to **12,800**. If you think that light levels you shoot in will remain relatively high, use a low **ISO Auto Setting**; set it to a higher value if you think that the light levels will vary widely and be less than ideal.

You can also set the rate of change between: **Slow**, **Standard**, and **Fast**. When set to **Fast**, the G16 will increase the ISO to a higher value than a **Slow** setting in the same lighting conditions.

› High ISO NR

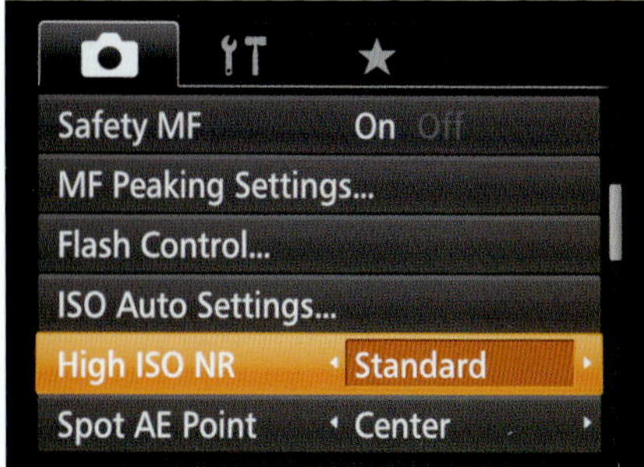

› HG Lamp Corr.

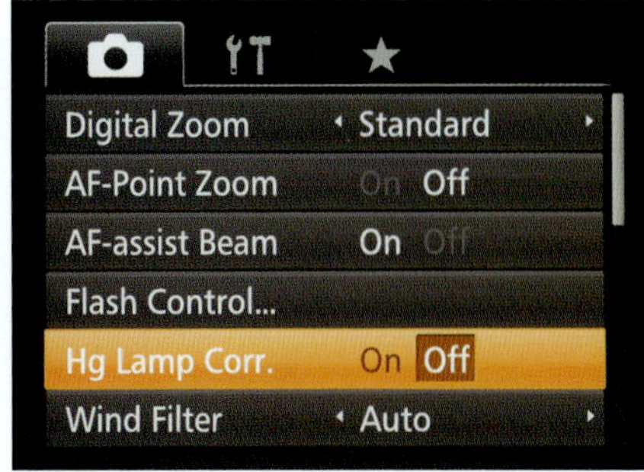

Applying in-camera noise reduction to tackle high ISO noise in JPEG images removes a step from the postproduction process, but the drawback is that there are only three levels of noise reduction available on the G16: **Low**, **Standard,** and **High**. This doesn't leave much scope for fine-tuning noise reduction.

High reduces noise aggressively, at the expense of fine detail in your images. This can leave images looking slightly too smooth and lacking texture. Set **High ISO NR** to **Low** if you prefer to combat noise during postproduction.

› Flash Control

The **Flash Control** submenu controls the G16's built-in and external (if fitted) flash units. The options available will depend on the Shooting mode you are using.

Mercury-vapor lighting is typically used outdoors in street lighting or sports arenas, and in large interior spaces such as warehouses. The lighting has a greenish tinge that is far from flattering to skin tones. **HG Lamp Corr.** automatically corrects this greenish tinge when set to **On**. When switched **On**, ⚘ will be displayed on the LCD. This option is only available when the mode dial is set to **AUTO**.

› Safety Shift

Setting **Safety Shift** to **On** forces the G16 to automatically adjust either the shutter speed in **Av** mode or the aperture in **Tv** mode to avoid exposure problems. So, for example, if you set an aperture in **Av** mode that requires a shutter speed faster than 1/4000 sec. for a correct exposure, the aperture will be reduced automatically to ensure that the exposure is correct.

› Spot AE Point

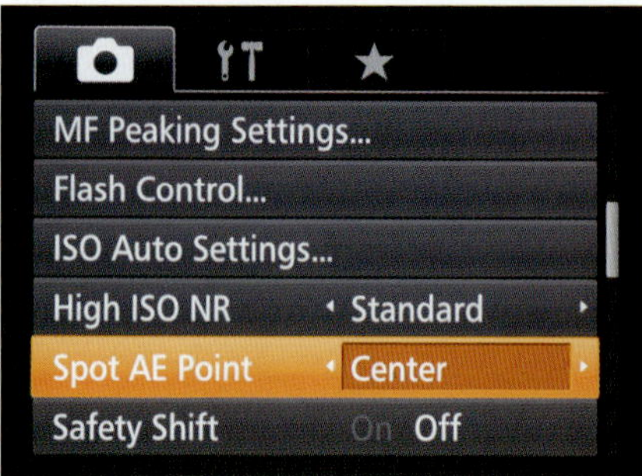

Spot metering is the most precise way of determining the exposure of a particular area of a scene. Spot AE Point offers you the choice of linking the spot metering either to the **AF frame** (when **AF Frame** is set to **FlexiZone**), or to the **Center** of the LCD. Generally, your subject would be where you focus so setting **Spot AE Point** to **AF frame** is a good way of combining accurate focus with accurate exposure. However, if your subject is not a midtone you should be prepared to apply exposure compensation if necessary.

› Blink Detection

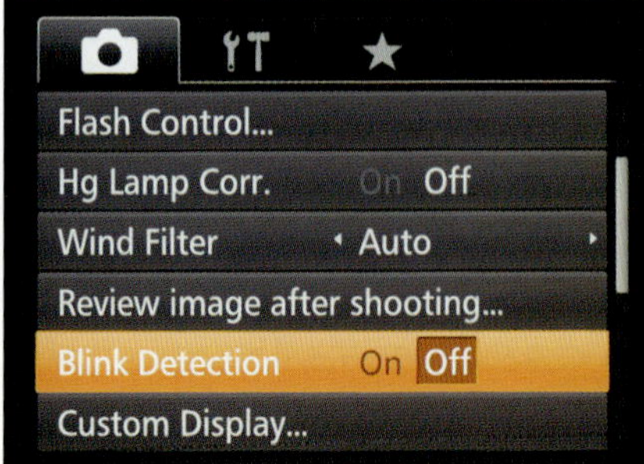

It's frustrating when you discover—too late—that your subject blinked just as you shot an image. When **Blink Detection** is set to On, your G16 will warn you if your subject had their eyes shut during an exposure by displaying a symbol on the LCD immediately afterward.

Turn **Blink Detection** to **Off** to disable this feature. One way to stop your subject(s) blinking is to ask them to count down from three on the understanding that you'll fire the shutter when they reach one. As your subjects are more in control of when the shot is taken they're less likely to blink at just the wrong moment.

> **Notes:**
> When the G16 is set to ○c, Blink Detection will only be activated on the final shot.
>
> Blink Detection is deactivated when you use mode.

› Wind Filter

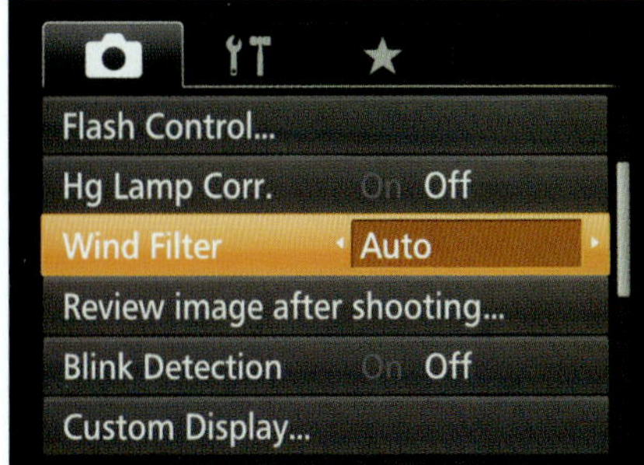

› Review image after shooting

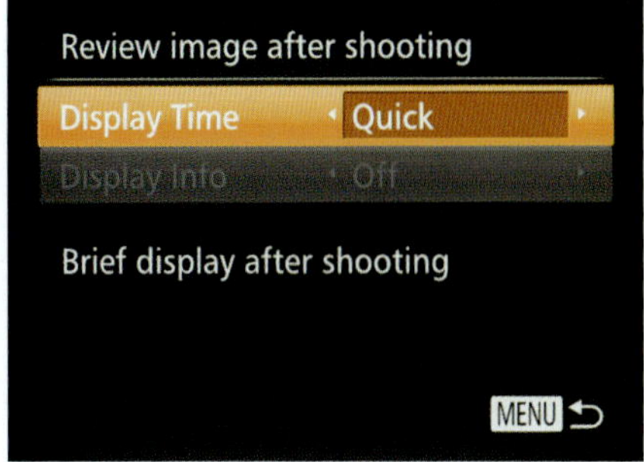

This option is only applicable to movie shooting. When set to **On**, the Wind Filter will try to digitally eliminate wind noise from your movie's soundtrack during recording. This is similar to the effect achieved by using a foam windshield on an external microphone. However, when shooting movies indoors or in calm conditions, Wind Filter should be set to **Off** to avoid degrading the quality of the recorded sound.

By default, once you've shot an image it's automatically displayed on the LCD. What happens next is set using the sub-options on **Review image after shooting**. See the tables below for the options available when setting either **Display Time** or **Display Info**.

Display Time	
Quick	The image is displayed momentarily.
2, 4 or 8 sec.	The image is displayed for the chosen length of time.
Hold	The image is displayed until you press the shutter-release button down halfway.
Off	No image is displayed after shooting.

Display Info	
Off	Image only is displayed.
Detailed	Information such as histogram and exposure settings will be displayed.

› Custom Display

There are three different display modes in shooting mode: you can jump between 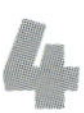 Custom Screen 1, Custom Screen 2, and Screen Off by pressing ▼ repeatedly. **Custom Display** allows you to choose what shooting information is shown on and . Add or remove **Shooting Info, Grid Lines, Electronic Level,** and **Histogram**, depending on which you find useful or distracting.

Setting Custom Display

1) Select **Custom Display**.

2) Use ✛ or ◉ to highlight the required option below or . Press (FUNC. SET) to add the shooting information to the left to the custom display—✔ will be displayed to confirm that you have added this information successfully.

3) If you want to disable a particular display mode, highlight either , , or at the top of the LCD and press (FUNC. SET). ⊘ is overlaid on the display symbol to indicate that it is no longer available. In Shooting mode, the disabled screen will not be shown when you press **DISP.** Highlight the display screen symbol again and press (FUNC. SET) again to re-enable it.

4) Press **MENU** to save your settings and return to ▣.

› Night Display

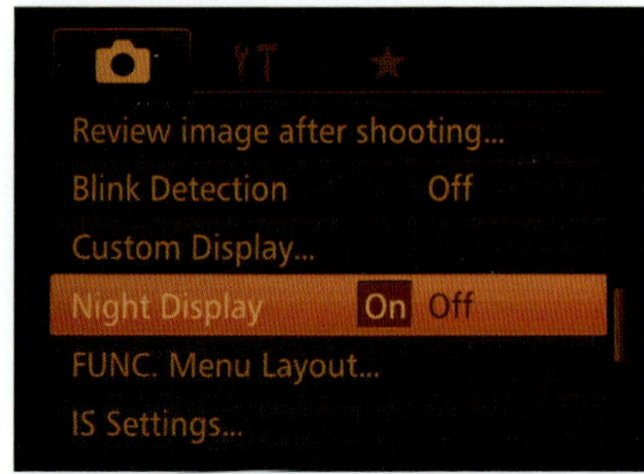

If you're shooting in dark conditions (particularly when using) your eyes will gradually adapt to the low light levels, enabling you to see details more easily. However, if you view a menu screen on your camera, the brightness of the LCD will cause you to lose your dark adaption. **Night Display** turns the menus screens (and text on the LCD in shooting mode) red, which prevent this from happening. However, don't whizz through your images in playback—if any of them were shot in bright conditions the screen may cause you to undo your dark adaption.

› FUNC. Menu Layout

This option allows you to select which options will be available on the FUNC. menu. All of the options are shown by default, but if there are options that you rarely use, removing them from the FUNC. menu will make it more efficient to use.

Setting FUNC. Menu Layout

1) Select **FUNC. Menu Layout** and press (FUNC/SET).

2) Use the directional buttons or the dial to highlight the required option. Options that are visible on the FUNC. menu will be shown with a ✓ next to the option icon. Press (FUNC/SET) to toggle the option **On** or **Off**.

3) Press the sort button to sort the order of options on the FUNC. menu. Turn the dial to highlight

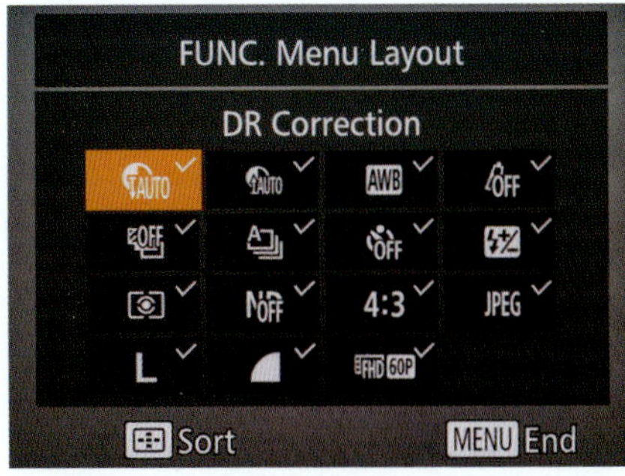

the required option and press (FUNC/SET). Press ▲ to move the option up the light or ▼ to move it down. Press (FUNC/SET) when you're happy with its position. Repeat as required.

4) Press **MENU** and select **OK** to apply your changes or select **Cancel** to return directly to Shooting mode without saving the changes.

IS Mode	
Continuous	Camera shake is corrected automatically when necessary. The effect will be visible on the LCD.
Shoot Only	IS will only activate when the shutter-release button is pressed.
Off	IS is switched off entirely. If you are shooting on a tripod set IS to **Off**.

Dynamic IS (for movie shooting)	
1	To stabilize the camera during movie recording this IS mode crops the image slightly so that there's a visible jump between your composition before and after you press the movie record button. This means that it's less easy to compose a shot correctly, but IS will be highly effective.
2	This IS mode doesn't crop the image, making it easier to accurately compose your movies. However, the IS isn't as effective as 1.

› IS Settings

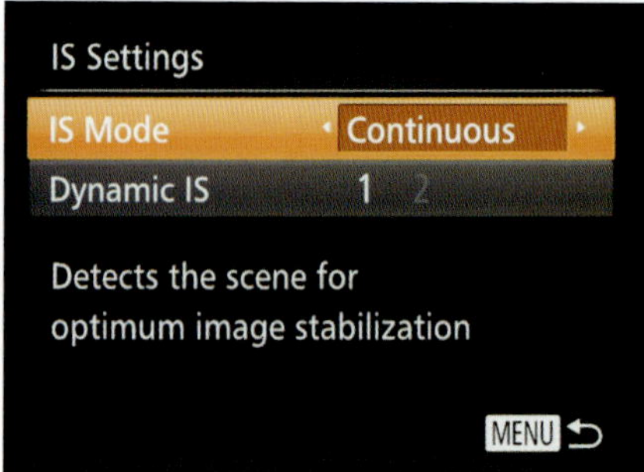

Camera movement during an exposure causes a visual phenomenon known as camera shake. The chances of it occurring increase with the length of the shutter speed (particularly so when the lens is set to [ ]), although it's worth noting that the actual shutter speed where camera shake occurs will vary from person to person: some people are steadier than others.

The G16 is equipped with lens-based image-stabilization (IS). When activated, and the camera detects movement, it will rapidly adjust elements within the lens to compensate for that movement. This works very well and allows you to handhold a camera at lower shutter speeds than would otherwise be possible.

If the IS system can't keep the camera steady at the selected shutter speed, will be displayed on the LCD. If you see the camera shake warning, increase the ISO to raise the shutter speed, or mount the camera on a tripod.

There are several different ways that IS is implemented on the G16. The one you use will depend on the shooting situation you are in.

› Date Stamp

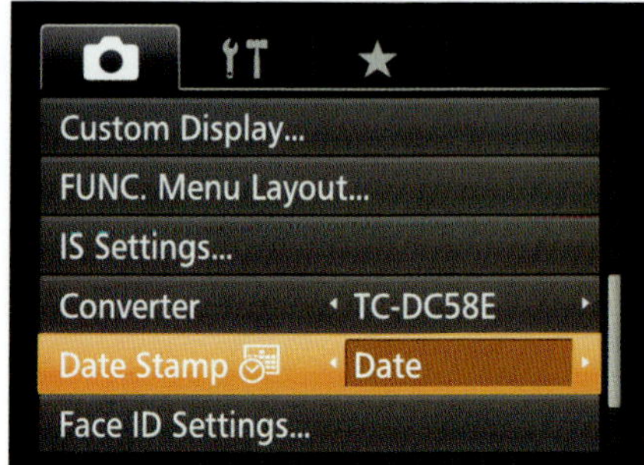

If you think it would be a good idea to brand your images with the date of shooting for ease of reference later, your G16 can do this without you asking. Every time you make an image, the date and time of shooting (and so much more) is embedded invisibly within the image's metadata. Metadata is data that is stored in an image file that is not part of the actual image data. The information contained in an image's metadata can be viewed in all good image-editing software or suitable image-browsers, and is also displayed on the G16's detailed playback screen.

However, your G16 also allows you to apply a permanent and visible reminder of the date, or date and time, every time a JPEG image is shot. This is useful if you ever need to demonstrate to a third-party that an image was shot when you say it was. **Date Stamp** can be set to either **Off**, **Date**, or **Date & Time**. When the latter two options are selected the date (and time) will appear at the bottom right hand corner of every image you subsequently shoot. Be sure that you want this information recorded on your images, though: it cannot be removed later, except by careful and time-consuming retouching using image-editing software.

› Converter

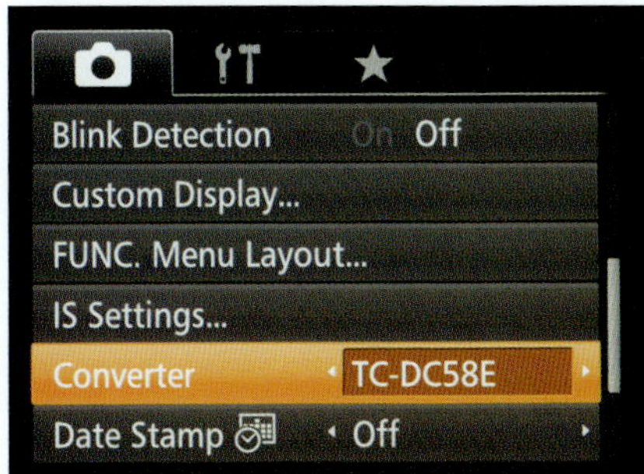

When you fit the optional TC-DC58E tele-converter you optically increase the focal length of the G16's lens, but you need to set **Converter** to **TC-DC58E**. Once it's been removed, set this option back to **None** (the default). If **IS Mode** is set to **Off**, the **Converter** setting does not need to be altered.

› Digest Type

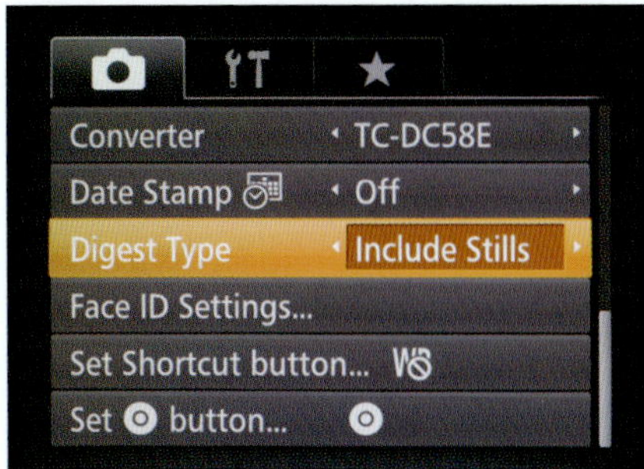

When is selected, both a movie and still image are recorded when the shutter-release button is pressed down (when **Digest Type** is set to **Include Stills**). You can choose to record the movie only by setting **Digest Type** to **No Stills**.

› Save Stills

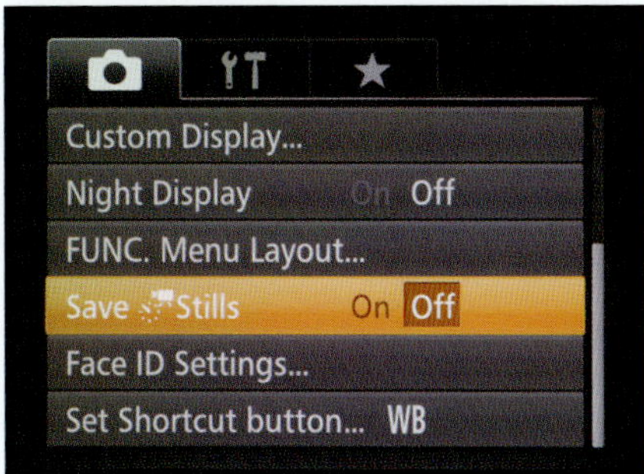

When you shoot using (available when is selected) your G16 shoots a sequence of still images. By default these still images are then processed into a movie and

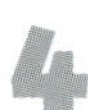

discarded (**Save** Stills is set to **Off**). If the sequence is lengthy this will save valuable memory card space.

You can, however, set **Save** Stills to **On**, which will save all the individual images for use later. The images are grouped together and, when viewed in playback, only the first image will be displayed. See page 39 about viewing individual images within a group.

› Star Emphasis

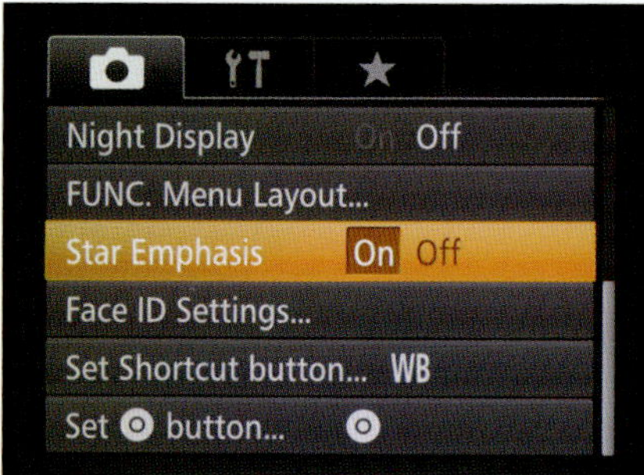

This option, when switched **On**, makes stars and star trails more obvious and prominent within your images (available when is selected). It's an extra level of processing that's applied after shooting, so it's worth experimenting to see whether or not you like the effect before you shoot seriously with . Switch **Star Emphasis** to **Off** if you don't like the effect.

› Face ID

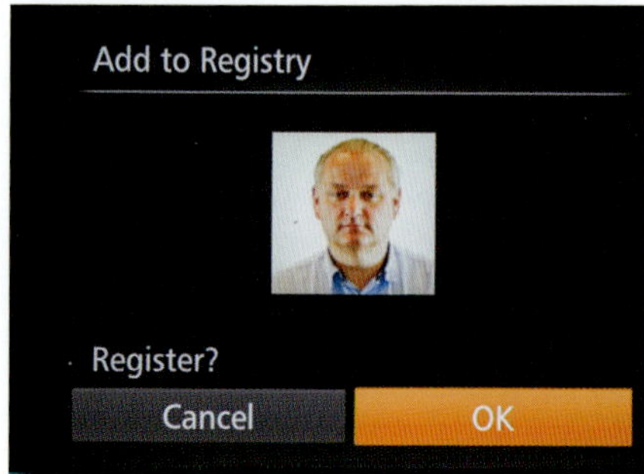

Face ID allows you to register the faces—and add the names and birthdays—of up to 12 people to your G16. Once you've registered a person's face, the camera will recognize them the next time you take their photo and adjust the exposure and focus automatically.

The information you've registered about each person can be used to find images of that person easily using the G16's filter function. It is also stored in the metadata of images featuring that person, which can be used in your own personal image database or when sharing images on social media websites. This information shouldn't be abused however: be sure to have a person's permission if you post a photo of them to the Internet. If you sell your camera later, make sure you delete all the personal data before you do so.

Registering a face

1) Select **Face ID Settings** followed by **Add to Registry**.

2) Select **Add New Face**.

3) Point your camera toward your subject and frame their face within the gray box at the center of the LCD. Once the G16 has determined that you are pointing it at a face the box will turn white. Press the shutter-release button.

4) Select **OK** to register the face or **Cancel** to go back to step 3.

5) On the **Edit Profile** screen select **Name**. Enter your subject's details on the **Input Name** screen. Press (FUNC/SET) to save the details.

6) Select **Birthday** and enter your subject's date of birth. Press (FUNC/SET) when finished.

7) Select **Save**.

8) Repeat the process by selecting **Yes** to register more facial angles of your subject. This will make the G16 more likely to recognize your subject's face. Otherwise select **No**.

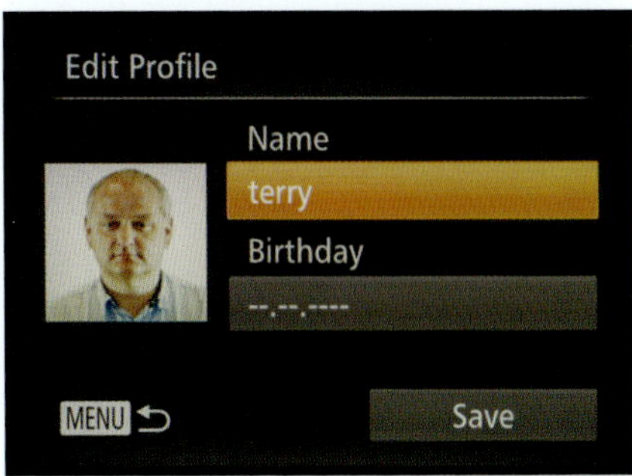

Other settings

1) Select **Face ID Settings**.

2) Select **Face ID** and set the function to **On** if you want name recorded in image metadata or to **Off** if you don't.

3) Select **Check/Edit Info** to check that the information for your registered faces is correct.

4) Select **Erase Info** to view the registered faces and delete unwanted information.

> **Note:**
> When the G16 recognizes faces when you're shooting, the names of up to three of those people will be displayed below the AF frame that surrounds the face.

› Set 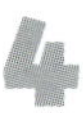 Func.

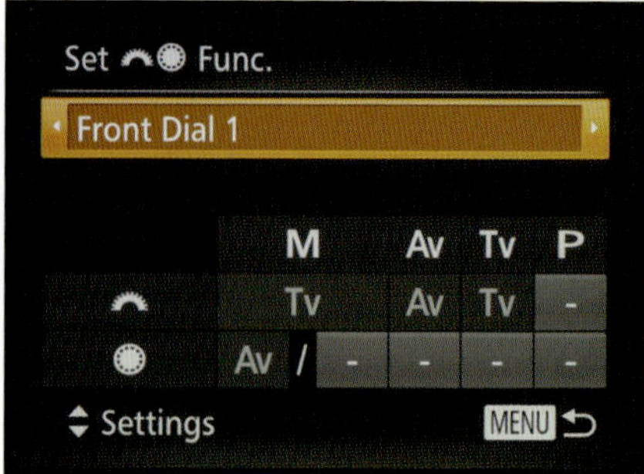

You can assign commonly used functions on the G16 to the and dials to make life easier when using **P**, **Tv**, **Av**, and **M** modes. By choosing carefully, you can quickly adjust your most used shooting functions by turning the appropriate control. The functions you can register are: aspect ratio switching, ISO speed, dynamic range correction, shadow correction, white balance, step zoom, or manual focusing. When multiple functions are assigned to , press **ISO** to toggle between them.

Setting functions

1) Select **Set Func.**

2) Press ◄ or ► to choose **Front Dial 1, Front Dial 2, Front Dial 3,** or **Control Dial**. Press ▲ or ▼ to start adding functions to the selected control.

3) Press ✦ or turn to highlight the various functions available in the different shooting modes and then turn to change that function.

4) Press **MENU** to save your new settings and return to the main Shooting menu.

› Set Shortcut button / Set ⊙ button

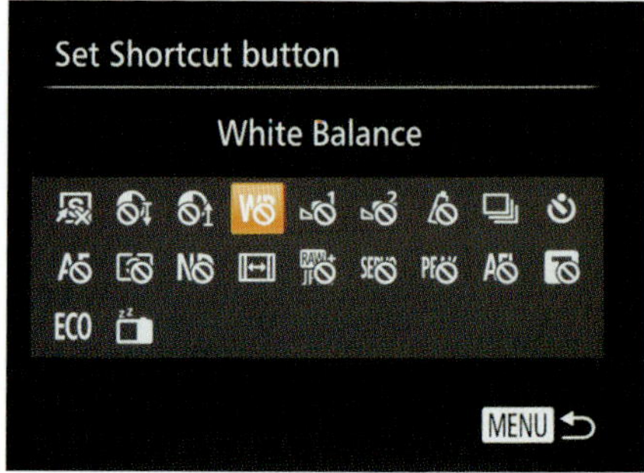

Everyone has different needs. The G16 caters for this by allowing you to quickly access two of your favorite shooting functions by assigning them to the and ⊙ buttons. If you choose carefully this will make using the G16 a far slicker experience, saving time and reducing the need to wade through countless menu screens.

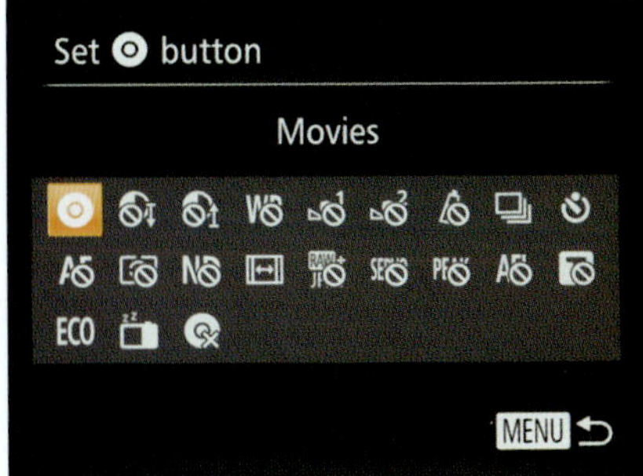

Setting the Shortcut / button

1) Select **Set Shortcut Button** or **Set button**.

2) Press ✛ or turn ⏣ to highlight the required function. Select if you'd prefer that no function be assigned to or . If is shown over a function symbol it means that function is not available in the shooting mode you are currently using, although you can still assign the function to the or buttons for use in modes when it is available. Press to assign the highlighted function to the relevant button.

3) In Shooting mode, press either the or buttons to call up the functions you have assigned.

› Save Settings

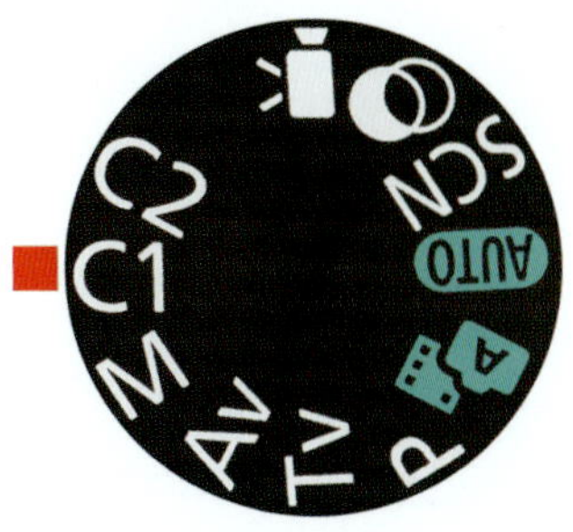

If you're using **P**, **Tv**, **Av**, or **M** you can save a particular combination of settings for future use. These settings can then be accessed quickly by turning the Mode dial to either **C1** or **C2**. Settings that can be saved include shooting menu functions, zoom and manual focus positions, and My Menu settings. If you regularly swap between different shooting styles (action and landscape, for example) saving the relevant settings for each will allow you to switch from one to the other with a turn of the mode dial.

Saving Settings

1) Select **Save Settings**.

2) Turn ⏣ to highlight either **C1** or **C2**. Press and your current settings will be assigned to the highlighted custom setting. Press **MENU** to return to the Shooting menu without assigning custom settings.

» ⚙ SET UP MENU

The ⚙ Set Up menu is where you go to alter the basic functions of your G16, whether that means changing the volume of operation sounds or configuring the power saving settings. As with 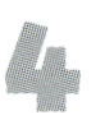, any option that is not available because you are using a certain shooting mode will be ghosted out and will not be accessible.

› Mute

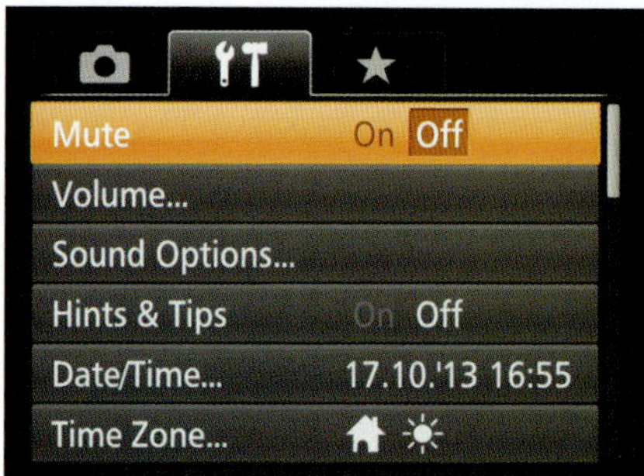

Mechanically, the G16 is a very quiet camera. This makes it ideal for those shooting situations where you don't want to draw attention to yourself or where noise would be unwelcome, but the G16 does make four distinct sounds when different operations are carried out. These can spoil your attempts at stealth, but fortunately, these noises can be switched **On** or **Off** using this menu option.

› Volume

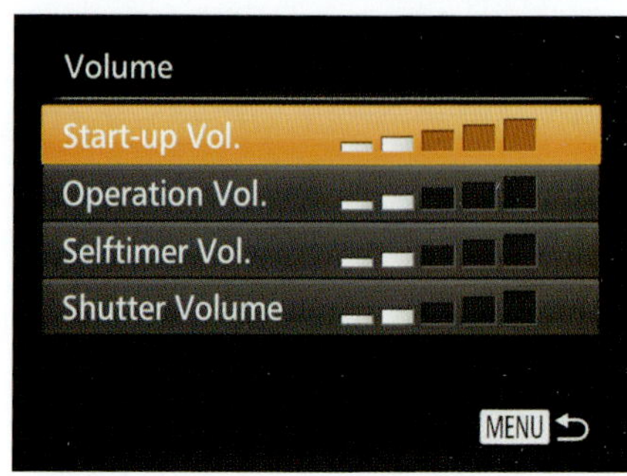

By default the G16 will make four different sounds when certain operations are performed. A sound is played at **Start-up** (when you first switch your G16 on); during an **Operation** (when a button is pressed when using the Menu system); when **Self-Timer** is activated (as the camera counts down); and when the **Shutter** fires to expose an image. You can deactivate these sounds entirely by setting **Mute** to **On** or by altering the **Volume** of each sound individually.

> **Notes:**
> **Volume** is not accessible when **Mute** is set to **Off**.
>
> You can also set **Mute** to **On** when you first turn your camera on by holding down ▼ as you do so.

Setting the volume

1) Select **Volume**.

2) Press ▲ / ▼ to highlight the sound that you wish to adjust the volume of.

3) Press ◄ / ► to adjust the volume down and up respectively. The highlighted sound will play once at the set volume or when you press (FUNC. SET).

4) Repeat to adjust the other volume settings if necessary. Press **MENU** to return to the main ᶠᵀ menu.

› Sound Options

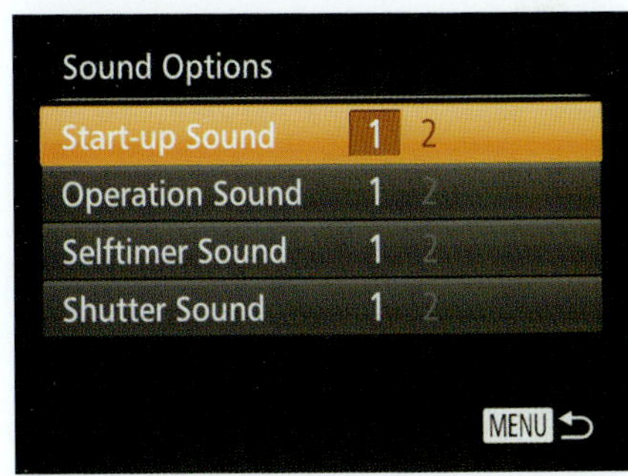

You can set your G16 to make one of two sounds at **Start-up**, **Operation**, **Self-Timer**, and **Shutter**. This is one of those choices that is purely personal preference.

Setting the desired sound

1) Select **Sound Options**.

2) Press ▲ / ▼ to highlight the sound you want to change.

3) Press ◄ / ► to highlight one of the two potential sounds. The highlighted sound will play once or when you press (FUNC. SET).

4) Repeat to adjust the other sound settings if necessary, and then press **MENU** to return to the main Settings menu.

› Hints & Tips

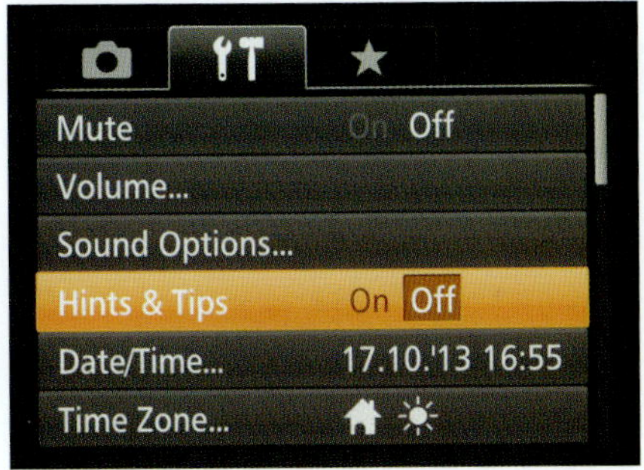

When you select a menu or FUNC. menu option, a short description of that option is displayed at the bottom of the LCD. This is useful, but it means that fewer options will be shown on the LCD at any one time. Setting **Hints & Tips** to **Off** will make your G16 slightly more efficient to use.

› Date/Time

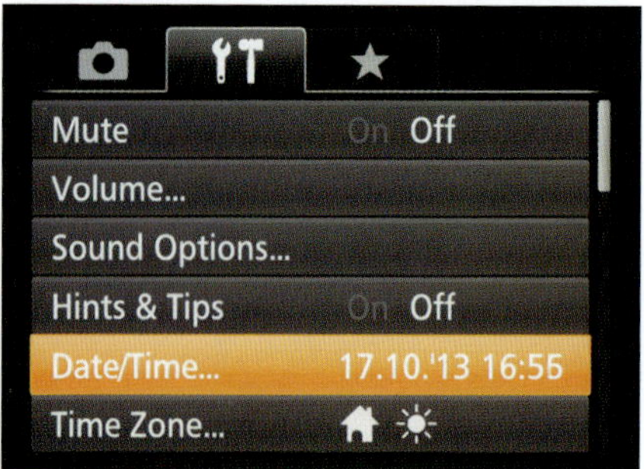

The date, time, date order method, and daylight savings are set using this option. The date order choices are dd/mm/yy, yy/mm/dd, or mm/dd/yy. When an image is created the date and time is written to the image metadata. See page 24 for detailed instructions on setting Date/Time.

› Time Zone

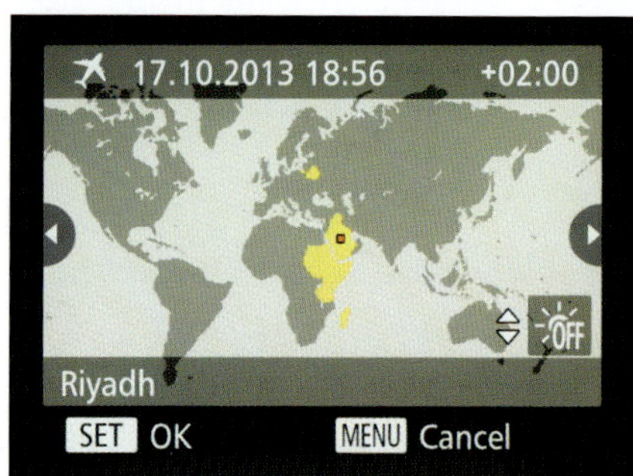

If you're a frequent traveler across time zones it can be a real bind altering your various timepieces to the correct local time. Unfortunately, the G16 doesn't automatically know which time zone it's in, so it's another device to add to the list. However, life is made easier by the Time Zone function.

To set the World Time Zone

1) Set the correct date and time for your current time zone if you have not already done so (see p26).

2) Select **Time Zone** followed by ✈ **World**. On the world map screen press ◀ / ▶ or turn ⬤ to select your destination time zone. Use ▲ / ▼ to apply ☀ daylight saving (+1 hour) if required.

3) Press ⬤ when you are happy with the settings.

Using the World Time Zone

1) Select **Time Zone**. Highlight ✈ **World** and press **MENU**. ✈ will be shown on the LCD to show that you've switched to the selected time zone.

2) Repeat step 1, this time selecting 🏠 **Home** to change the time settings back to your home time zone.

› Lens Retract

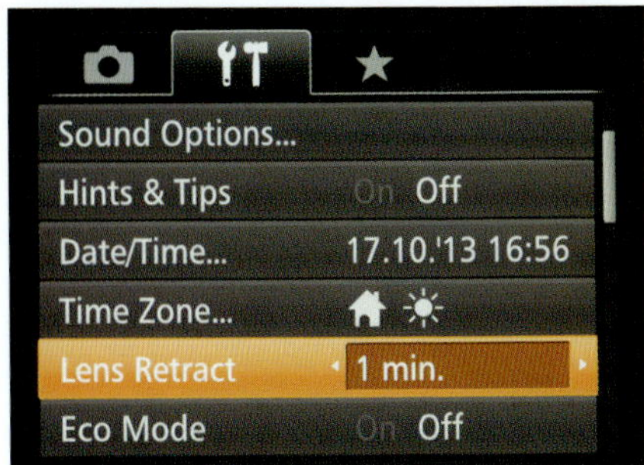

The default for lens retraction on the G16 is **1 min.** after you've pressed ▶ in Shooting mode. If you prefer that the lens retracts as soon as you press the ▶ button, set this function to **0 sec.** The main reason you'd want to retract the lens is to avoid it getting damaged as you're reviewing images—this is a greater risk if the camera is being passed around a group of people.

The downside of setting the lens to retract as soon as you press the ▶ button is that it will take a few seconds for your camera to be ready when you want to start shooting again.

› Eco Mode

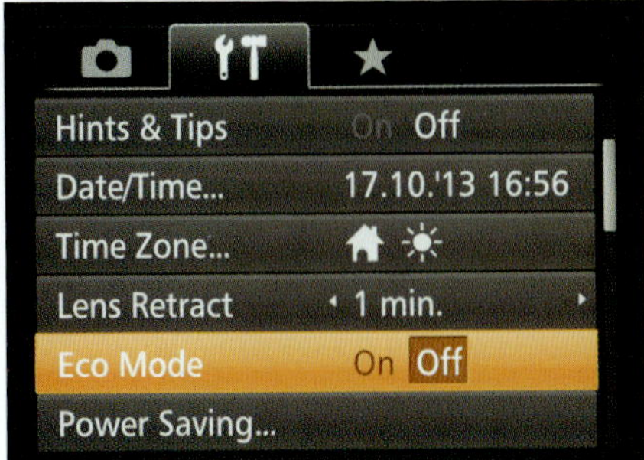

When **Eco Mode** is switched **On**, the G16's LCD screen will dim 2 seconds after you've pressed or turned a control on the camera. After 10 more seconds (providing you don't press or turn a control during that time) the LCD will turn off entirely (the power light will still be lit however, so it's easy to see that the camera hasn't merely switched itself off). Pressing any button on the camera instantly switches the LCD back on again.

Eco Mode will save battery power and for that reason it's worth considering (as long as you're happy to keep pressing buttons every time the LCD switches off).

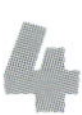

› Power Saving

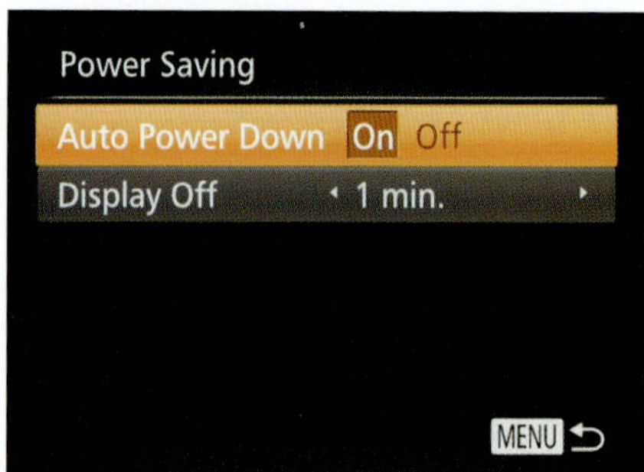

› LCD Brightness

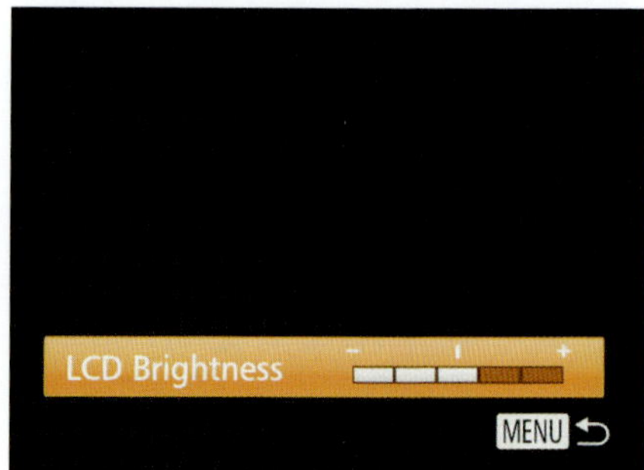

The G16 has a two-stage process to conserve power when in Shooting mode. By default, the LCD turns off **1 min.** after you touch any of the controls. Then, approximately three minutes after you last touched a control, the lens retracts and the camera switches off completely.

Pressing the shutter-release button down lightly will reactivate the G16 anytime during the period between the screen switching off and the lens retracting. Once the lens has retracted you will need to switch the G16 back on using the power button.

If you prefer the G16 not to shut down, set **Auto Power Down** to **Off**, which ensures you are always ready to shoot.

The length of time taken for the LCD to switch off can be set using **Display Off** on the Power Saving submenu. The choice is **10**, **20**, or **30 sec.**, or **1**, **2**, or **3 min**. Use a setting that suits your style of shooting, but does not use battery power needlessly.

The G16's LCD can be set to one of five levels of brightness. Generally you would use a lower brightness level when ambient light levels are low, and a higher brightness level when ambient light levels are high.

However, using the LCD at maximum brightness will drain the battery more quickly and potentially lead you to think that images are not exposed correctly. Set the brightness to a level that allows you to see the screen easily, but use the histogram as a more objective way to assess the exposure of your images.

> **Note:**
> Hold down ▼ for 1 second or more to set brightness to maximum in shooting or single image Playback mode. To restore brightness to the level set on LCD Brightness hold down ▼ again for 1 second or more or switch the camera off and on again.

CANON POWERSHOT G16

› Start-up Image

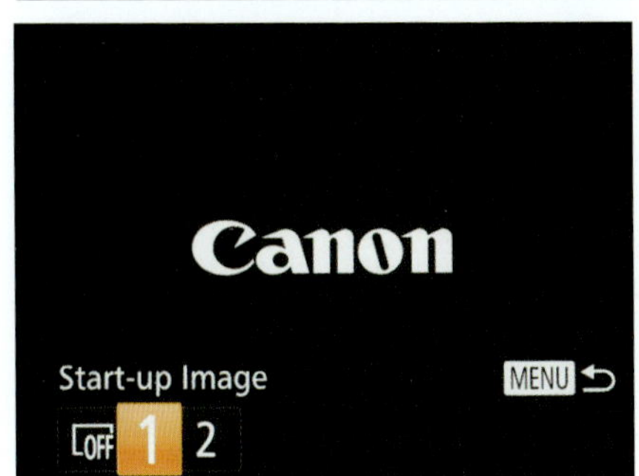

When your G16 is first turned on a start-up image is briefly displayed. This option lets you choose another image to display, or set no start-up image at all for a more minimalist approach.

Setting the Start-up Image
1) Select **Start-up Image**.

2) Use ◄ / ► or ⊙ to highlight ⊡OFF (no image), **1**, or **2** to choose what you prefer to see at start-up.

3) Press **MENU** to return to the ℹ️ menu.

› Format

See chapter 2 for more details.

› File Numbering

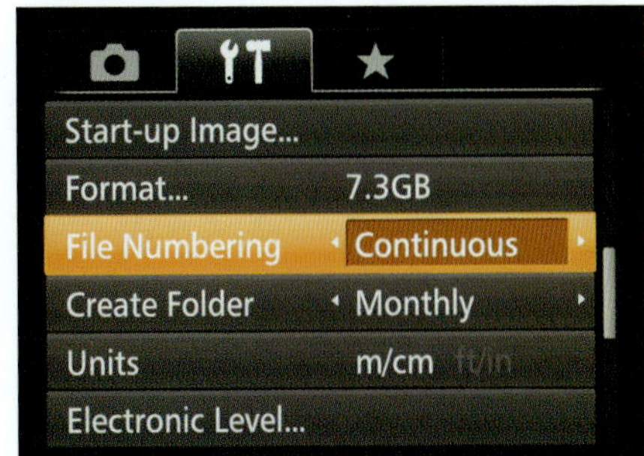

Every time a still image or movie is created on your G16 it is assigned a file name. A still image file name is composed of the letters IMG_ and then a four-digit number. After the main file name is a suffix denoting the file type (.JPG for a JPEG, or .CR2 if the file is in Raw format). A movie file name starts with MVI_, follows the same numbering convention as a still image, and ends with the .MOV suffix.

The four-digit number is a count of the number of images (both still and movie) that you've shot with the G16, starting from 0001. The count is reset depending on which of the two File Numbering options you've selected.

If you choose **Continuous**, the count continues up to 9999, even if you swap between different memory cards.

If you select **Auto Reset** the count is reset to 0001 every time a new memory card is used or a new folder is created.

› Create Folder

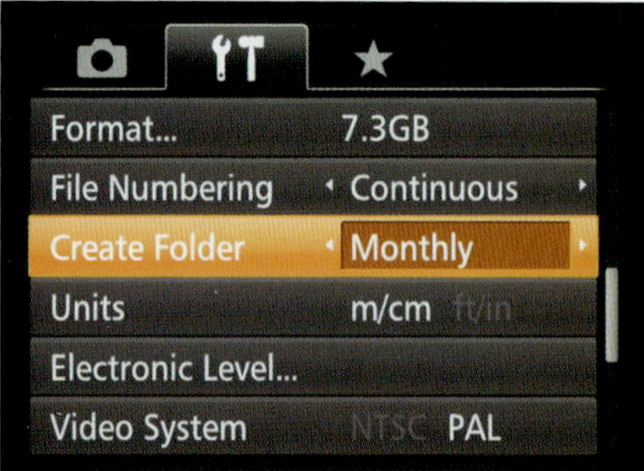

› Units

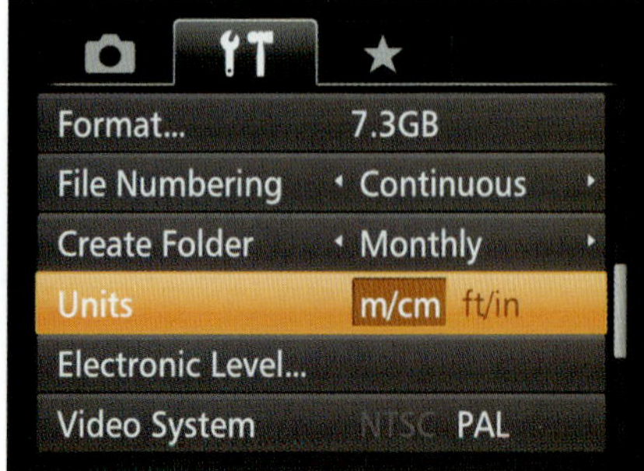

When a memory card is first formatted, the G16 creates a folder in which image files will be stored by default. However, you can also choose whether a new default folder is created **Daily** (every new day that you use your camera) or on a **Monthly** basis.

If you use your G16 regularly, setting the folder creation to **Daily** will very quickly result in a large number of folders on your memory card (unless the card is emptied on a regular basis). This could be confusing if you are looking to find an exact picture, but don't know what date it was shot.

However, creating a new folder **Daily** is useful if you have very specific projects that need to be kept separate from other images on the memory card.

This option allows you to choose which unit of measurement you prefer when focus distance is displayed on the LCD: **m/cm** or **ft/in**. Arguably, metric is the more accurate for measuring smaller distances, but which you choose is a matter of personal preference.

Distance measurements are particularly important when you're using **MF** combined with 🌷. For increased accuracy you could physically measure the distance from the camera to your subject and set that as the focusing distance.

> **Notes:**
> If there are already images on a memory card, the count may continue from the file number of the last image on the card.
>
> You can store a maximum of 2000 images in a folder. A new folder will be created automatically if this is reached.

› Electronic Level

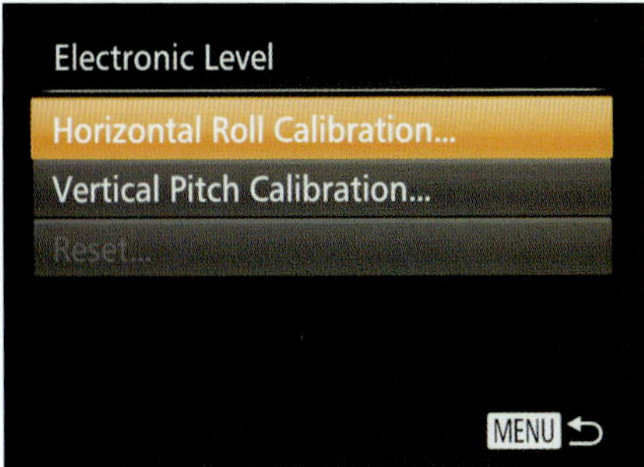

The **Electronic Level** is essentially an electronic spirit level that can be displayed on the LCD. This is particularly useful when shooting subjects such as large bodies of water (water never slopes!).

When the horizontal roll bar is green, the camera is perfectly horizontal, and when the vertical pitch bar is centered, the camera is free from forward or backward tilt. The **Electronic Level** should be accurate straight away, but if you feel that it isn't there is the option to calibrate it.

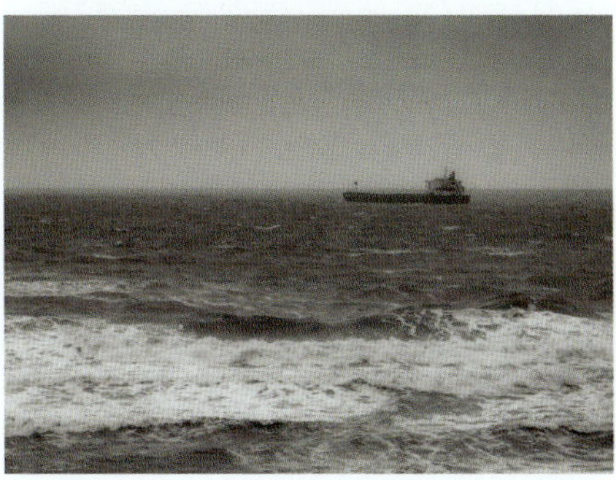

Calibrating the Electronic Level

1) Attach your G16 to a tripod, or a horizontal and stable surface. Ensure that the camera is level and stable before you begin. Some tripods have a spirit level built into the head, so use this to confirm that the camera is level. Alternatively, use a hotshoe-mounted spirit level, available from most good camera shops.

2) Select **Electronic Level** followed by **Horizontal Roll Calibration**. Select **OK** to continue.

3) Calibration will take a few seconds, after which the G16 will return to the main ⚙ menu automatically.

4) Repeat steps 1 and 2, this time selecting **Vertical Pitch Calibration.**

> ***Notes:***
> If you want to reset the default level calibration, select **Reset** from the Electronic Level screen.
>
> Electronic Level can be activated using **Custom Display** on the 📷 menu.

SEASCAPES «
A level of some sort is almost a necessity when shooting seascapes. Another method of keeping horizons level is to align them with the LCD grid.

› Video System

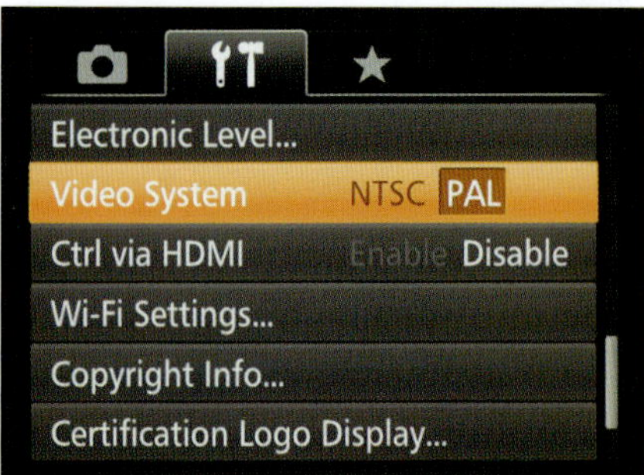

There are two main standards for analog TV transmission, so if you want to connect your G16 to an analog TV you'll need to set it to the correct standard (although most modern TVs should be able to switch automatically between the two formats).

The choices are: **NTSC** (used in Japan and North America) and **PAL** (used in the United Kingdom and other European countries). If you connect your G16 to an analog TV and no image is displayed, it may simply be that the **Video System** is set incorrectly. Switching between **NTSC** and **PAL** should work and, if not, you'll at least have narrowed down the list of potential problems.

› Wi-Fi Settings

See chapter 9.

› Ctrl via HDMI

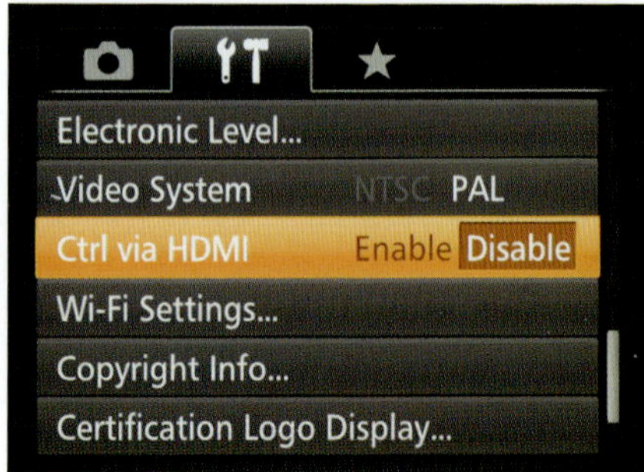

When the G16 is connected to an HDMI CEC-compatible television, the television's remote control can be used to control some of the camera's playback functions. See chapter 9 for further information.

› Copyright Info

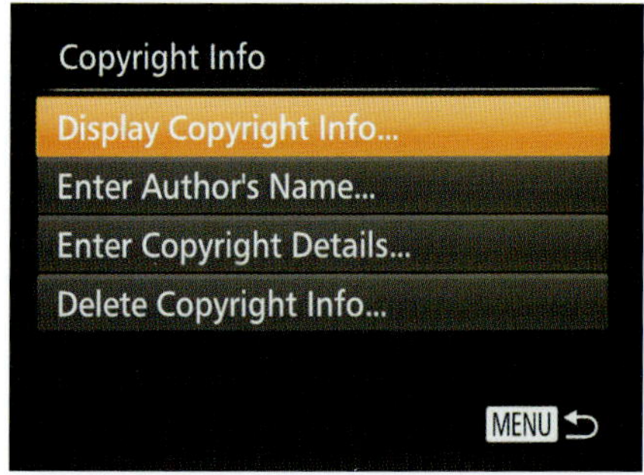

An image for which there is no information about ownership is known as an "orphan work." This is proving to be a big problem for photographers who make their living from licensing their photography. Without ownership (copyright) information, there is increased likelihood that an image might be used without attribution and, more importantly, without payment to the original photographer.

You can reduce the likelihood of this happening to you by embedding copyright information in the image metadata. When copyright information has been entered on your G16, it will be embedded automatically into the metadata of every image you create.

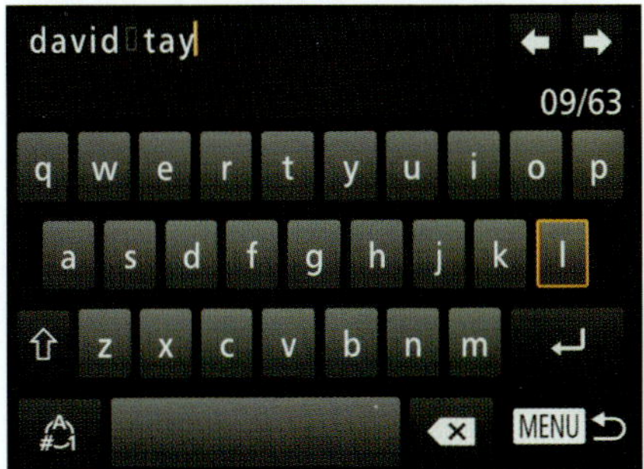

Setting Copyright Info

1) Select **Copyright Info**, then choose either **Enter Author's Name** or **Enter Copyright Details**.

2) On the text entry screen enter the required copyright details.

3) Press **MENU** and select **Yes** to save the copyright details and return to the main **Copyright Info** screen. Select **No** to return to step 1.

Other copyright options

Selecting **Display Copyright Info** shows the currently set copyright information. Selecting **Delete Copyright Info** removes all the copyright information set on the camera (but not from any images saved on the card previous to this).

> **Note:**
> You will probably want to use the same information in Enter Author's Name and Enter Copyright Details. However, you can assign copyright in an image to anyone you wish, so you could conceivably have another person's name or even a company as the copyright owner.

› Certification logo display

This option allows you to view the logos of any third-party imaging technology that has been licensed by Canon for use on the G16. However, it doesn't display all of the technology that has been used in the camera—those logos can be found in the PDF manual that comes with the G16. This is an option you may look at once (if at all) and then never view again.

› Reset All

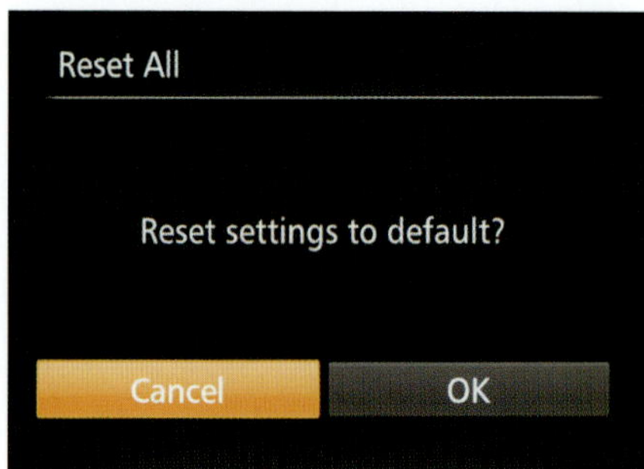

The G16 can be reset to the default factory settings, which is useful if you want to set your camera back to its original state. Once the G16 has been reset you will lose any changes you have made to any settings. The only settings that are not changed and need to be adjusted manually are:

⁝T settings
Time Zone
Language
Date and time
Video System
Registered **Copyright Info**
Electronic Level calibration settings
Wi-Fi settings
Registered Face ID information
Custom white balance settings
Color Accent and Color Swap choices
The current **SCN** or ◓ shooting mode
Exposure compensation settings
Movie mode

› Language

The G16 can display information on the menu screens in a bewildering range of languages. For the sake of amusement it's tempting to set the G16 to an unfamiliar language, but you may regret this—finding your way back to reset the **Language** may prove more difficult than you think!

» ▶ PLAYBACK MENU

The ▶ Playback menu allows you to set how images are displayed on your G16, as well as delete and protect them. You can also run slideshows and change images by applying a variety of color and contrast effects, and by cropping them.

› List/Play Digest Movies

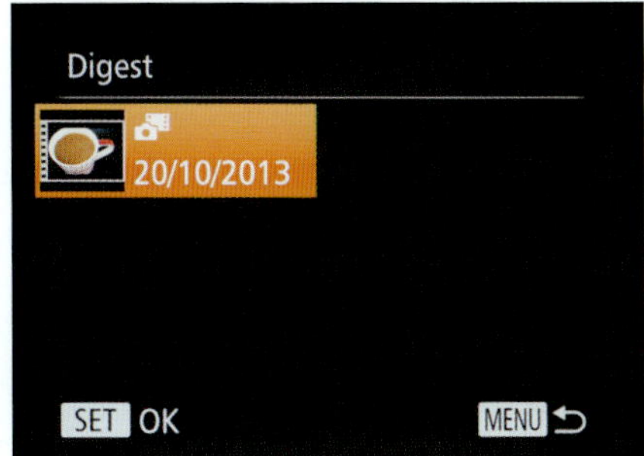

Allows movies shot using ⏷ mode, to be played back by date.

Viewing Movie Digest clips
1) Highlight **List/Play Digest Movies** and press (FUNC. SET).

2) Use ▲ / ▼ or ⏺ to highlight the date of the clip(s) you want to see. Press (FUNC. SET) to view the clip(s) or **MENU** to return to standard playback.

3) The G16 will return to standard playback once the clip has been viewed.

› Smart Shuffle

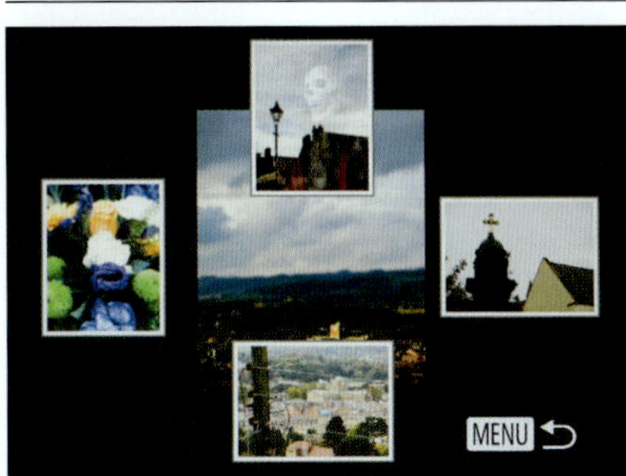

Smart Shuffle selects four images that your G16 thinks you may want to view based on the current still image. These four images are displayed as thumbnails arrayed around the larger main still image.

Using Smart Shuffle
1) Select **Smart Shuffle**. Four small thumbnail images are displayed. Press ✛ to select one of these four images.

2) The selected image will replace the current still image and four new images will be displayed around the main image.

3) Press (FUNC. SET) to toggle between thumbnail view and displaying the current still image on its own.

4) Press **MENU** to return to standard single image display.

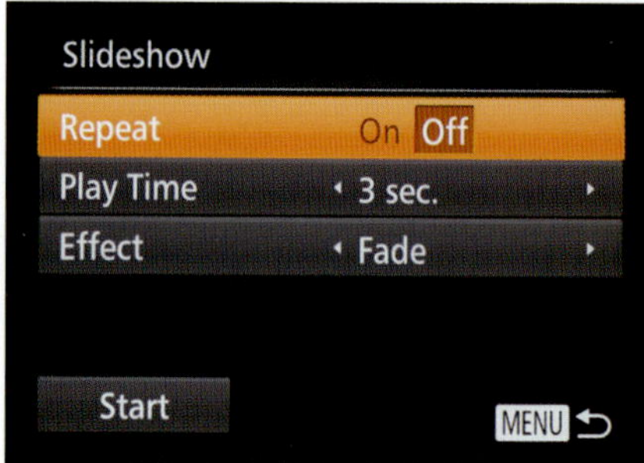

Using Slideshow

1) Select **Slideshow**.

2) From the Slideshow submenu change any or all of the settings listed below.

3) Select **Start** to begin playing the slideshow or press **MENU** to return to the main ▶ menu.

Still images recorded on the memory card can be played back automatically using the **Slideshow** function. For extra impact, why not show your images with the camera connected to a TV (see chapter 9)?

4) When the Slideshow is running, press (FUNC SET) to pause and restart the show, or **MENU** to stop the slideshow.

Setting	Description
Repeat	Set to **On**, the slideshow restarts after the final image has been displayed. When set to **Off**, the slideshow stops after the last image has been displayed.
Play Time	Sets the length of time an image is displayed on screen (between **3 sec.** and **30 sec.**).
Effect	The transition effect used when images are swapped. Choose between **Off** or **Fade**.

› Erase

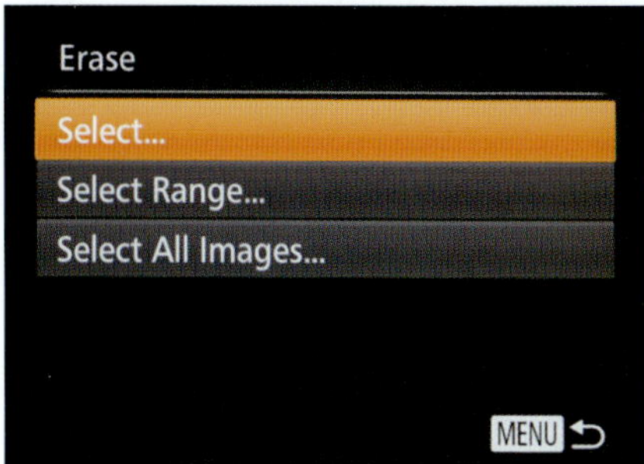

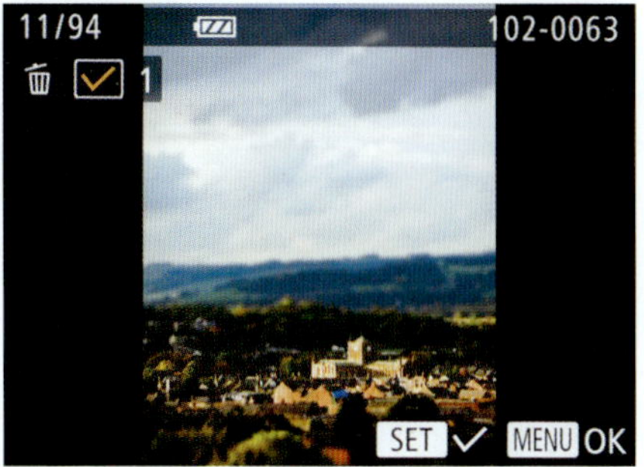

You can erase one image at a time during playback by pressing the ISO/🗑 button. The **Erase** option on the ▶ menu gives you more control over the number of images that are erased at any one time (unless the write-protect tab on the card is set or images have been protected).

Selecting individual images for deletion

1) Highlight **Erase** and press (FUNC. SET).

2) Highlight **Select** on the **Erase** submenu and press (FUNC. SET).

3) The last image you shot will be displayed. Press (FUNC. SET) to mark this image for

deletion if required. An orange ✔ will be displayed in the top left corner to confirm the image has been marked. If you change your mind, press (FUNC. SET) again to remove the ✔ so that the image is no longer marked for erasure.

4) Use ◄ / ► or ⊛ to choose additional images for deletion. Repeat until you have selected all the images to be deleted. The number of images set for deletion will be shown to the right of the ✔.

5) Press **MENU** and select **OK** to erase the selected images; **Stop** to cancel erasure; or **MENU** to return to step 4.

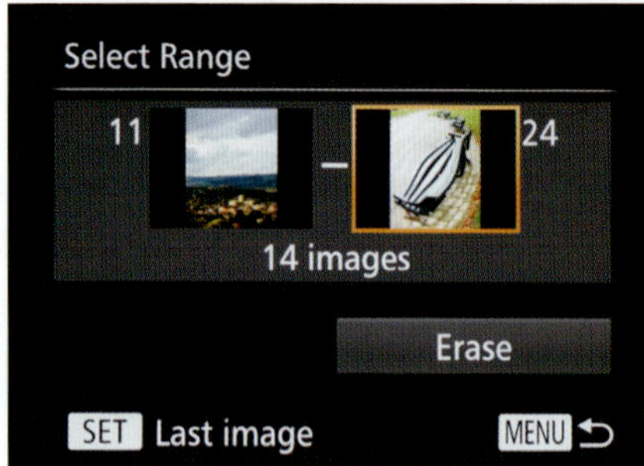

Selecting a range of images for deletion

1) Select **Erase** followed by **Select Range**.

2) Turn ⬤ to navigate to the desired **First image** in the range. Press (FUNC. SET) to view the image full screen and again to return to the Select Range screen.

3) Press ▶. Turn ⬤ to navigate to the desired **Last image**. Press (FUNC. SET) to view the image full screen and again to return to the Select Range screen. You will not be allowed to choose an image that comes before the first image chosen in step 3.

4) Press ▼ to highlight **Erase** and then press (FUNC. SET) to confirm deletion or press **MENU** to return to the Erase submenu without erasing any images.

Selecting all images for deletion

1) Select **Erase** followed by **Select All Images**.

2) Select **OK** to delete all the images on the memory card or **Cancel** to return to the Erase submenu without erasing all the images on the memory card.

› Protect

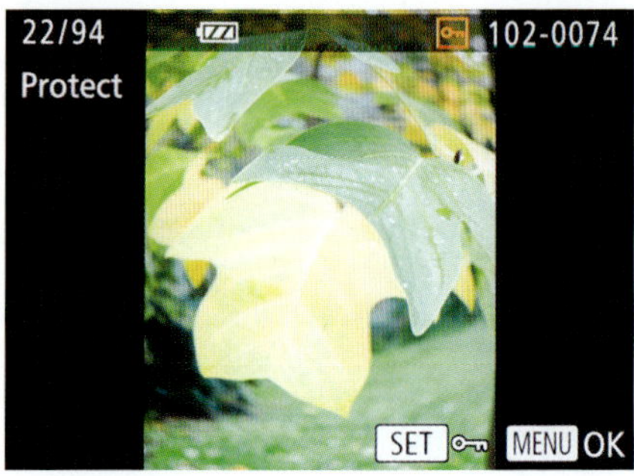

You can shield the images on your G16 from accidental erasure by using **Protect**. You can specify protection for one image only, a range of images, or all the images on the memory card. If you erase images from the memory card only those without protection will be erased.

Selecting individual images for protection

1) Select **Protect** followed by **Select**.

2) The last image you shot will be displayed. Press (FUNC/SET) to protect this image. [O⌐] will be displayed in the bottom left corner of the LCD to confirm that protection is set. Press (FUNC/SET) again to remove the protection.

3) Press ◀ / ▶ or turn ⚙ to select additional images for protection. Repeat this process until all the required images are protected.

4) Press **MENU** and then select **OK** to protect the selected images, **Stop** to cancel protection, or **MENU** to go back to step 3.

> ### Tip
>
> *If you accidentally erase images it's still generally possible to recover them using commercially available data-recovery software. The most important thing is not to shoot any more images using that particular memory card—once you start adding more files to a memory card the chances of successfully recovering images are reduced.*

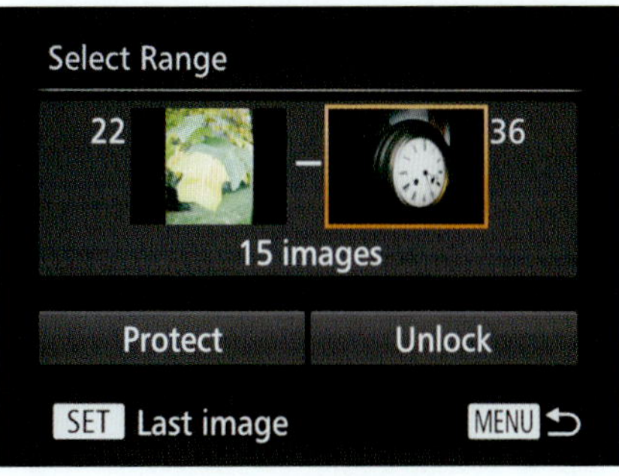

Selecting and deselecting protection for a range of images

1) Select **Protect**, then **Select Range**.

2) Turn ⚙ to navigate to the desired starting image in the range. Press (FUNC/SET) to view the image full screen, and then again to return to the **Select Range** screen.

3) Press ▶. Turn ⚙ to navigate to the desired last image. Press (FUNC/SET) to view the image full screen, and then again to return to the **Select Range** screen. You will not be allowed to choose an image that comes before the first image chosen in step 2.

4) Press ▼ to highlight **Protect** followed by (FUNC/SET) to confirm.

5) To remove protection on the selected range of images press ▼ and then ▶ to highlight **Unlock**, followed by (FUNC/SET).

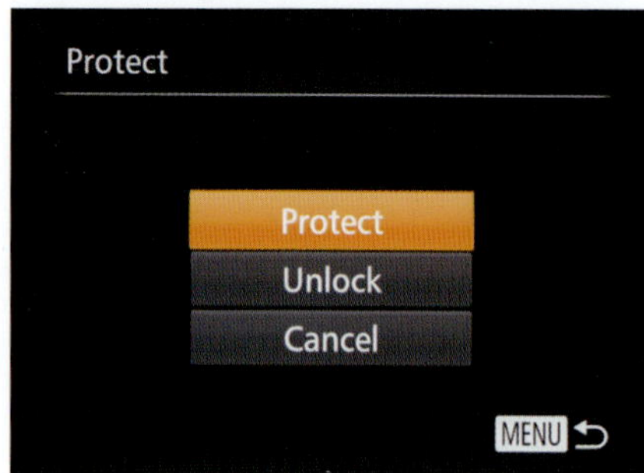

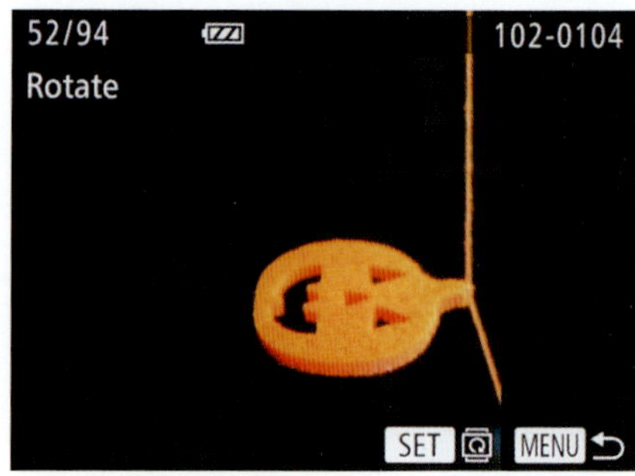

Selecting and deselecting protection for all images

1) Select **Protect** followed by **All Images**.

2) Select **Protect** to set protection on all the images saved to the memory card. Select **Unlock** to remove protection from all the images on the memory card. Press **MENU** or select **Cancel** to return to the **Protect** submenu.

> **Note:**
> If you format a memory card all images will be erased, regardless of whether protection has been applied.

› Rotate

If the G16 can't determine the angle it is being held at when an image is made, there's a chance the image can be saved in the wrong orientation. This is most likely to happen if you shoot an image with the G16 pointing directly down or straight up. If an image has been saved in the wrong orientation you can rotate it using the **Rotate** option.

You can also use Rotate for a more subtle reason: it's often easier to see whether a composition has worked when an image is viewed upside-down. It may sound odd, but it works. This is due to the fact that you're able to look at an image more objectively when it's upside-down.

Rotating images

1) Select **Rotate**.

2) Press ◀ / ▶ or turn ⊙ to navigate to the image you want to rotate. Press (FUNC SET) to rotate the image 90-degrees clockwise. Each time you press (FUNC SET) the image is rotated another 90-degrees clockwise until it returns to its original orientation.

3) Press **MENU** to return to the main ▶ Playback menu.

› Favorites

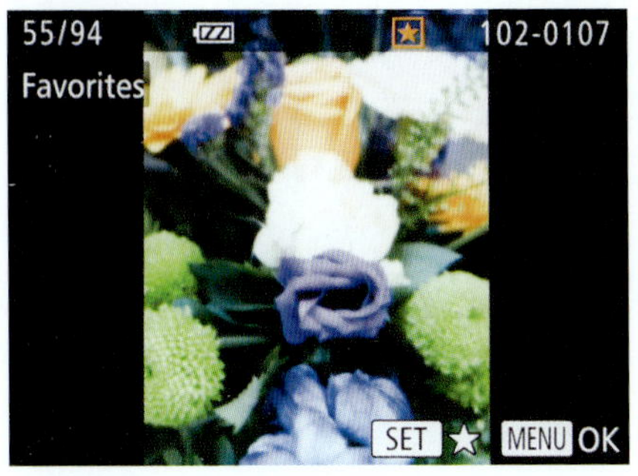

You can tag images shot by the G16 as Favorites. Tagging images this way can be used as a method of viewing certain images using the G16's filtered playback, making the creation of slideshows, viewing, protecting, erasing images, and setting DPOF far more efficient.

Notes:
Rotate is not available if **Auto Rotate** is set to **Off**.

Movies saved using 60P, 30P, or HD 30P can't be rotated.

JPEGs that have been tagged as favorites will have a rating of ★★★ when transferred to a computer running Windows Vista, 7, or 8.

Selecting images as favorites

1) Select **Favorites**.

2) Press ◀ / ▶ or turn ⬤ to navigate to the image you want to tag as a favorite and press ⒮. An orange ★ will be displayed at the top of the LCD as confirmation. Press ⒮ again to untag the image.

3) Continue navigating through your images until you have tagged all the images that you want to set as favorites and then press **MENU**.

4) Select **OK** to set all the selected images as favorites, **Stop** to return to the ▶ menu without tagging, or press **MENU** to go back to step 2.

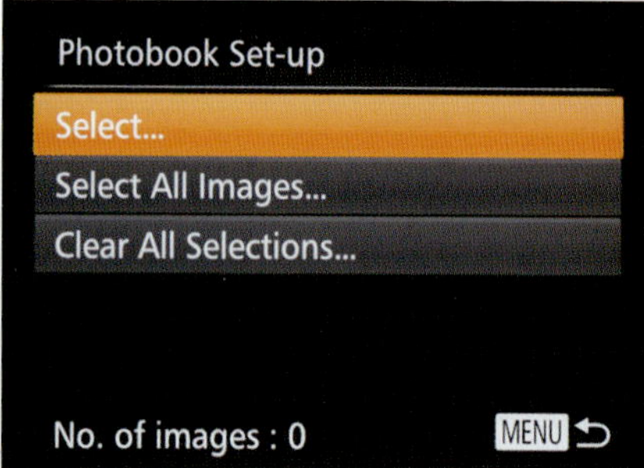

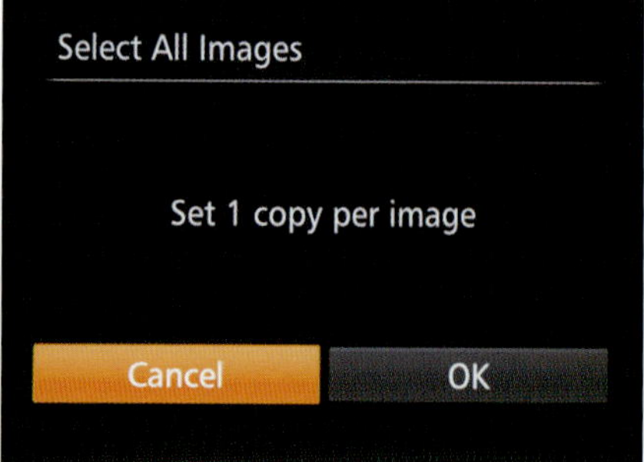

Although images can look good on a screen, there's nothing like seeing them reproduced as a print or even in a book. One of the revolutions brought about by digital imaging technology is the ability to create and publish professional-looking photobooks using your own images. These books can be ordered from companies such as Blurb and Lulu in any quantity from a single copy upward.

Photobook Set-up lets you select up to 998 images for use in a photobook. With Canon's software installed you can then transfer the selection to your computer, where they will be saved into a dedicated folder. With Photobook Set-up you can: **Select** individual images, **Select All Images**, or **Clear All Selections**.

Adding individual images to Photobook Set-up

1) Select **Photobook Set-up** followed by **Select**.

2) Press ◀ / ▶ or turn ⬤ to navigate through the images on the memory card. Press (FUNC SET) to add the currently displayed image to the photobook set. An orange ✓ will be displayed in the top left corner to show that the image has been selected. Press (FUNC SET) again to remove it from the set.

3) Continue to select other images. When you're finished, press **MENU** and select **OK** to create the set and return to the **Photobook Set-up** submenu.

> **Note:**
> Raw files cannot be added to the photobook set.

› i-Contrast

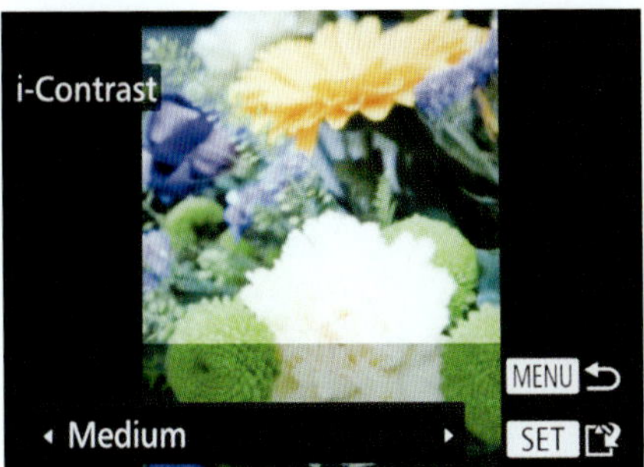

i-Contrast applies automatic brightness and contrast adjustments to an image to try and recover highlight or shadow detail (in a similar way to the DR Correction and Shadow Correct functions).

As with DR Correction or Shadow Correct, your G16 can't work miracles. In fact, the results using this option should only be seen as a last resort—far better image quality will be achieved by activating either DR Correction and Shadow Correct at the time of shooting, rather than applying i-Contrast to fix things later. There are four levels of adjustment to choose from, and the results are saved as a new image.

Using i-Contrast

1) Select **i-Contrast.**

2) Press ◄ / ► or turn ◉ to navigate to the desired image. Press ⬛ to continue.

3) Use ◄ / ► or ◉ to choose a level of correction. **Auto** will apply correction automatically, while **Low**, **Medium**, and **High** alter the strength of correction. Press ⬛ to set the level of correction or press **MENU** to go back to step 2.

4) Select **OK** to save a new image with correction applied, or **Cancel** to return to step 3.

› Red-Eye Correction

Automatically removes red-eye caused by flash from your images. See chapter 4 for more details.

> **Notes:**
> Adjusting the brightness of an image with **i-Contrast** may increase the overall noise levels in the image, particularly in areas of shadow.
>
> Raw files cannot be adjusted using **i-Contrast**.
>
> Functions such as **i-Contrast**, which save a new version of an altered image, can only be used when there is sufficient space on your memory card.

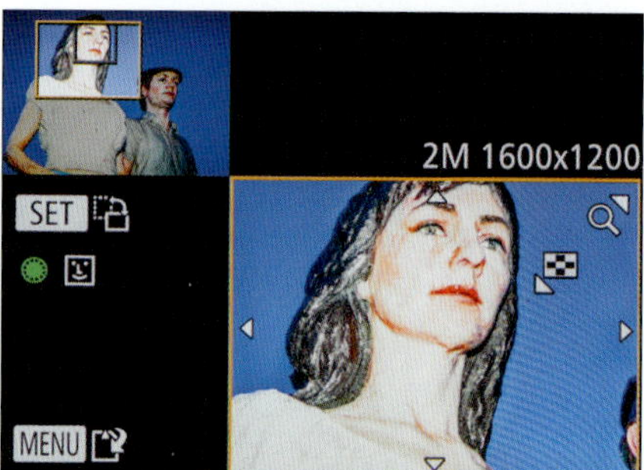

You can crop your images after shooting if you believe a bit of judicious pruning will help to improve a composition. When an image is cropped the original is retained and a new image file is created.

Notes:
Raw files and JPEGs recorded as **S** or saved as **XS** cannot be trimmed.

A cropped image will have the same aspect ratio as the original.

Cropping your photos
1) Select **Cropping**.

2) Use ◀ / ▶ or ● to navigate to the image you want to crop and press (FUNC SET).

3) The original image is displayed at the top left corner of the LCD and a preview of the cropped image appears at the bottom right. A frame is displayed inside the original image showing the area that will eventually be cropped.

4) Use the zoom lever to increase or decrease the area to be cropped, pushing to the left to increase the crop area or to the right to decrease it.

5) Use ✚ to move the crop box around the image or (FUNC SET) to change the orientation of the frame.

6) If your G16 detects a face (or faces) in the original image, a gray box will be drawn around the face(s). You can use these boxes as a basis for cropping. Switch between the different boxes by turning ●.

7) Press **MENU** and select **OK** to save a new image with trimming applied, or **Cancel** to return to step 2.

› Resize

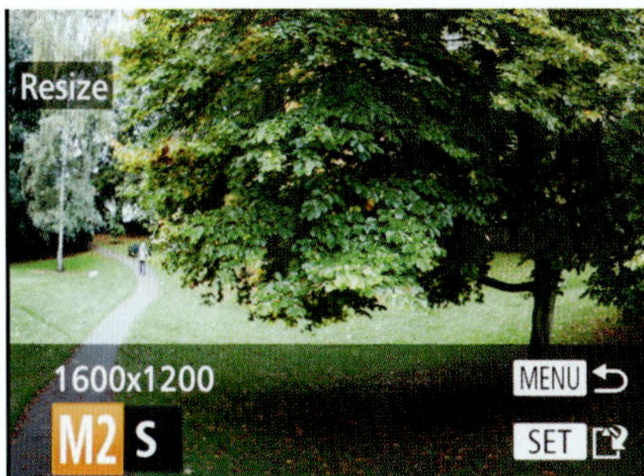

Resize allows you to shrink JPEG images in-camera, reducing the pixel resolution of the image, and then saving the result as a new file. This is useful if you want to shrink an image to email or upload to a web site, but don't have any image-editing software on your computer, tablet, or smartphone.

Resizing your images

1) Select **Resize**.

2) Use ◀ / ▶ or ⬤ to find the image you want to shrink and press (FUNC/SET).

3) Use ◀ / ▶ or ⬤ to highlight one of the resize options. There are two options: **M2 (1600x1200)** and **S (640x480)**.

4) Press (FUNC/SET) and select **OK** to save the new image or **Cancel** to return to step 3.

› My Colors

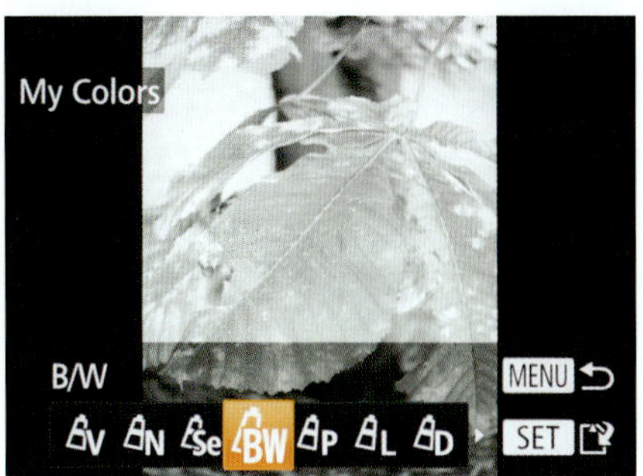

This option allows you to apply My Colors options (see p50) to the currently displayed image after capture, saving the results as a new file. As with i-Contrast, this can reduce the image quality compared to choosing the required My Colors option at the time of capture.

Applying My Colors to images

1) Select **My Colors**.

2) Use ◀ / ▶ or ⬤ to navigate to the desired image and then press (FUNC/SET).

3) Use ◀ / ▶ or ⬤ to highlight a **My Colors** option and press (FUNC/SET).

4) Select **OK** to save a new image with the selected **My Colors** option applied, or **Cancel** to return to step 3.

› Face ID Info

Use this option if you've previously set Face ID information, but the name shown during playback is incorrect (registered names will only be shown in playback when **Name Display** on the Face ID Info submenu is set to **On**).

Changing Face ID Info

1) Highlight **Face ID Info** and press (FUNC. SET).

2) Highlight **Edit ID Info** and press (FUNC. SET).

3) Press ◄ / ► or turn ⊛ to navigate to the image with the incorrect name shown (if it's not already displayed) and press (FUNC. SET) once more.

4) An orange frame will be drawn around the face. If there is more than one registered face press ◄ / ► or turn ⊛ to select the face with the incorrect name. Press (FUNC. SET).

5) Select the option you want to edit and then follow the procedure on page 132 to **Overwrite** or **Erase** the information. **Cancel** will take you back to step 4.

› Transition Effect

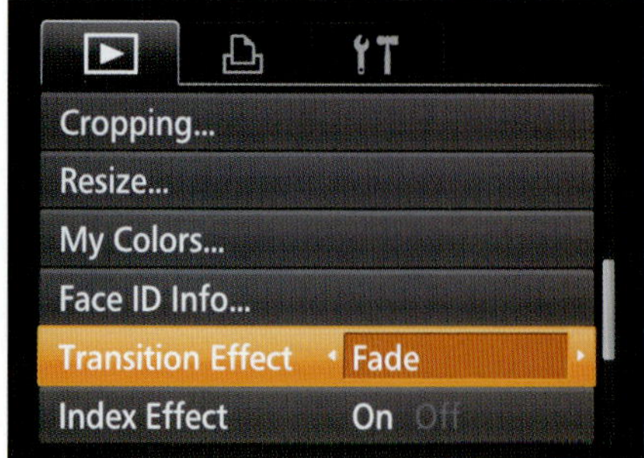

You can set your G16 to use a variety of effects to clear the screen when jumping between images in Playback mode. There's no right answer to what setting you use, it's very much personal preference. **Off** is the most time efficient (as there's no delay between images), while **Fade** is arguably more aesthetically pleasing.

› Group Images

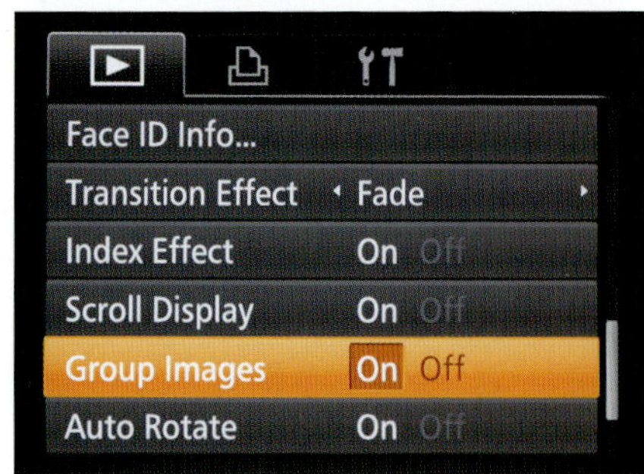

When a sequence of still-images is shot using continuous shooting or 💥, they will be grouped together when **Group images** is set to **On**. Set to **Off**, images are not saved as a group, so you can view them individually once they've been saved to the memory card.

› Index Effect

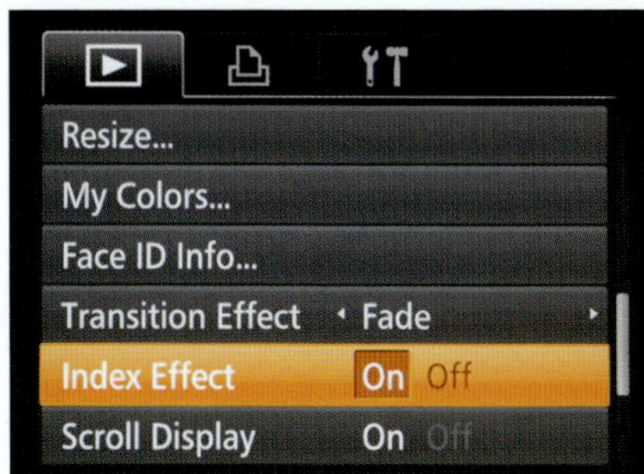

If you're viewing images in index mode (so that there's more than one image on the screen) you can choose how the images are displayed as you quickly scroll through the thumbnails.

When **Index Effect** is set to **On**, the index display will tilt into the screen as you scroll. The faster you scroll, the greater the tilt. When you stop scrolling the index display returns to normal. When **Index Effect** is set to **Off** the display sticks strictly to two dimensions. It's a non-essential option, but fun for a few minutes.

› Scroll Display

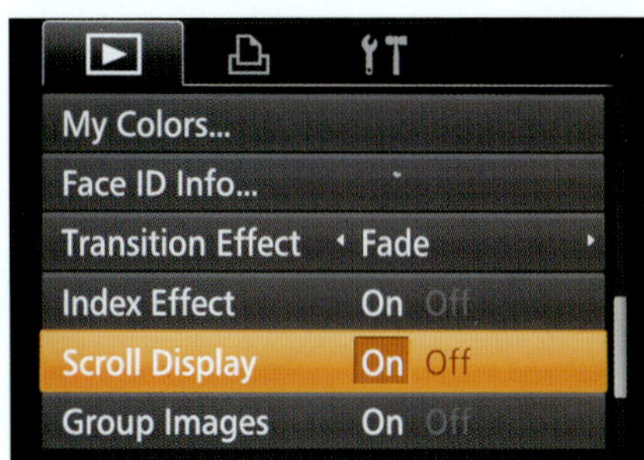

Turning ⬤ allows you to scroll quickly through the images on your memory card in Playback mode. As you turn ⬤, three images are displayed on screen: a thumbnail of the current image flanked by smaller thumbnails of the previous and next images.

To view the main image full screen you need to press ⊙. If this seems a bit clunky, set **Scroll Display** to **Off**. Now, when you turn ⬤ only one image is displayed (full screen) at a time, removing the need to press ⊙.

Set **Scroll Display** to **On** to restore the three-image view.

› Auto Rotate

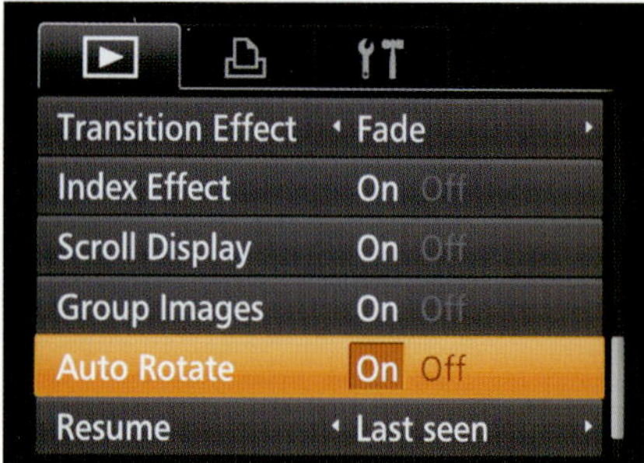

If **Auto Rotate** is set to **On**, the current image on the screen changes orientation so that it is always the right way up as you turn the camera. This means that when the camera is held vertically, horizontal images no longer fill the screen. Conversely, vertical images don't fill the screen when the camera is held horizontally (but they do when the camera is held vertically).

Switching **Auto Rotate** to **Off** stops the image automatically rotating, so vertical and horizontal images always fill the screen, but will be displayed in the wrong orientation when the camera is held in the opposite orientation.

› Resume

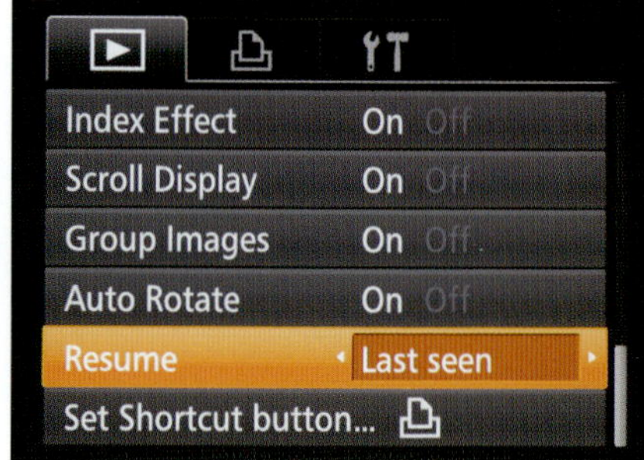

When you press ▶, the default setting is that the **Last seen** image will be displayed. However, this can be changed to **Last shot**, which will always display the last image you shot.

› Set Shortcut button

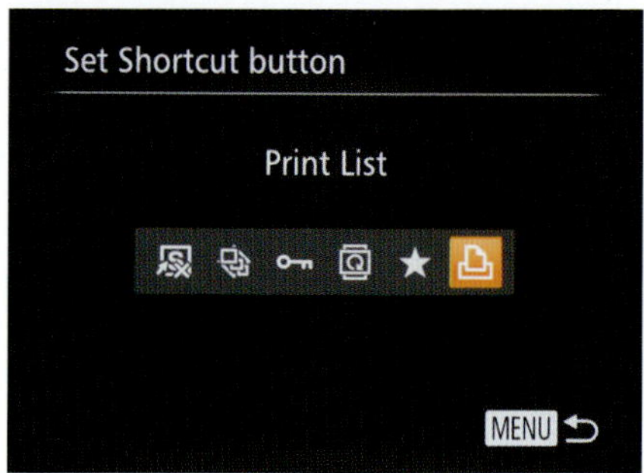

Set Shortcut button allows you to assign a playback function to the 🅢 button. Choose between: Slideshow, On Protect, Rotate, ★ Favorites, and Print List.

» 🖨 PRINT MENU

The G16's Print menu allows you to specify print settings for images saved to the memory card. These include setting the range of images set for printing, and the number of pages to be printed of each image. Print settings comply with the commonly used DPOF standard (JPEG files only). See chapter 9 for more information.

» ★ MY MENU

It can be a chore wading through menus, so if there are options on the 📷 menu that you find yourself altering regularly, you can assign them to the more succinct My Menu. Up to five menu items can be assigned to My Menu.

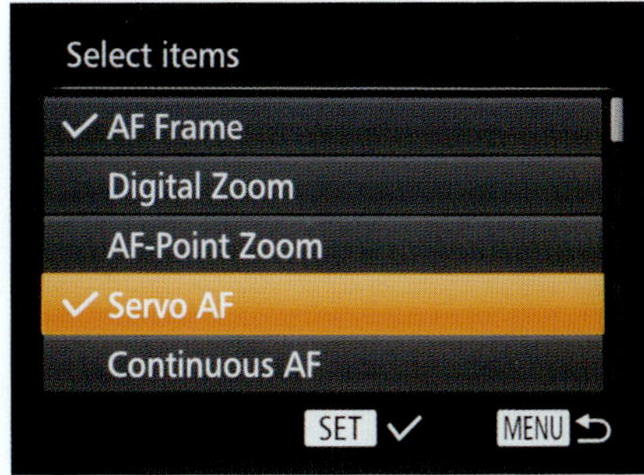

Adding menu options to My Menu
1) Select **My Menu settings** on the ★ menu screen, followed by **Select items**.

2) Use ▲ / ▼ or ⚙ to move up and down the 📷 function list. Press (FUNC.SET) to add a function to ★. A ✓ will be displayed next to the function to confirm selection. Press (FUNC.SET) again to deselect it. If a function is grayed out it can still be selected, but may not be available in the Shooting mode you are currently using.

3) Press **MENU** to return to the ★ submenu and save your selection.

Changing the order of functions on My Menu
1) Select **My Menu settings** followed by **Sort**.

2) Use ▲ / ▼ or ⚙ to navigate up and down the ★ list. Highlight a function and press (FUNC.SET) to select it so it can be moved up or down the list. Press ▲ / ▼ or turn ⚙ and the item will jump one place up or down the list order. Press (FUNC.SET) to confirm the function's new position in the list.

3) Press **MENU** to return to the ★ submenu and save the new order.

The G16 has a built-in, pop-up flash for those occasions when extra illumination is needed. It is also compatible with Canon's EX Speedlite range, as well as other third-party flash units.

The G16's built-in flash is usually hidden inside the top plate of the camera to the left of the lens. To release the flash, move the ▶ᔍ switch to the right; to stow the flash, push it down gently until it clicks back into place.

Some of the more automated modes will raise the flash automatically if light levels are low, but in the less automated modes you'll be warned when flash may be necessary with **Raise the Flash** appearing on the LCD (it's up to you whether you take heed of this advice). The flash will not fire when movies are being recorded.

With the lens set to [wide], and using maximum aperture, the effective range of the flash is 1.6–23ft (50cm–7m), but at [tele] the effective range of the flash is reduced to 1.6–15ft (50cm–4.5m). The reason for this difference is that the aperture you use affects the effective distance of the flash, and at [tele] the maximum aperture available is f/2.8 compared to f/1.8 at [wide]. It is the smaller maximum aperture at [wide] that accounts for the reduction in the effective range of the flash.

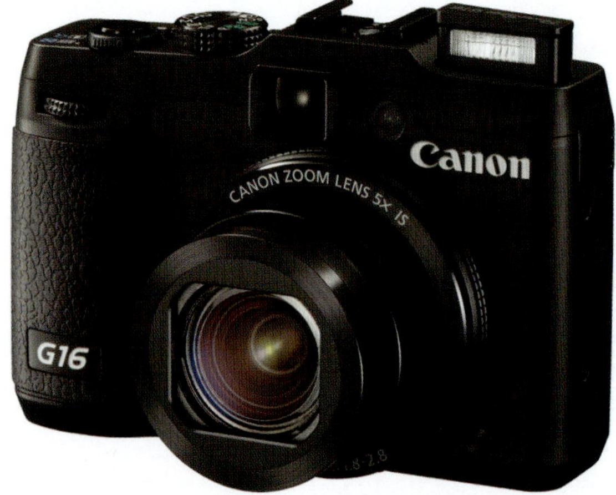

RAISED «
The power of the G16's flash power is low compared to an external flash, but it still has its uses.

FILL IN »
One of the built-in flash's uses is its ability to light foreground objects that are backlit, which helps prevent them being rendered as silhouettes.

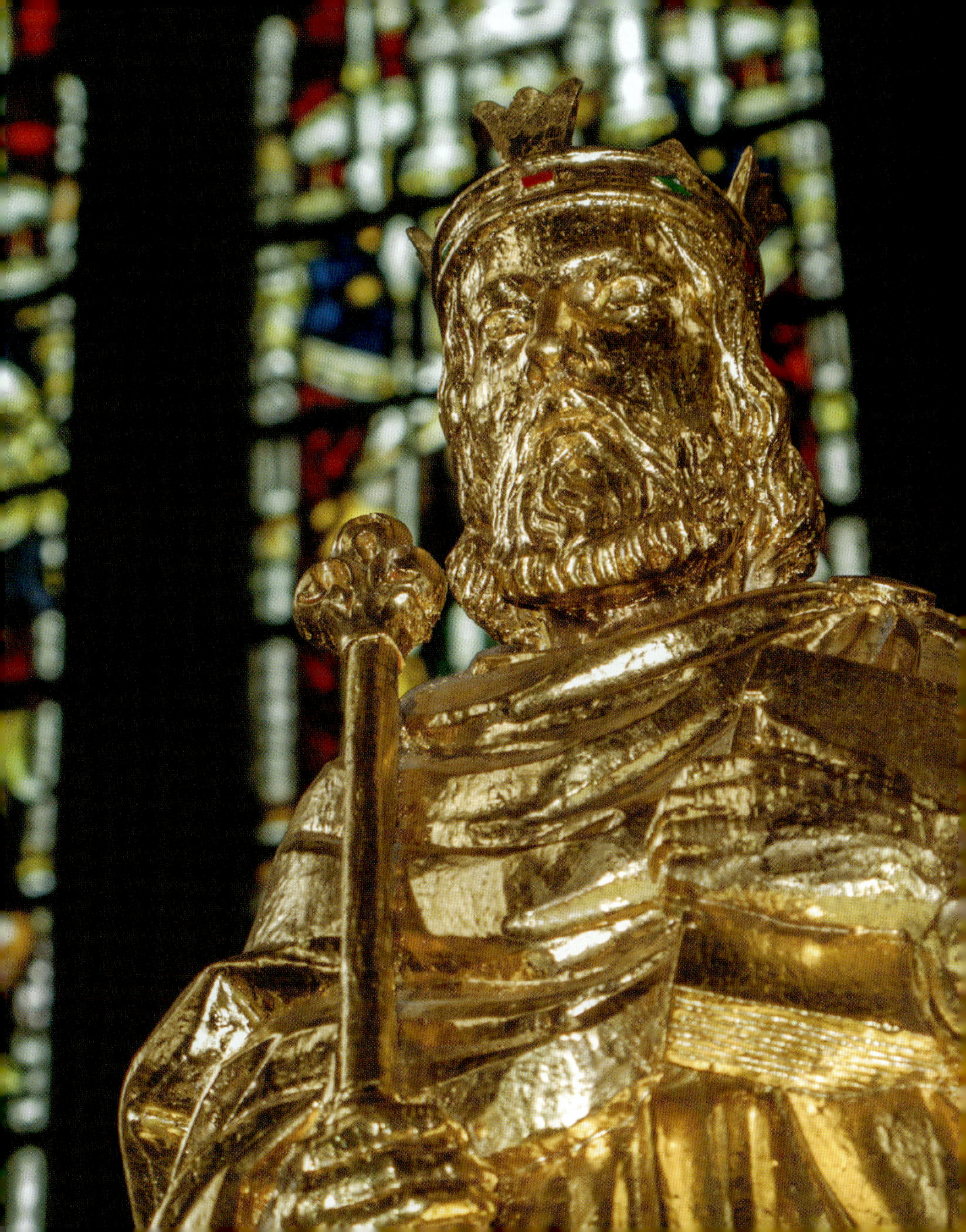

5

» CONFIGURING THE BUILT-IN FLASH

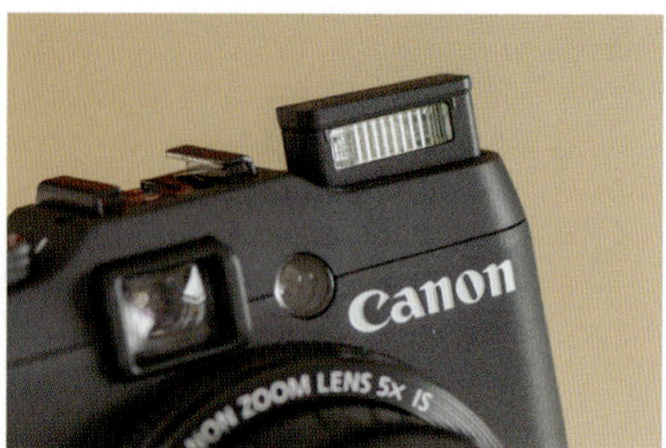

Flash wouldn't be that useful if it always just fired regardless. Fortunately, the G16 has a number of different options to configure the built-in flash. The most obvious option is for it not to fire at all (⚡). This is useful for situations when flash wouldn't be appropriate, such as during a wedding ceremony. At the other extreme is Flash On ⚡, where the flash fires every time you press the shutter-release button. Between the two is a more subtle option—Auto Flash ⚡ᴬ—where the flash only fires if the G16 deems it necessary.

Which of the latter two you'd use would depend on the shooting situation: ⚡ is arguably better for situations when a reliable light source is desirable, while ⚡ᴬ would be better suited to times when you're moving between scenes with different levels of ambient light, where flash may or may not always be necessary. The final option available is ⚡ Slow Synchro (see right).

Setting the flash options

1) Raise the flash by pushing the ▶⚡ switch to the right.

2) Press ▶/⚡ and then quickly press ◀ / ▶ or turn ⬤ to highlight the required flash option. Press (FUNC SET) to select the option.

3) Depending on the flash mode you've chosen, the relevant mode symbol will appear at the top left corner of the LCD.

4) Once you've taken your shot, the flash may take time to recharge. If ⚡ blinks on the LCD the flash is still charging. No further shots can be taken until the flash is fully charged.

5) Repeat step 2, this time highlighting ⚡ to turn the flash off. Push the flash gently back into the body of the camera.

› ⚡ Slow Synchro

The G16's built-in flash is very useful for illuminating subjects that are close to the camera, but it is generally not powerful enough to illuminate an entire scene (this applies to external Speedlites too, even though they are more powerful than the built-in flash).

This often leads to images where the (relatively close) subject is exposed correctly by the flash, but the background is grossly underexposed. This typically happens when ambient light levels are low, such as at dusk or outdoors at night.

The answer to this problem is a technique known as "slow synchro" flash. No matter what shutter speed you select it will have no effect on the flash exposure. What it does affect however, is how well (or otherwise) the areas not lit by flash are exposed.

Slow synchro is the technique of using as slow a shutter speed as is necessary to correctly expose the background. In low light this may mean a shutter speed of several seconds or longer. Using slow synchro will often mean mounting your camera on a tripod and asking your subject (if it's a person!) to keep as still as possible during the exposure.

› Flash Control...

The flash options described previously are set by pressing the ⚡ button. However, many options are found on the **Flash Control...** screen, which is accessed via the ◉ menu. The options available on the **Flash Control...** screen change depending on the shooting mode you're currently

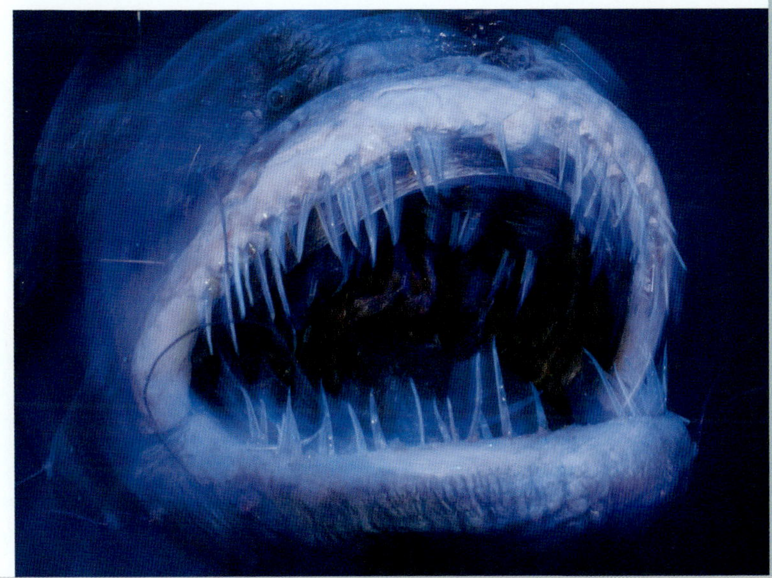

SLOW SYNCHRO »
Moving the camera during long flash exposures can create interesting effects: the flash part of the exposure will be pin-sharp, but areas lit by the ambient light will be blurred.

using. As a rule, the less automated the shooting mode, the greater the number of options. The description at the top of the **Flash Control...** screen changes depending on whether you're altering the **Built-in Flash Settings** or the **External Flash Settings** when a Speedlite is fitted.

> **Note:**
> Canon uses the word Speedlite as a synonym for an external flash and that's the convention used here.

› ◉ Red-Eye Correction

Red-eye is a commonly seen phenomenon when a camera's built-in flash is used. It's caused by light from the flash bouncing off the back of a subject's eyes (the flash light being tinted red by the color of the eye's blood vessels as it does so). Red-eye is exacerbated by the fact that flash is generally used in low light when the pupils of the eyes are at their widest.

You can correct red-eye in one of three ways with the G16: at the time of shooting through the use of the red-eye lamp (this lights before the shutter, causing your subject's pupils to reduce in size); by removing it automatically as the image is written to the memory card (JPEG only); or in postproduction when viewing an image in playback mode (also JPEG only).

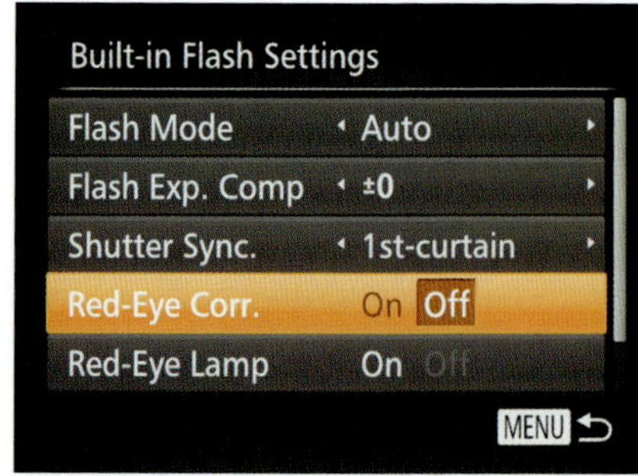

Enabling Red-Eye Correction

1) Select **Flash Control...** from the 📷 Shooting menu.

2) Highlight **Red-Eye Corr.** and set it to **On**. Press the shutter-release button down lightly to return to Shooting mode. ◉ is displayed on the LCD to show that red-eye correction is active.

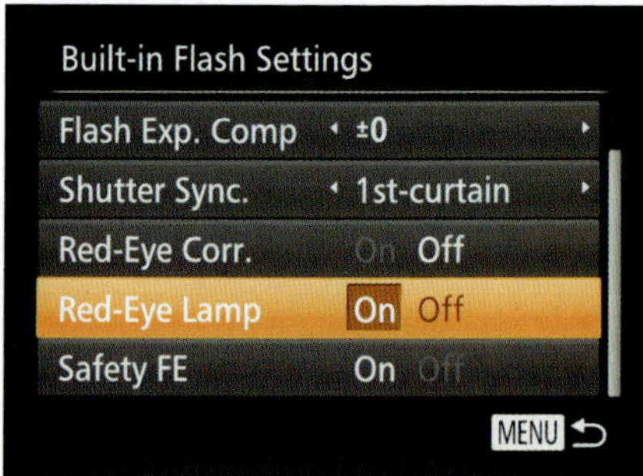

Enabling Red-Eye Lamp

1) Select **Flash Control...** from the 📷 Shooting menu.

2) Highlight **Red-Eye Lamp** and set it to **On**. Press the shutter-release button down lightly to return to Shooting mode. ⊚ is displayed on the LCD to show that red-eye correction is active.

> **Notes:**
> If you're shooting Raw, **Red-Eye Lamp** is the only way to correct red-eye in-camera.
>
> The red-eye lamp is very bright, which makes it very distracting if it's not required. Set **Red-Eye Lamp** to **Off** if you're not photographing people.

Fixing red-eye after exposure

1) In playback mode press **MENU** and select **Red-Eye Correction...** from the ▶ menu.

2) Press ◀/▶ or turn ⦾ to find the image you want to correct and press ⓕⓤⓝⓒ to start the red-eye reduction process. The G16 will detect any faces in your image, reduce red-eye, and draw a box around the altered area. You can use the zoom lever at this point to magnify the image and check the results more closely.

3) Select **New File** to create a new image with the alterations applied, **Overwrite** to replace the original, or **Cancel** to exit without making any changes.

› Shutter Sync.

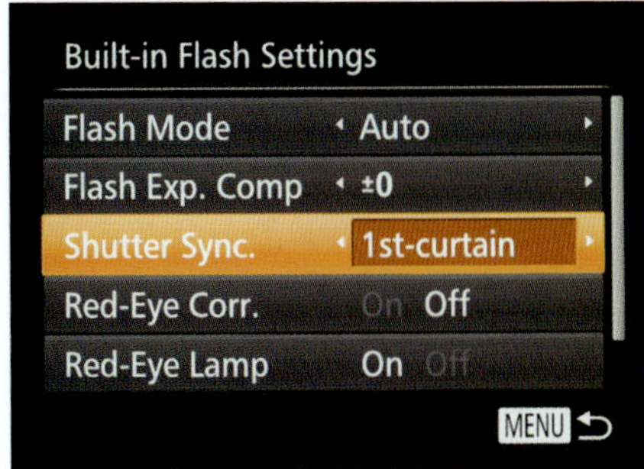

The duration of the light fired from a flash—whether built-in or external—is far shorter than the fastest shutter speed on the G16.

This poses an interesting question: When should the flash fire? At the start of the exposure, when the shutter first opens, or at the end, just before the shutter closes?

By default, the G16 fires the flash when the shutter first opens (also known as 1st-curtain shutter sync). However, you can also choose to fire the flash when the shutter closes (known as 2nd-curtain sync).

You'd be forgiven at this point for wondering what difference this would make to a photograph. Generally, the answer is "very little," and you may never notice a difference between the two settings. However, if your subject is moving across the image frame during an exposure, the setting you choose becomes more important.

When **1st-curtain** is selected, the flash will freeze the movement of the subject at the start of the exposure. If the shutter speed is relatively lengthy, the movement of your subject will then be recorded as a blur that appears in front of it.

When **Shutter Sync.** is set to **2nd-curtain**, the light freezes the movement of the subject at the end of the exposure, which results in your subject's movement being recorded as a blur behind it. Of the two, 2nd-curtain usually appears more natural, although there's no reason not to experiment with both settings for effect.

Setting 2nd-curtain sync

1) Select **Flash Control...** from the 📷 Shooting menu.

2) Highlight **Shutter Sync.** and press ▶ to select **2nd-curtain**. Press **MENU** to return to the main 📷 menu or lightly press the shutter-release button to go directly to Shooting mode.

3) Repeat these steps, selecting **1st-curtain**, to return to the default setting.

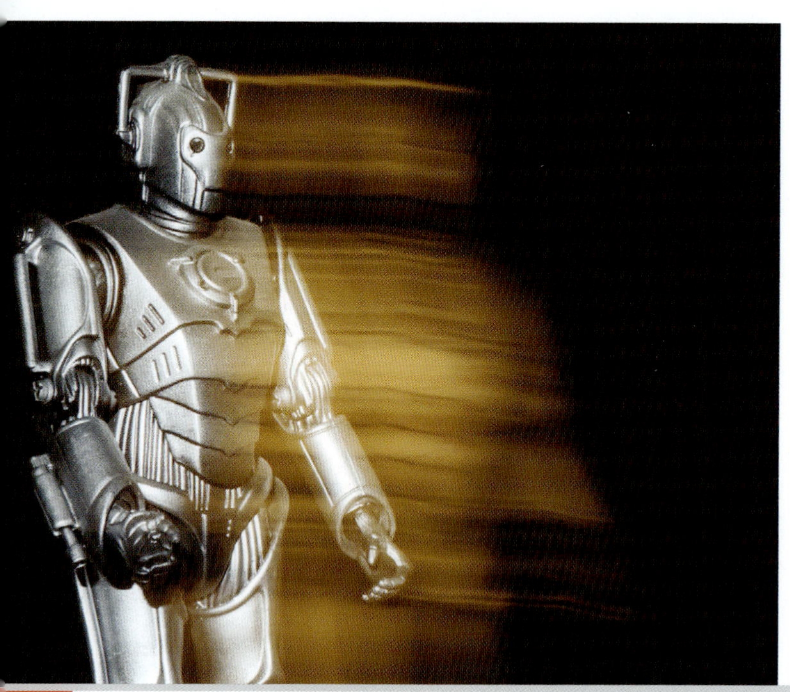

MOVEMENT «
When flash is set to 1st-curtain sync, any movement after the flash fires is recorded as a blur that appears in front of the subject. This will make the subject look as though it's traveling backward.

» FLASH EXPOSURE

Getting flash exposures right is often seen as a dark art. However, once you've grasped a few basic concepts the mystery lessens considerably. One of the most important concepts is the idea of a flash's guide number, or "GN." This number specifies the maximum power output of the flash at a given aperture and ISO setting. To avoid confusion ISO 100 is the standard used when quoting the GN of a flash.

If you know the GN of a flash, you can use this to calculate the aperture value needed to illuminate your subject correctly, or to work out the effective range of the flash at a specific aperture. The formula to calculate both is:

GN/distance=aperture
GN/aperture=distance

By varying the aperture, you alter the effective range of the flash. The wider the aperture, the greater the effective range; the smaller the aperture, the smaller the effective range. Using the Canon 270EX II Speedlite (which has a GN of 89ft/27m), as an example, at an aperture setting of f/2.8 and ISO 100, the effective flash distance is 31.6ft/9.64m. If you change the aperture to f/4, the effective flash distance is reduced to 22.1ft/6.75m.

If you double the ISO, the GN increases 1.4 times, so using the example above, at an aperture setting of f/2.8 and ISO 200, the effective flash distance would be increased to 44.8ft/13.64m.

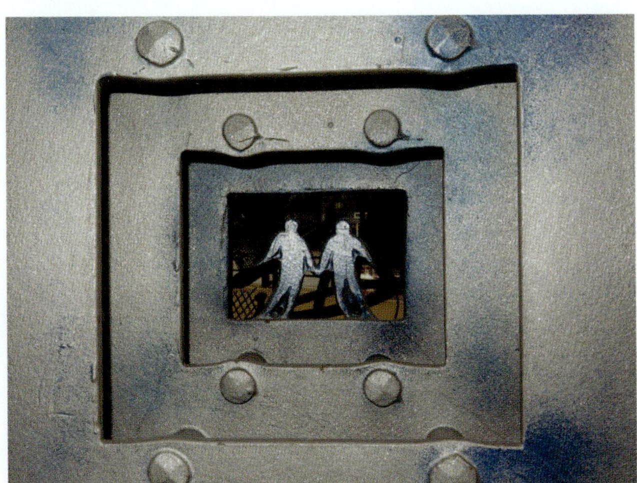

CLOSE «
This sculpture was lit by flash. As it was so close to the camera I used the G16's minimum aperture of f/8 to avoid flash overexposure.

› E-TTL and Manual flash

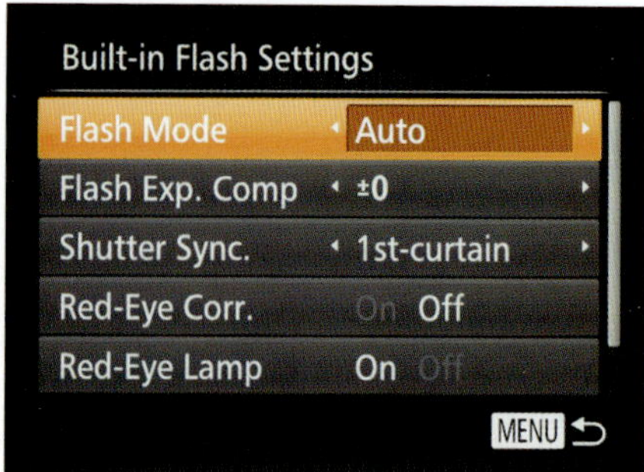

The G16 uses Canon's E-TTL flash exposure system (E-TTL stands for "evaluative through-the-lens metering"). This means that the camera determines the required flash exposure rather than the flash. This has the advantage that accurate exposure is possible even when a light-reducing filter is fitted to the camera.

E-TTL works by firing two bursts of flash. The first is a "test flash," which fires before the image is exposed. The brightness of the second flash is then modified (if necessary) to create an accurate exposure. This all happens in a fraction of a second, so it's impossible to tell that two bursts of flash were fired. This system is generally very accurate, but if necessary you can step in and alter the flash's output.

Manual flash is simple, but trickier to master than E-TTL. With manual flash, the flash is fired at maximum power (1/1) by default. This means that you need to work out the correct aperture to set the camera

to, depending on the distance of your subject from the flash (using the formula on the previous page) or, alternatively, determining the exposure by adjusting the power output of the flash.

Setting the flash mode

1) Select **Flash Control...** from the ◘ Shooting menu.

2) Highlight **Flash Mode** and select **Auto** (so the camera uses E-TTL) or **Manual**.

3) Press **MENU** to return to the ◘ Shooting menu or lightly press the shutter-release button to go to Shooting mode.

> *Note:*
> You can only choose **Manual** when shooting in the **Tv**, **Av**, and **M** modes.

› Flash exposure compensation

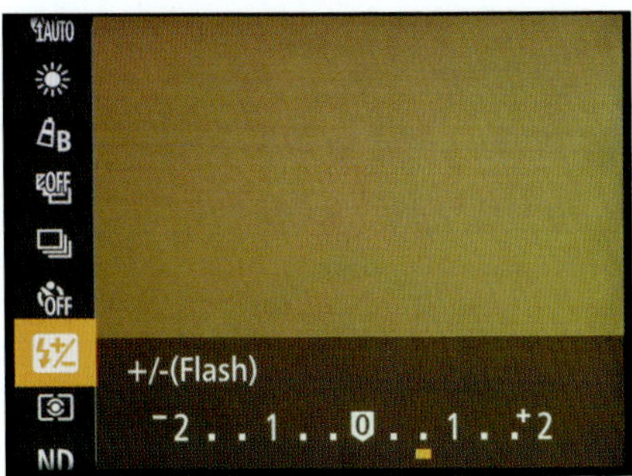

Generally, E-TTL is reliable and your flash exposures should be correct. However, no device is infallible and there may be times when you need to step in and override the flash exposure. This is often necessary when a scene has a higher or lower than average reflectivity.

When flash exposure compensation has been applied, ▦ is displayed on the LCD, but note that the flash can't ever exceed the effective range for the selected aperture/ISO combination, no matter how much positive compensation has been applied. There are three ways to adjust flash exposure compensation.

> **Note:**
> Flash exposure compensation is only available when shooting in the **P**, **Tv**, and **Av** modes.

Method 1

1) In shooting mode, raise the flash (if it's not raised already) and set it to ⚡, or any option other than ⊘.

2) Immediately turn ⟅ to set the flash exposure compensation. You can alter flash exposure by ±2 in $1/3$-stop increments. The amount of compensation is shown at the bottom right corner of the LCD.

3) Make an exposure and check the histogram to see if the flash compensation level was correct. Adjust the flash exposure compensation and reshoot if necessary.

Method 2

1) In shooting mode, raise the flash (if it's not raised already) and set it to ⚡, or any option other than ⊘.

2) Press (FUNC SET) and then use ▲ / ▼ to highlight ▦.

3) Use ◄ / ► or ◉ to adjust the flash exposure.

4) Press (FUNC SET) to set the exposure and return to Shooting mode.

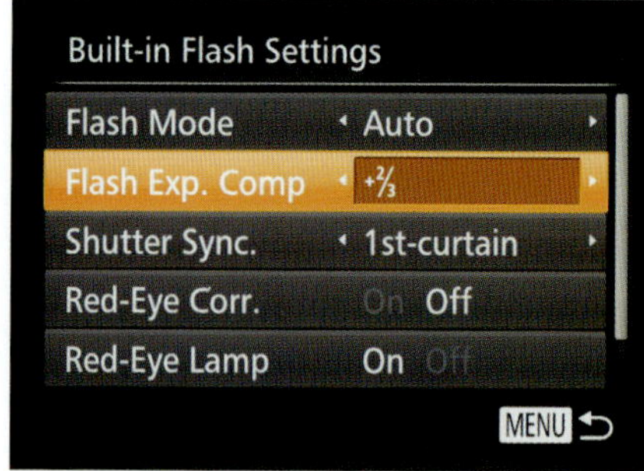

Method 3

1) In shooting mode, raise the flash (if it's not raised already) and set it to ⚡, or any option other than ⚡̷.

2) Select **Flash Control...** from the 📷 Shooting menu.

3) Highlight **Flash Exp. Comp** and use ◄ / ► to adjust the flash exposure. The flash exposure can be altered ±2 stops in $1/3$-stop increments.

4) Press **MENU** to return to the main 📷 Shooting menu or lightly press the shutter-release button to return to Shooting mode.

› FE lock

You can lock the flash exposure in a similar way that non-flash exposures can be locked using AE lock; rather logically, locking the flash exposure is referred to as FE lock. Before the flash exposure is locked, the G16 needs to fire a test flash to determine the exposure that will be locked. If you only get one chance to shoot a particular subject don't use FE lock, as this will announce your intention of shooting and will give the game away.

Setting FE lock

1) In Shooting mode, raise the flash and set it to ⚡.

2) Press ✳. The G16 will fire the flash, determine and lock the flash exposure, and display ✳ on the LCD.

3) Compose your shot if you haven't already, and press the shutter-release button to focus and take your shot.

4) FE lock is deactivated once you've taken the shot, and normal flash exposure operation resumes.

› Safety FE

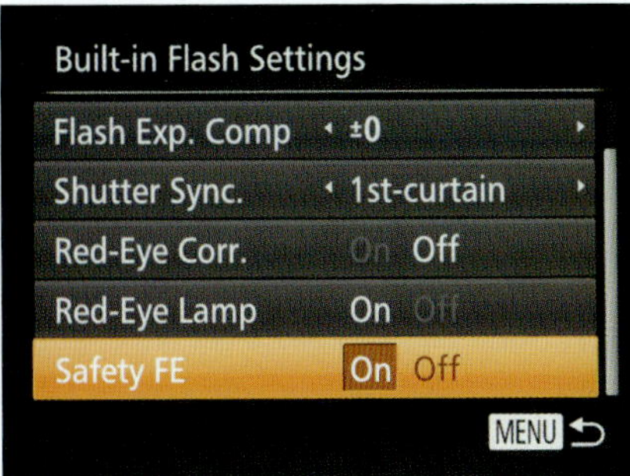

Another safety net to avoid incorrect flash exposure is **Safety FE**. When set to **On**, your G16 automatically changes the shutter speed or aperture to avoid flash overexposure and prevent washed-out highlights. When **Safety FE** is set to **Off**, the shutter speed or aperture will not be adjusted. Safety FE is particularly useful when shooting backlit portraits, as it helps to avoid the faces of your subjects being overexposed.

Setting Safety FE

1) Select **Flash Control...** from the 📷 Shooting menu.

2) Highlight **Safety FE** and set it to **On**.

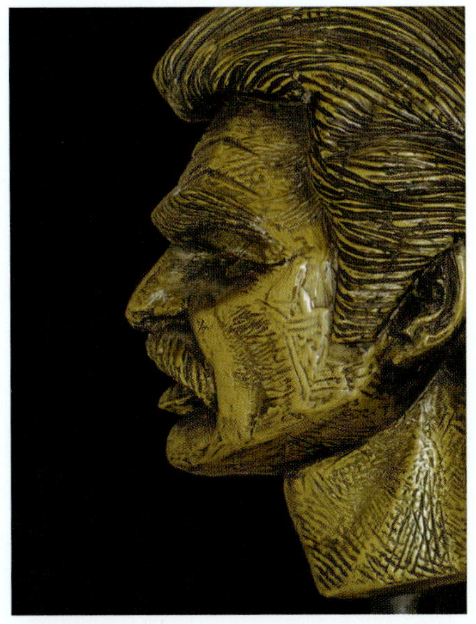

SAFETY FE ⌃
You lose a little bit of control over your flash exposures when Safety FE is activated, so if your flash images don't look as expected turn Safety FE **Off**.

» EXTERNAL SPEEDLITES

Canon's current Speedlite EX flash units are all compatible with the G16, although certain functions may not be available on some Speedlite models. The functions that can be altered are set using the G16's **Flash Control** menu. Non-Canon flash units are not recommended for use with the G16.

Flash isn't a particularly flattering type of illumination when it is fired directly from the camera, and this applies as much to the light from a hotshoe-mounted Speedlite as it does to the G16's built-in flash. A more pleasing light comes from using a Speedlite "off-camera." This will require an OC-E3 Off-Camera Shoe Cord (with optional BKT-DC1 Bracket), or you can fit a "master" Speedlite to the G16's hotshoe and use this to wirelessly trigger an off-camera Speedlite.

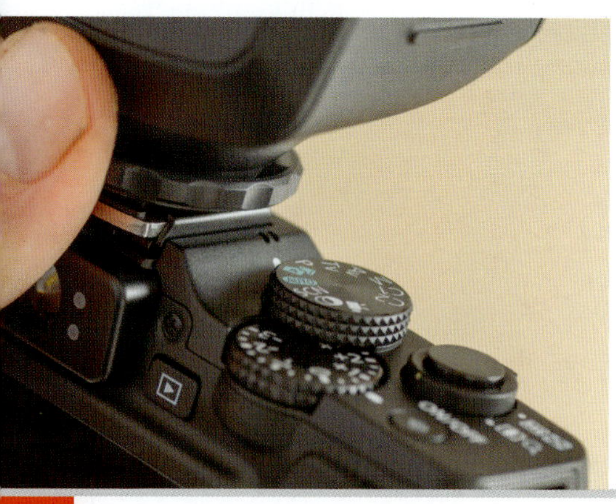

Fitting an external flash

1) Make sure both the G16 and Speedlite are switched off.

2) Slide the Speedlite shoe into the hotshoe of the G16. If the Speedlite has a locking collar, press the locking button and slide the collar round until it clicks into the "locked" position.

3) Turn the Speedlite on first, followed by the G16.

4) Use one of the following modes on your G16: **P**, **Tv**, **Av,** or **M**.

5) To alter the Speedlite's settings press **MENU**, highlight **Flash Control** on the ◯ menu, and press (FUNC SET). The options currently set on the Speedlite will be shown. Alter the settings as required. Anything you change on this menu will automatically be applied to the Speedlite.

6) To remove the flash, switch off the G16 and Speedlite, and reverse the procedure in step 2.

› Configuring an external Speedlite

The options below can be altered on the **Flash Control...** screen when your G16 is set to **P**, **Tv**, **Av,** or **M**. In all other modes only **Red-Eye Corr.** and **Red-Eye Lamp** can be set.

Option	Settings	Shooting mode			
		P	Tv	Av	M
Flash Mode	Auto[1]	Y	Y	Y	N
	Manual[2]	Y	Y	Y	Y
Flash Exp. Comp[3]	-3 to +3	Y	Y	Y	N
Flash Output[4]	1/128 to 1/1 (in 1/3 steps)	Y	Y	Y	Y
Shutter Sync.	1st-curtain/2nd-curtain/Hi-Speed	Y	Y	Y	Y
Slow Synchro	On	Y	Y	Y	Y
	Off	Y	N	Y	N
Wireless Func.	On/Off	Y	Y	Y	Y
Red-eye Corr.	On/Off	Y	Y	Y	Y
Red-eye Lamp	On/Off	Y	Y	Y	Y
Safety FE[6]	On	Y	Y	Y	N
	Off	Y	Y	Y	Y
Clear flash settings[7]		Y	Y	Y	Y

1 Speedlite is set to E-TTL mode.
2 Speedlite is set to Manual.
3 Can only be set on Speedlite when **Flash Mode** is set to **Auto** and flash exposure compensation is [+0].
4 Can be set when **Flash Mode** is **Manual**.
5 Flash output can only be reduced to 1/64 on the Speedlite 220EX, 270EX, 320EX, 430EX II, Macro Ring Lite MR-14EX, and Macro Twin Lite MT-24EX.
6 Can only be altered when **Flash Mode** is set to **Auto**.
7 Resets to default settings.

Notes:
In modes other than **P**, **Tv**, **Av**, or **M** the Speedlite is set and fired automatically unless flash is not available in that mode.

The G16's built-in flash is disabled when an external flash is fitted and switched on.

» CANON SPEEDLITES

› SPEEDLITE 90EX

The 90EX is the newest Speedlite in the range. It's also the smallest, lightest, and the least powerful. Designed for the Canon EOS M camera, the 90EX is compatible with the G16 and its most useful function is as an inexpensive master flash to trigger other compatible Speedlites wirelessly.

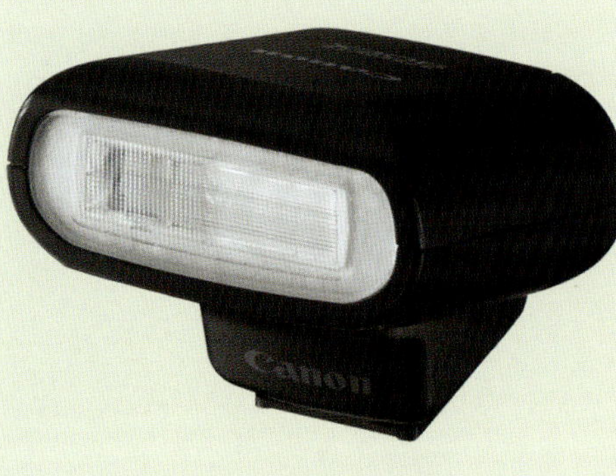

Guide number (GN)
29ft/9m (at ISO 100)

Tilt/swivel
No

Focal length coverage
Min. 24mm*

AF-assist beam
Yes

Flash metering
E-TTL II/E-TTL

Approximate recycling time
5.5 seconds

Batteries
2 x AAA/LR03

Dimensions (w x h x d)
1.7 x 2 x 2.5in./44 x 52 x 65mm

Weight
1.8oz./50g (without batteries)

*35mm equivalent

› SPEEDLITE 270EX II

Next in size, weight, and power is the 270EX II. It's not a particularly powerful flash, but it is still more powerful than the G16's built-in unit. Although the 270EX II is small, it features a zoom and bounce head, and rapid, near-silent recharging. The 270EX II can be used wirelessly as a slave flash in conjunction with a suitable master Speedlite or the built-in flash. However, unlike the 90EX it cannot be used as a master flash to fire other Speedlites.

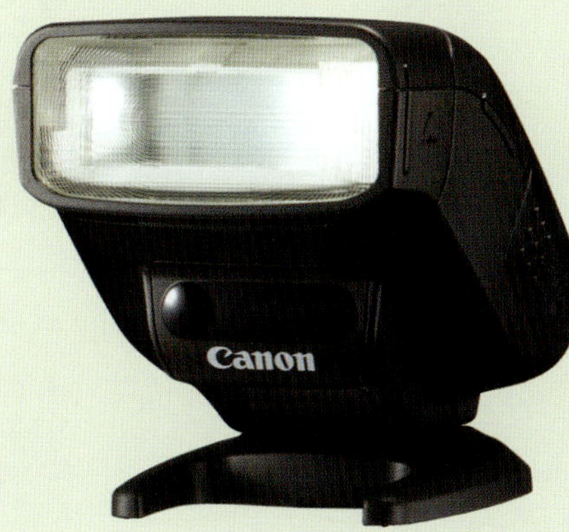

Guide number (GN)
89ft/27m (at ISO 100)

Tilt/swivel
Tilt only

Focal length coverage
28–50mm*

AF-assist beam
Yes

Flash metering
E-TTL II/E-TTL

Approximate recycling time
0.1–3.9 seconds

Batteries
2 x AA/LR6

Dimensions (w x h x d)
2.5 x 2.6 x 3.0in./64 x 65 x 72mm

Weight
5.1oz./155g (without batteries)

Included accessories
Soft case, shoe stand, manual

*35mm equivalent

› SPEEDLITE 320EX

The 320EX is a relatively recent addition to the Speedlite range, and is larger and more powerful than the 270EX II. The most distinctive aspect of the 320EX is the built-in LED light in addition to the main flash head. The LED light is there to provide a constant light source when shooting movies. In theory this is a good idea, but in practice the light isn't that powerful, so your subject needs to be very close to the camera. Like the 270EX II, the 320EX can be used as a slave flash but does not have master flash capability.

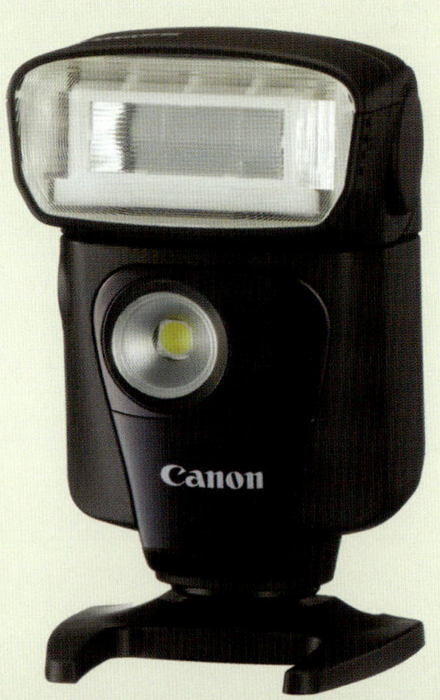

Guide number (GN)
104ft/32m (at ISO 100)

Tilt/swivel
Yes

Focal length coverage
24–50mm*

AF-assist beam
Yes

Flash metering
E-TTL II/E-TTL

Approximate recycling time
0.1–2.3 seconds

Batteries
4 x AA/LR6

Dimensions (w x h x d)
2.75 x 4.5 x 3.09in./70 x 115 x 78.4mm

Weight
9.7oz./275g (without batteries)

Included accessories
Soft case, shoe stand, manual

*35mm equivalent

› SPEEDLITE 430EX II

The Speedlite 430EX II is the smaller, less powerful sibling to the top-of-the-range 600EX-RT. However, with a GN of 43m, it is far more powerful than the G16's built-in flash. The drawback to the 430EX II (and more so for the Speedlite 600EX-RT) is size: fitted to a G16 the setup becomes top heavy and unwieldy. The 430EX II features high speed, 1st- and 2nd-curtain sync, has comprehensive exposure compensation options, and nine custom functions.

Guide number (GN)
141ft/43m (at ISO 100)

Tilt/swivel
Yes

Focal length coverage
14–105mm*

AF-assist beam
Yes

Flash metering
E-TTL II/E-TTL

Approximate recycling time
0.1–3.7 seconds

Batteries
4 x AA/LR6

Dimensions (w x h x d)
2.8 x 4.8 x 4.0in./72 x 122 x 101mm

Weight
11.6oz./320g (without batteries)

Included accessories
Soft case, shoe stand, manual

*35mm equivalent

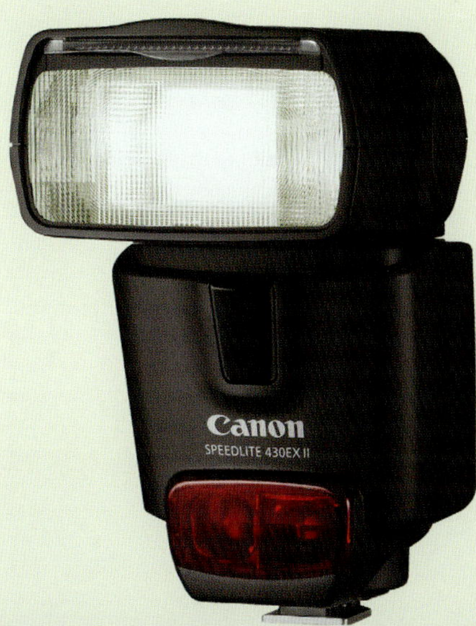

5

› SPEEDLITE 600EX-RT

The Speedlite 600EX-RT is the largest, heaviest, and highest specified flash in the Canon range. It has integrated radio-triggering, as well as infrared wireless flash control, improved weather sealing, high-speed sync, and 18 custom functions. However, as noted, it is perhaps too big and heavy to use in the G16's hotshoe.

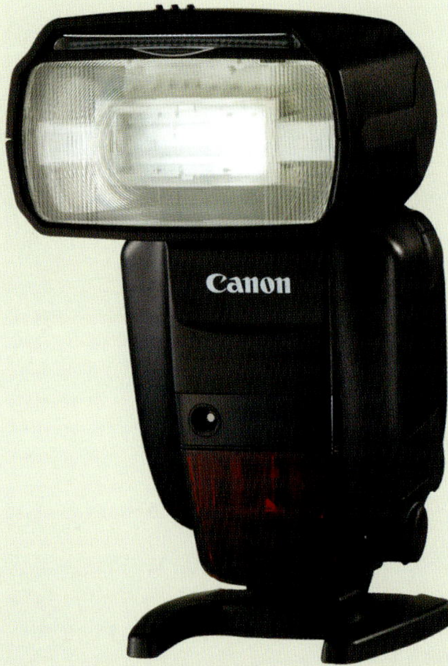

Guide number (GN)
196.9ft/60m (at ISO 100)

Tilt/swivel
Yes

Focal length coverage
14–200mm*

AF–assist beam
Yes

Flash metering
E-TTL II/E-TTL/TTL/Manual

Approximate recycling time
0.1–5.5 seconds
(0.1–3.3 seconds using quick flash)

Batteries
4 x AA/LR6

Dimensions (w x h x d)
3.1 x 5.6 x 4.9in./79.7 x 142.9 x 125.4mm

Weight
15oz./425g (without batteries)

Included accessories
Soft case, shoe stand, color filters
(with case and holder)

*35mm equivalent

› Bounce flash

With the exception of the 90EX, all of Canon's Speedlites allow you to angle the flash head, which means you can use a technique known as bounce flash. Bounce flash is a very simple way of modifying the light from a flash, making it a more sympathetic way to illuminate your subject.

The simplest way to use bounce flash is to angle the Speedlite upward, so that the light bounces from the ceiling down onto your subject. You can achieve the same effect by holding a large piece of white card above the Speedlite and angling it toward your subject.

The surface you bounce the light from must be neutral in color (pure white is ideal as it won't absorb as much light as a light neutral gray surface would). If the surface has a color tint, the light from the Speedlite will pick up the tint, coloring your subject. However, this may be no bad thing—a yellow or cream-colored surface can be used creatively as a way to warm the light when creating portrait images.

It is worth noting that some of the light will be absorbed by the surface you bounce from and the flash-to-subject distance will be increased too. These two factors make your flash less effective, so you will need to use a wider aperture and/ or a higher ISO. The more powerful the Speedlite, the better it will be when it comes to using bounce flash.

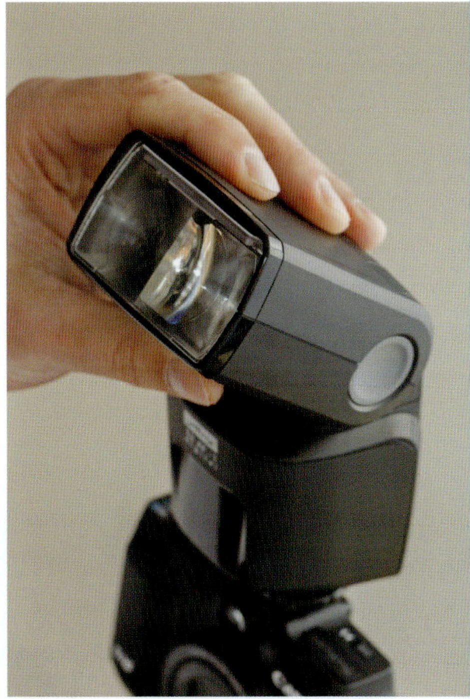

VARIABLE ⌃
To use bounce flash, you need a Speedlite with a head that can be angled up or down. Some also swivel left or right, allowing you to bounce the flash off a wall.

6 IN THE FIELD

Despite the G16's diminutive size compared to Canon's DSLRs it still has many features in common with these cameras. The key is learning to use the camera so that its operation is instinctive.

The body of the G16 is small, but reassuringly solid. As long as you don't abuse it, your camera should be able to withstand many years of active use, but that doesn't mean you should be complacent. If you're shooting in heavy rain, keep your camera covered when not in use, and if it gets wet, wipe it dry as best you can before covering it up again. Once you're back indoors, check the camera thoroughly, and dry it again if necessary.

The lens will also need to be checked and you can remove any moisture on the lens' surface with a lint-free lens cloth.

The ambient temperature at which you shoot is a potential source of problems too. Canon recommends 104°F (40°C) as the maximum operating temperature of your G16. Try to avoid using your camera in temperatures hotter than this, or at least keep the camera cool in the shade when it is not in use.

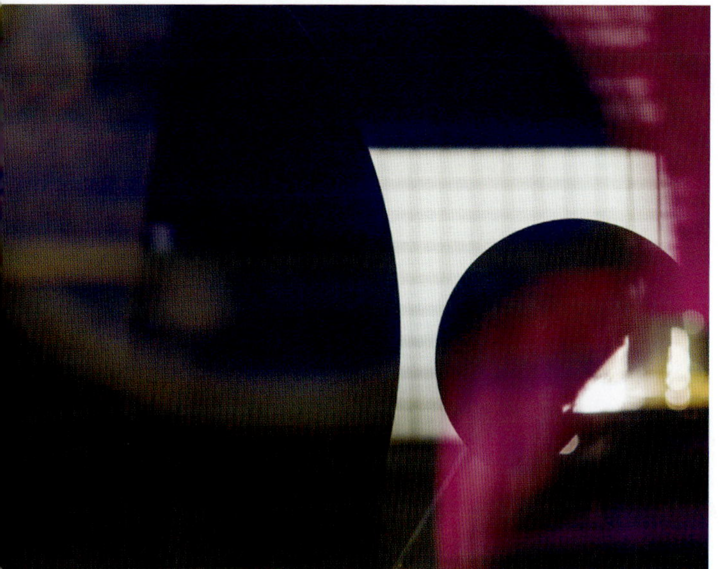

ABSTRACT «
A camera is a powerful tool for self-expression. You can be as literal or as creative as your mood takes you.

SEEN »
This was a "grab" shot, taken on the spur of the moment while walking along a street.

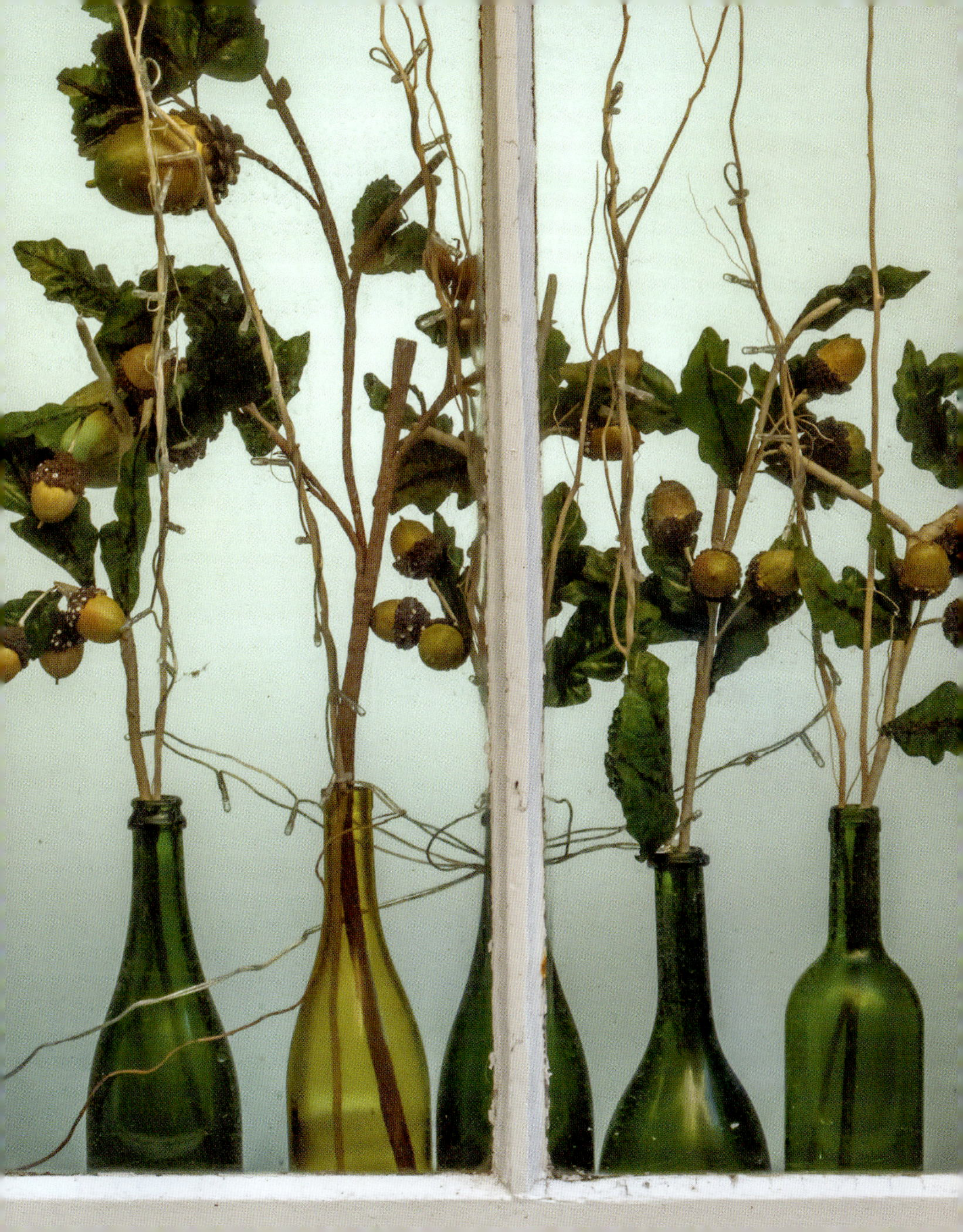

» EXPOSURE

The exposure meter in the G16 works on a very simple principle. It's a reflective meter, so called because it measures the amount of light that has been reflected by the scene being metered (handheld meters are incident meters that measure the amount of light that falls onto a scene; a subtle, but important difference).

Reflective exposure meters aren't perfect. They assume that the scene being measured has an average amount of reflectivity, so it reflects roughly 18% of the light that falls on it. This equates to a mid-gray tone (a pixel in an image that has an RGB value of 127, 127, 127). In the cover of this book is a gray card that reflects that precise amount of light. Real-world examples of subjects that have average reflectivity include grass and stone.

Reflective meters trip up when a scene has a higher- or lower-than-average reflectivity. A scene that is lighter than average (such as a scene dominated by brightly lit snow) will cause the meter to underexpose. This means the snow is darkened as the overall range of tones in the image is brought down to a midtone average. A darker than-average scene will cause the opposite problem; overexposure. In these scenarios it's often necessary to apply exposure compensation to obtain the correct exposure. A snow scene, for example, often requires +1 to +2 stops of exposure compensation.

Your G16 also takes account of where the lens is focused, biasing the exposure to the focus point. This is easily seen by using FlexiZone AF and moving the AF frame around the LCD. If the area under your AF frame isn't a midtone, be prepared to apply exposure compensation.

AVERAGE «
This was a surprisingly easy scene to expose correctly. The light and dark tones effectively balance each other out, creating an "average" scene overall.

CANON POWERSHOT G16

» UNDEREXPOSURE

The large areas of white in this composition initially caused the G16 to underexpose slightly. This was seen on the histogram on the LCD screen before shooting and by applying 1-stop of positive exposure compensation the exposure was corrected.

Settings
> Focal length: 7.4mm
> Exposure: 5 sec. at f/3.5
> ISO: 80

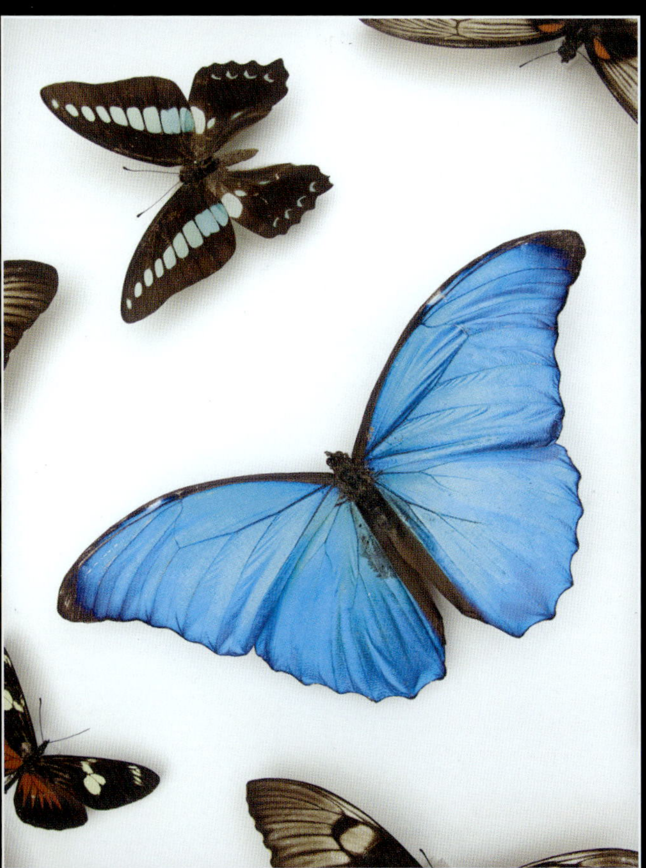

Looking at an image on the G16's LCD is not a good way of assessing the exposure of an image. It is far more accurate if you look at the image's histogram, either before exposure or during playback (note that histograms can't be used to assess the exposure of movies).

A histogram is a graph showing the range of tones in an image, from pure black at the left edge to pure white at the right (with the midtones in the middle). Despite what some people say, there is no "right" shape for a histogram, but a good rule of thumb is that an image with a histogram skewed far to the left is probably underexposed, while a histogram that is skewed far to the right is likely to mean the image is overexposed. However, it's important to remember that a histogram is only showing you the range of tones in an image: it's up to you to decide if the exposure is what you are after. The height of a histogram as you move from left to right shows the proportion of pixels in the image that match a particular tonal value.

To accurately interpret a histogram you need to think of the scene in front of the camera as a range of tones. It's particularly useful to recognize subjects that correspond to the midtone area of a histogram as this also has a bearing on how your camera meters a scene. A good example of a subject that is generally a

midtone is green grass. If you were to take a correctly exposed picture of grass (with nothing else in the picture) you would expect to see a "hump" in the middle of the histogram, which would indicate a

STONE   ⌄

Flatly lit stone is often roughly equivalent to a midtone. The histogram for this image confirms this for this particular stone carving.

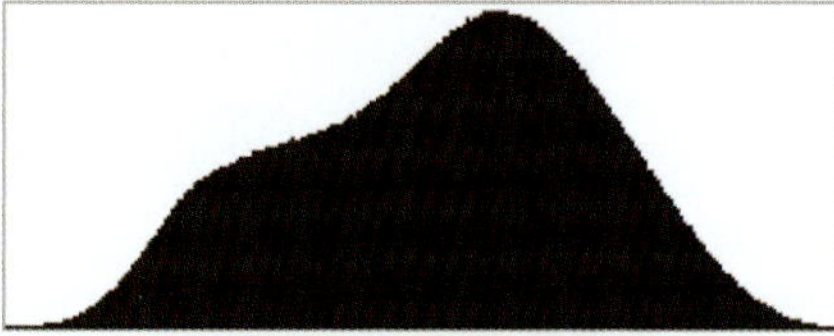

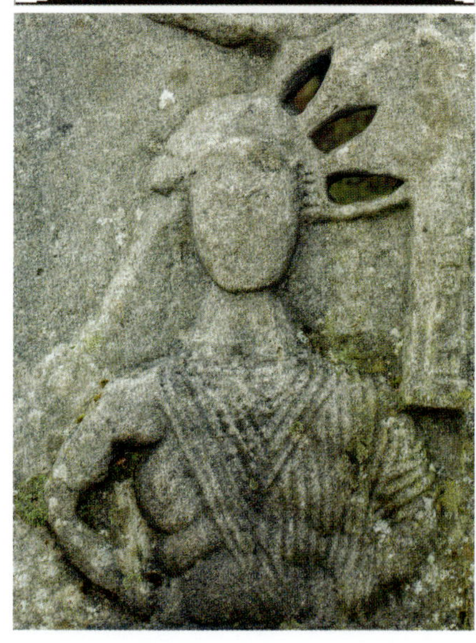

predominance of pixels in the image that have a midtone value.

When a histogram is skewed so far left or right that it "leans" against either edge it is described as being clipped. When a histogram is clipped there will be no tonal detail in the shadows (when clipped at the left edge) or in the highlights (when clipped at the right). The pixels in these areas will be pure black or pure white respectively and you'll never be able to recover this lost detail, no matter how you alter your image in postproduction. However, there will be times when the contrast of a scene means clipping is unavoidable. In these situations you will need to decide where it is least desirable to lose information detail—in the shadows or in the highlights—and set exposure compensation accordingly.

CLIPPED

There is no "correct" shape for a histogram. However, this histogram is from an image with overexposed highlights. It's clipped on the right edge, which means that there are pixels in the image that are pure white. The solution would have been to darken the exposure, perhaps by applying negative exposure compensation.

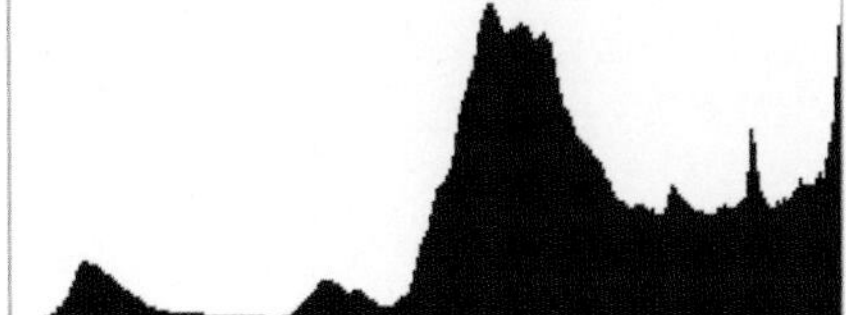

Checking the histogram

1) In image playback, press ▼/**DISP.** until the detailed image review screen is displayed. Initially only a monochrome histogram is displayed, showing the range of tones in an image as if they were converted to shades of gray. However, you can view an RGB histogram by pressing ▼.

2) If the histogram is clipped, reshoot the image if required and adjust the exposure compensation. If the image has been underexposed (the left edge is clipped), add positive exposure compensation. If the image is overexposed (the right edge is clipped) employ negative exposure compensation instead.

Notes:
If an image has been overexposed, the clipped highlight areas will also blink in the image thumbnail on the detail image review screen.

The RGB histogram shows how the reds, greens, and blues in an image are exposed. This is particularly useful when determining the correct white balance. If an image is too warm, it is likely that the red channel will be skewed to the right; too cool and it will be the blue channel that is skewed to the right.

There are two different functions that can be used to control the amount of light reaching your camera's sensor: the shutter speed and aperture (a third function—ISO—sets how much light is actually needed to make a successful exposure).

Shutter speed is a measure of time. On the G16 you can set the shutter speed from 1/4000 sec. all the way down to 250 seconds in a set series of steps. The difference between each of these values is $\frac{1}{3}$ of a stop. A 1-stop difference between shutter speeds represents either a halving (as the shutter speed gets faster) or a doubling (as it gets slower) of the amount of light that reaches the sensor. For example, a shutter speed of 1/1000 sec. allows through twice as much light as 1/2000 sec., but half that of 1/500 sec.

The aperture is part of the lens. An aperture is an iris that can be varied in size. The wider the aperture, the more light it will let through. The size of the aperture is measured in f/stops, represented by f/ and a suffix number, and as with the shutter speed, the aperture is also adjusted in $\frac{1}{3}$-stop increments. On the G16 the aperture range is f/1.8–f/8 (when the lens is set to ▲▲▲); the larger the suffix number, the smaller the aperture. Each whole f/stop difference on a lens also represents either a doubling or halving of the amount of light, so f/5.6 will allow in half as much light as f/4, but twice that of f/8.

Shutter speed, aperture, and ISO are linked: if one is changed, one or both of

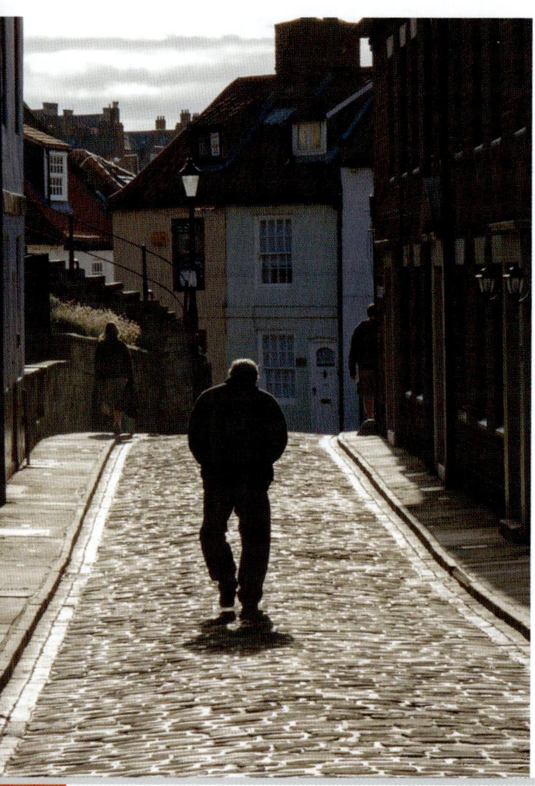

MOVEMENT «

In order to "freeze" movement you need to use a relatively fast shutter speed. In this instance a shutter speed of 1/160 sec. was fast enough to "freeze" this man mid-stride.

the other two must also be changed to maintain the same exposure.

As an example, if the suggested exposure is 1/25 sec. at f/4 with an ISO setting of 100 and you change the ISO to 200, either the shutter speed needs to change to 1/50 sec. or the aperture must be altered to f/5.6. This is because you've increased the sensitivity of the sensor, so you need less light to make an image, which can be achieved either by making the shutter speed faster or by making the aperture smaller.

When you're using an automatic shooting mode this is all done for you, but when you're shooting using **M** mode you need to be aware that altering one control will affect the overall exposure unless another exposure control is altered also.

› Shutter speed

Controlling the shutter speed allows you to determine how movement is conveyed in your images. When an image is created, it records a moment in time; how long this moment is will depend on the shutter speed you use.

Freezing movement requires a fast shutter speed, and the faster the movement is (particularly if the movement is across the image space), the faster the shutter speed will need to be. Sports photography is one area that typically requires the use of fast shutter speeds.

However, freezing movement can sometimes make a subject appear too still. We expect to see blur and softness as that's closer to how we perceive

Freezing movement	
Subject speed	Suggested shutter speed
Slow walk	1/125 sec.
Fast walk	1/250 sec.
Waves	1/250 sec.
Running person	1/500 sec.
Cyclist	1/500 sec.
Galloping horse	1/1000 sec.
Automobile (on urban road)	1/500 sec.
Automobile (on highway)	1/1000 sec.
Train	1/2000 sec.
Fast jet	1/4000 sec.

fast movement. For that reason it's sometimes aesthetically more pleasing to use a slightly slower shutter speed so that images don't look too static.

The G16 is the most flexible G-series camera to date when it comes to the range of shutter speeds you can use. Although, the fastest shutter of 1/4000 sec. hasn't changed compared to the G15, the longest shutter speed available is now 250 seconds (when using **M** mode). This capability is due to the addition of the new Starry Nightscape mode, which is a clue to when extremely long shutter speeds are useful: when light levels are extremely low.

This would typically be at night, but in a dense forest, cave, or tunnel are other situations when extremely long shutter speeds might be necessary.

It's also possible to simulate low light by using extremely dense neutral density (ND) filters. These are often used by landscape photographers to blur moving subjects such as water or clouds. The key to using these filters with the G16 is to focus manually before fitting the filter—once it's fitted, the G16's AF system may not be able to cope. The following list is a guide to using longer shutter speeds when shooting moving subjects.

Subject	Suggested shutter speed
Waterfall	1/4 sec.
Waves (retaining detail)	1 second
Moving clouds	8 seconds
Waves (smoothed out)	15 seconds
Fireworks	30 seconds
Wind-blown foliage	30 seconds
Traffic trails	30–60 seconds
Waves (misty quality)	1–2 minutes

» SPEED

Blur helps to give the impression of speed. This image was shot from the window of a moving train using a long shutter speed. This has created a more impressionistic image that conveys movement far more readily than if I'd "frozen" the scene with a fast shutter speed.

Settings
› Focal length: 15.7mm
› Exposure: 1 sec. at f/8
› ISO: 80

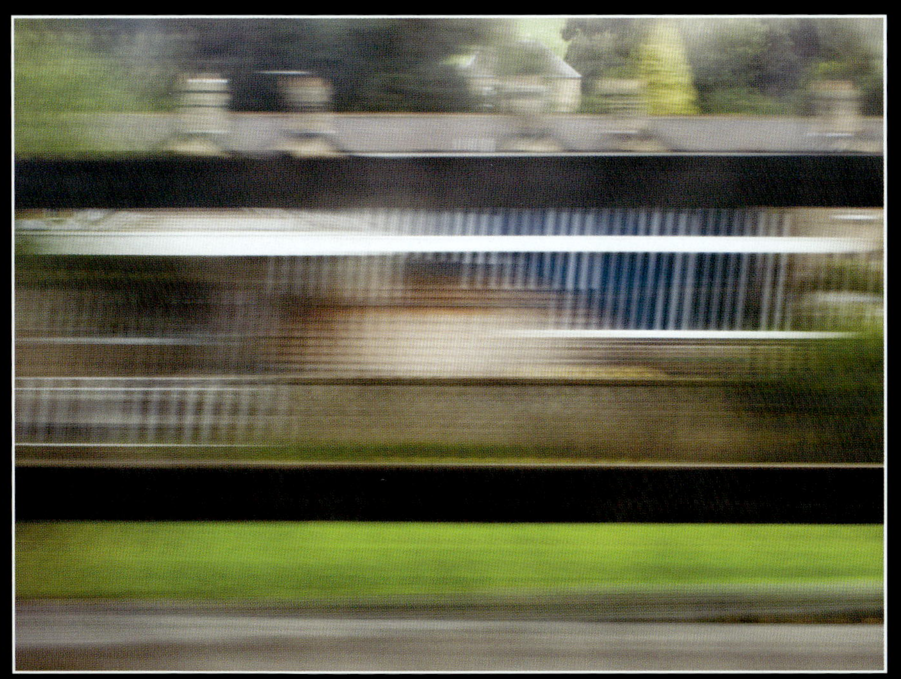

› Aperture

The aperture in the lens can be varied in size, helping to control the amount of light reaching the sensor. It also controls an effect known as "depth of field." The shorter the focal length of a lens, the more inherent depth of field there will be. The lens on the G16 is extremely short in comparison to a DSLR—even at [▲] (maximum zoom) the focal length is only 30.5mm. This means that achieving maximum depth of field (for non-macro shots) is relatively straightforward.

What is more difficult is shooting so that areas of an image are out of focus, a technique that is often used to isolate a subject from a background. Fortunately, the G16 has a large maximum aperture at both ends of the focal length range. If you want to try this technique, first set the lens to maximum zoom and the aperture to f/2.8 (the largest aperture at [▲]). Focus precisely on your subject (you may need to step back quite a way to frame your subject correctly). You should see the background behind your subject appears soft. If not, move closer to your subject if possible without adjusting the lens' focal length. Take the shot when you're happy with the effect.

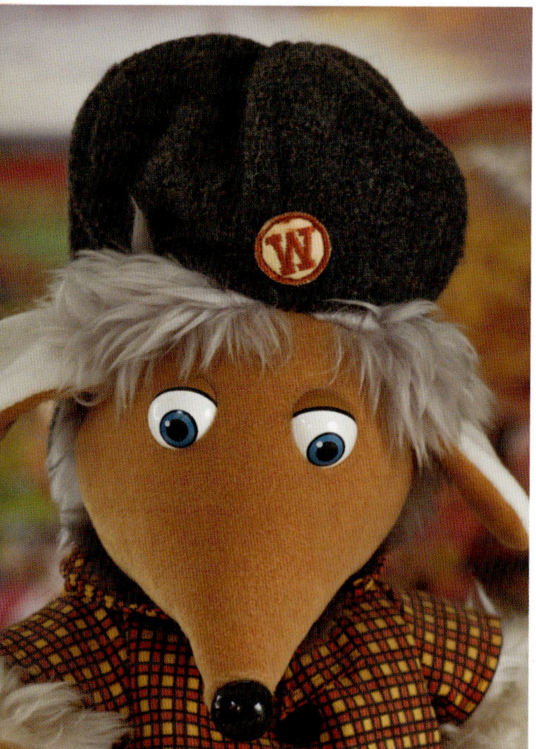

BACKGROUND 〈〈
Using maximum aperture and the lens set to [▲] was the only way I could keep the background out of focus when shooting this image.

» DEPTH

The greater the distance between the foreground and the background in a scene, the more important it is to be aware of depth of field. This image required an aperture setting of f/5.6 to ensure that everything from front to back was sharp.

Settings
> Focal length: 14.6mm
> Exposure: 1/125 sec. at f/5.6
> ISO: 80

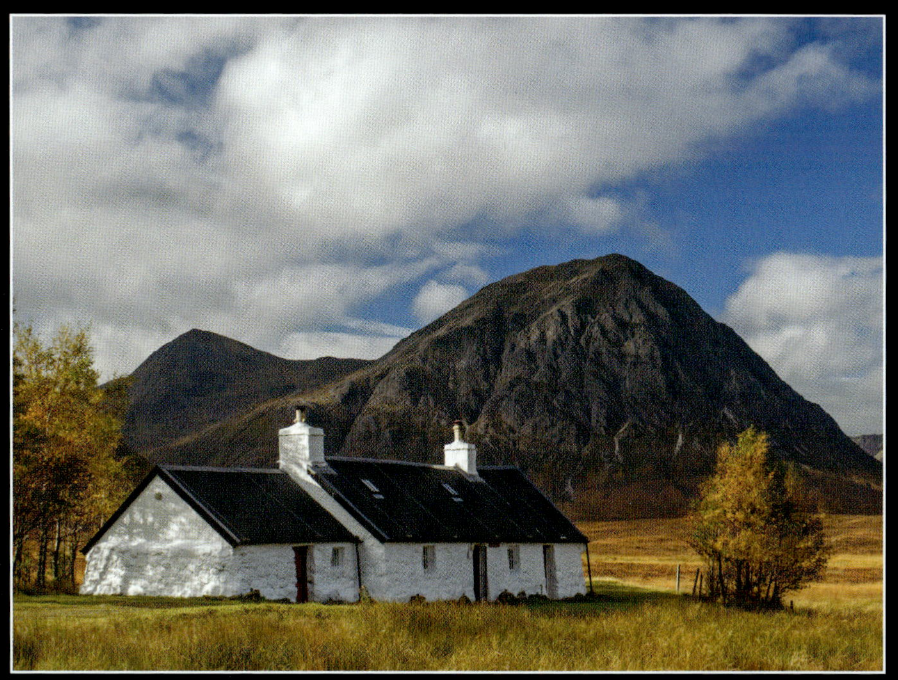

» OPTICAL PROPERTIES

› Flare

Lens flare is seen in images as either unwanted colored blobs or streaks and/or as a reduction in overall image contrast. It is caused by light from a point light source being scattered and bounced around the various glass elements that make up a camera lens. Lens flare occurs either when you point your camera directly toward a point light source or when light enters the lens obliquely from the side when the light source is just out of shot.

The latter cause of lens flare can be reduced through the use of a lens hood, although at present Canon don't make a lens hood for the G16 (one is supplied with the TC-DC58E Tele-converter, though). Another solution is to hold the G16 with one hand and shade the lens with the other, although a better answer is to mount the camera on a tripod and shade the lens with your entire body, being careful not to end up in the shot yourself. Keeping the G16 lens clean will also help to keep flare under control; greasy fingerprints or dust on the lens will only exacerbate flare.

› Distortion

No lens is perfect and all display distortion to some degree. Distortion refers to the way a lens bends an image out of shape, causing straight lines to curve. There are two types of distortion: pincushion and barrel. Pincushion distortion causes straight lines to appear to bow in toward the center of an image, while barrel distortion makes straight lines appear to bow outward. The G16 exhibits some barrel distortion at the setting, but is relatively distortion free at and often not noticeable except on big enlargements.

FLARE «
The easiest way to reduce flare when shooting toward a light source is to partially hide it behind your subject.

» DIGITAL PROPERTIES

› Dynamic range

The dynamic range of a camera (often shortened to DR) is the ratio of the minimum and maximum level of light intensities that camera can record. On a practical level, the DR affects how much detail can be retained in both the shadow and highlight areas of an image.

The G16's DR is very respectable for a camera with a relatively small sensor, but in high contrast scenes there's generally a need to consider carefully how you expose an image. It's generally preferable to expose for the highlights, particularly when shooting JPEG. This is because there is little or no latitude to recover highlight detail in a JPEG later on: once a highlight has blown, it's gone for good. When shooting Raw there is often a little more latitude for recovering highlight detail (as long as the histogram isn't too clipped).

Exposing for the highlights will mean that shadow detail may be lost, but as we expect shadows to be dark this is generally more acceptable than losing highlight detail. If you're shooting Raw, it's easier and more effective to recover shadow detail later than when shooting JPEG, although as this will introduce noise into the shadows, it's not a perfect solution.

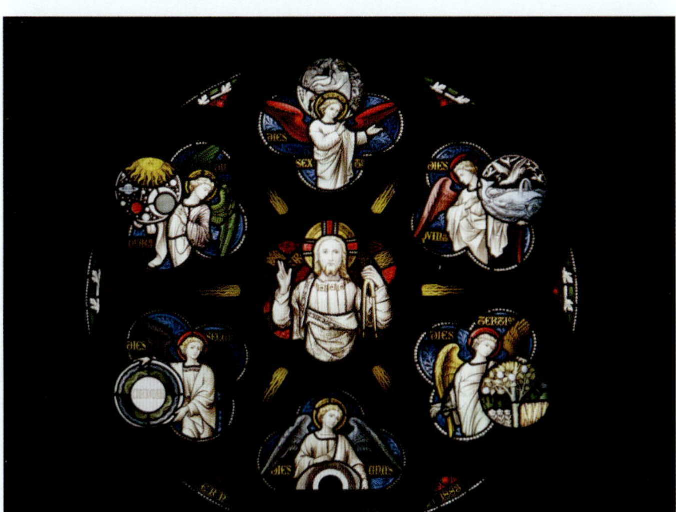

COMPROMISE «
The compromise when shooting this stained-glass window was losing all detail in the shadow areas of the shot. Exposing to retain detail in the shadows would have meant overexposing the window, which would have been less acceptable.

› Sharpening images

Strange as it may seem, the sensor in your G16 is designed to soften your images slightly at the moment of exposure. This is done to reduce the occurrence of an effect known as moiré, which causes odd visual effects with high-frequency subjects such as tightly woven fabrics. Because of this, images have to be sharpened to some degree after capture. In the case of JPEG images, this is done in-camera, as the file is processed; Raw files do not have any sharpening applied, so this must be done during postproduction.

Sharpening an image involves increasing the contrast between edges, which fools the eye into thinking the image is sharper. The more an image is sharpened, the greater the edge contrast.

However, this is easily overdone, resulting in unusual-looking halos around the edges in the image. Once sharpening has been applied in camera it cannot be undone, so if you plan to alter your JPEG images during postproduction, it's a good idea to set your G16 to apply as little sharpening as possible (sharpening can be reduced by using θ_C in My Color).

If you shoot Raw files, you will need to sharpen them in postproduction. Most good photo-editing software (such as Canon Digital Photo Professional) will have the facility to sharpen an image, but the amount of sharpening an image needs will depend on how it is to be used: an image that is to be printed will require more sharpening than one used on a web site.

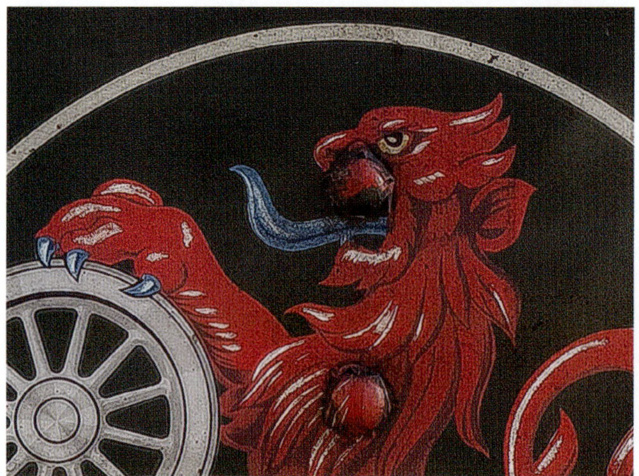

SHARP «
The effects of sharpening have been exaggerated in this image. One big problem with sharpening is that it can make image noise more noticeable. Arguably, images shot at higher ISO settings should be sharpened less.

› Noise

All images created by digital cameras suffer from noise, to one degree or another. There are two types of noise: luminance and chroma. Of the two, luminance is the least objectionable, as it often resembles film grain in structure, making an image appear "gritty." Chroma noise, on the other hand, creates ugly patches of random color and is considered to be less aesthetically pleasing. It is also more difficult to remove successfully.

Noise is caused by random fluctuations in the electrical signal as the digital image is captured. It is generally more visible in areas of even tone, such as large expanses of blue sky or in the shadow areas of images, and regardless of where it is seen it can obscure fine detail.

If you're shooting Raw, noise can be removed during postproduction, while high ISO noise is reduced in-camera when shooting JPEG. Be warned, though: if you reduce noise too aggressively your images can begin to look artificially smooth and cartoon-like.

The visibility of noise increases the higher the ISO used (and the longer the shutter speed after 1 second or so). It's an unfortunate fact that the smaller the sensor in the camera, the greater the likelihood of noise becoming apparent even at modest ISO settings.

Fortunately, although it has a relatively small sensor size, the G16 has above-average noise characteristics. If you use an ISO setting below 1600, it's possible to create very usable images, even with JPEG (JPEGs do suffer slightly from a loss of detail due to noise suppression, but it's an acceptable trade-off). It's only when ISO settings above 3200 are used that the G16 starts to struggle. It is still recommended that you use the lowest ISO possible, though, and use the higher ISO settings only as a last resort.

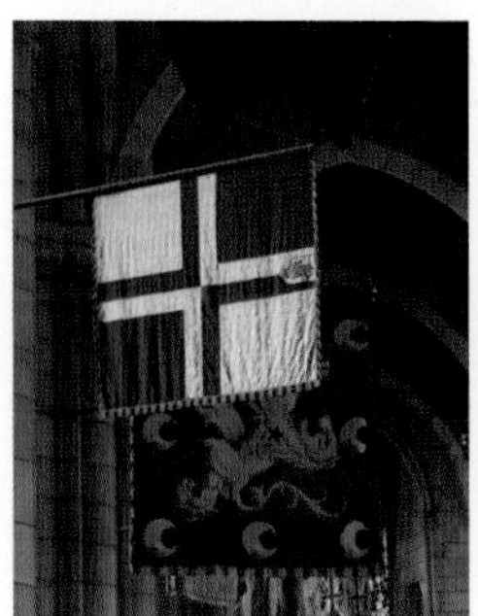
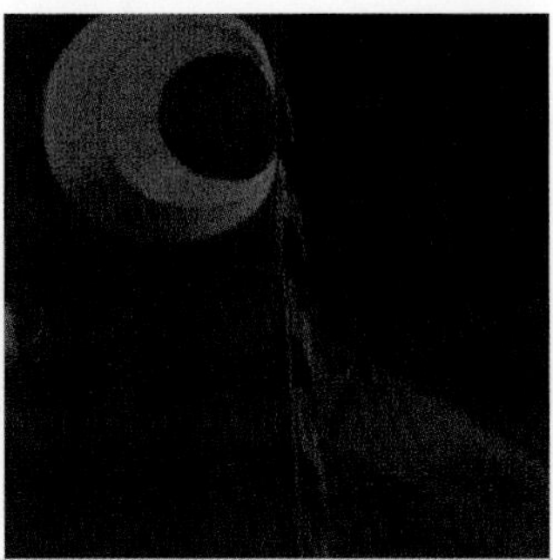

NOISE «
Reduced in size, the noise in this image (shot at ISO 3200) is difficult to see. However, view a close-up, and noise is readily apparent.

6

» CARING FOR YOUR G16

Although the G16 isn't a delicate camera that doesn't mean that it can be thrown about with abandon. Treated with care, your camera should provide you with years of trouble-free operation.

Conditions to avoid (or at least be aware of) are dusty conditions, excessive moisture, and extreme heat. You should also be careful to avoid your camera receiving sharp knocks.

Dust and sand

Dust and sand can easily get into places they shouldn't on your G16, so if you are shooting in these conditions try to keep the camera inside a bag when not in use. Before retracting the lens, make sure there isn't dust coating the lens surface or the blades that protect the lens when

retracted. If there is, don't use a cloth to clean it. Instead, use a blower brush and avoid touching the lens' surface.

Wet conditions

Although the G16 isn't weather sealed, there's no reason—with care—not to be out in wet conditions. Keep the camera covered when not in use (an umbrella is a useful addition to a camera bag) and carry a cloth with you so that you can wipe your G16 dry as best you can before covering it up again. When you're back indoors check the camera over and dry it again if necessary. Check the lens and make sure there is no moisture on the lens surface; the lens cover can stick if moisture gets between the blades.

Take special care if you are using your G16 near salt water. Salt is very destructive and will be left as a residue on your camera as the salt water evaporates. Dry your G16 immediately if it is splashed with salt water and wipe it down again when you get home.

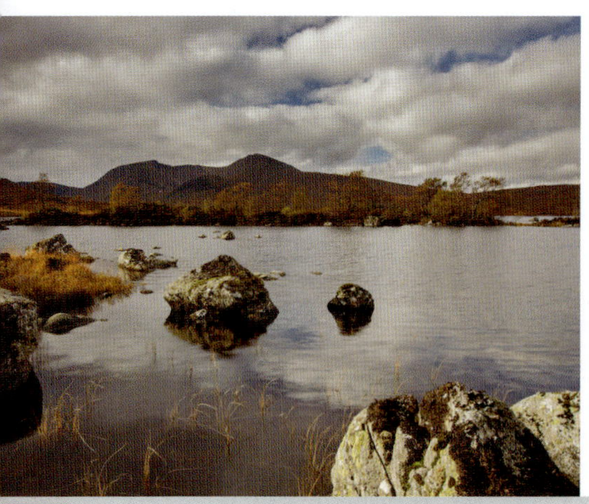

WET   «
Water and cameras aren't a good mix. Near bodies of water keep the G16 around your neck using the strap.

Hot conditions

Excessive heat can damage your G16, which is why Canon recommend that the camera should not be used for long periods in temperatures above 104°F (40°C). Keep the G16 in shade as much as possible to keep it cool, and never leave it lying in strong sunlight.

Cold conditions

Cold conditions can affect battery life: the lower the ambient temperature, the less efficient a battery becomes. Even a new, fully charged battery will power your camera for less time than normal in temperatures below 41°F (5°C). If you have a spare battery, keep it inside your jacket for warmth and be prepared to swap over. Use power-saving techniques such as using the viewfinder rather than the LCD to prolong the life of your batteries.

When you return indoors, allow your G16 to return slowly to room temperature and check that condensation hasn't built up on the lens or LCD. Keeping a packet of silica gel in your camera bag will help prevent excessive moisture building up.

General care

The G16's rear LCD screen is robust, but it will scratch if mishandled. There are third-party plastic films that can be used to protect screens, and they are a worthwhile investment. Try to avoid touching the screen and leaving marks: if you do mark the screen then use a soft, lint-free cloth to gently wipe the surface. If there is dust or grit on the screen use a blower brush to remove the dirt.

Don't point the G16 toward a strong light source such as the sun. This can damage the sensor and could cause excessive internal heating.

Take care not to knock the lens, especially when it is fully extended in telephoto mode. Set the lens retract period to as short a time as possible, so that the lens is safely out of the way when not in use.

CLOTH »
Only use a cloth designed specifically for cleaning LCDs when wiping your G16's screen.

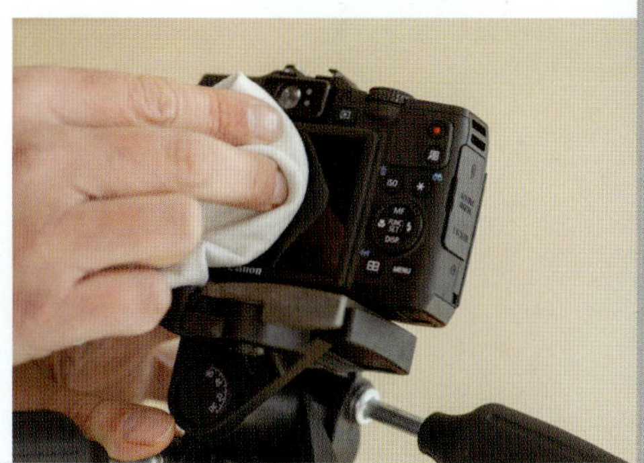

Colors that harmonize are particularly pleasing.
One interesting color harmony is known as a
complementary color scheme. This is when colors
that are on opposite sides of a standard color wheel
are placed together. In this image the complementary
colors of orange and blue dominate.

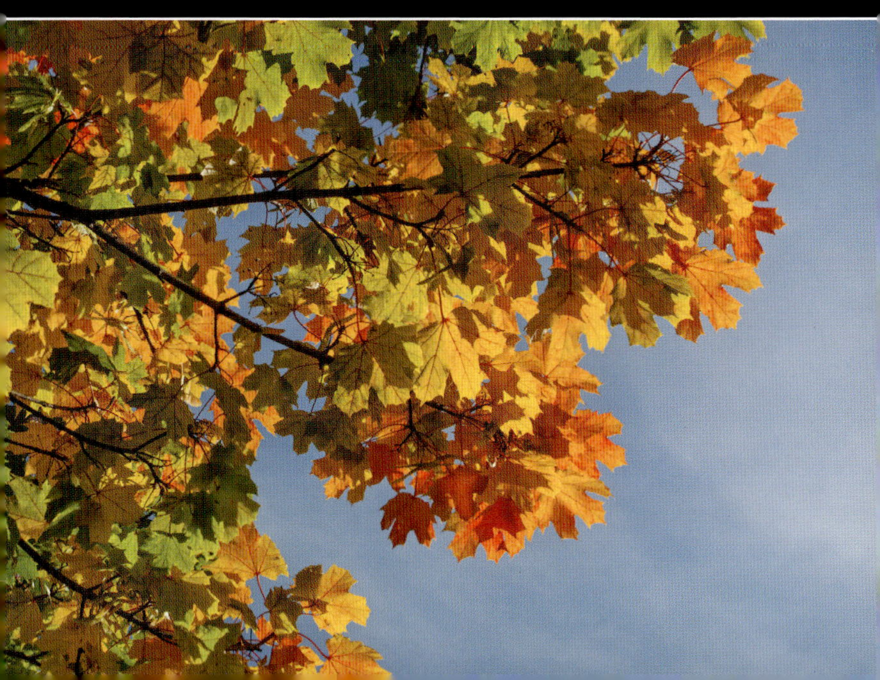

» SILHOUETTE

Exposing for the background when a subject is backlit will record the subject as a silhouette. The key to shooting successful silhouettes is to keep it simple. Don't have too many competing shapes in the image and try to avoid different elements overlapping if possible.

Settings
> Focal length: 8.9mm
> Exposure: 1/50 sec. at f/3.2
> ISO: 200

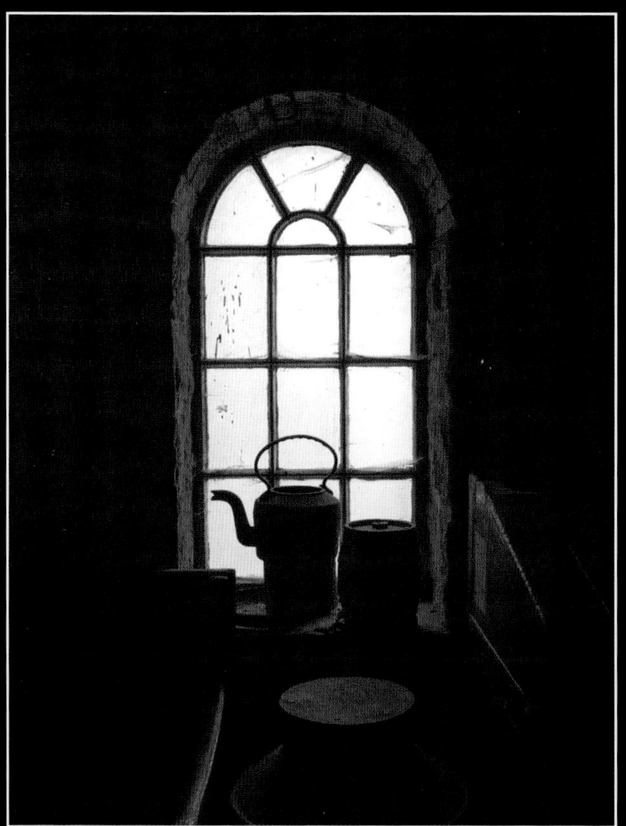

7 CLOSE-UP

One of the real benefits of compact cameras like the G16, compared to a DSLR, is the ease with which striking close-up images can be shot.

The world of the small is as fascinating a subject as the widest vista, and it often requires more thought and imagination to photograph well. A drawback with the G16 in comparison to previous G-series models (such as the G12) is the lack of a flip-out screen. This means that shooting at ground level is slightly more difficult. However, no one ever said that photographers must always be comfortable, so you shouldn't be put off getting down low if it's physically possible. Fortunately, digital photography also allows you to review your images immediately, so if a shot hasn't worked there's no excuse for not persevering.

When shooting close-ups you need to be aware that your subject could be disturbed easily by your camera's close proximity. This disturbance can either take the form of your camera knocking the subject or, if your subject is alive and aware, frightening it so that it moves out of the way. Although you can't focus as close, using a longer focal length is often preferable for these reasons.

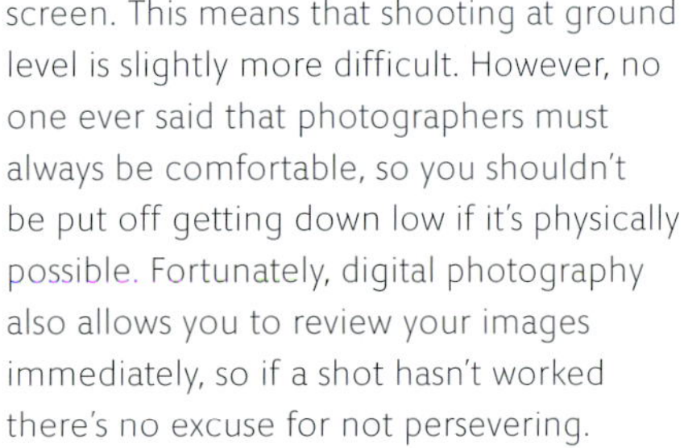

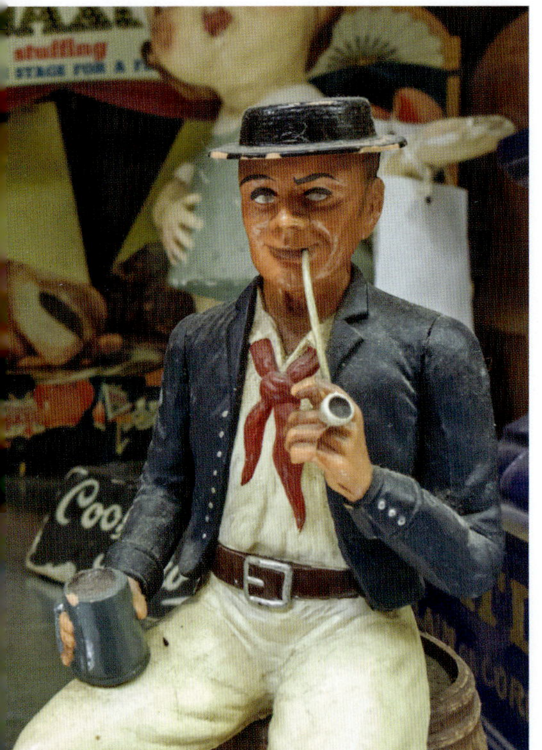

EXHIBIT «
Museums are good places to find interesting details. If an exhibit is inside a glass case, lightly press the G16's lens against the glass to cut out reflections.

EQUIPMENT »
The G16's ✿ mode means that you don't need expensive equipment to create interesting close-up images.

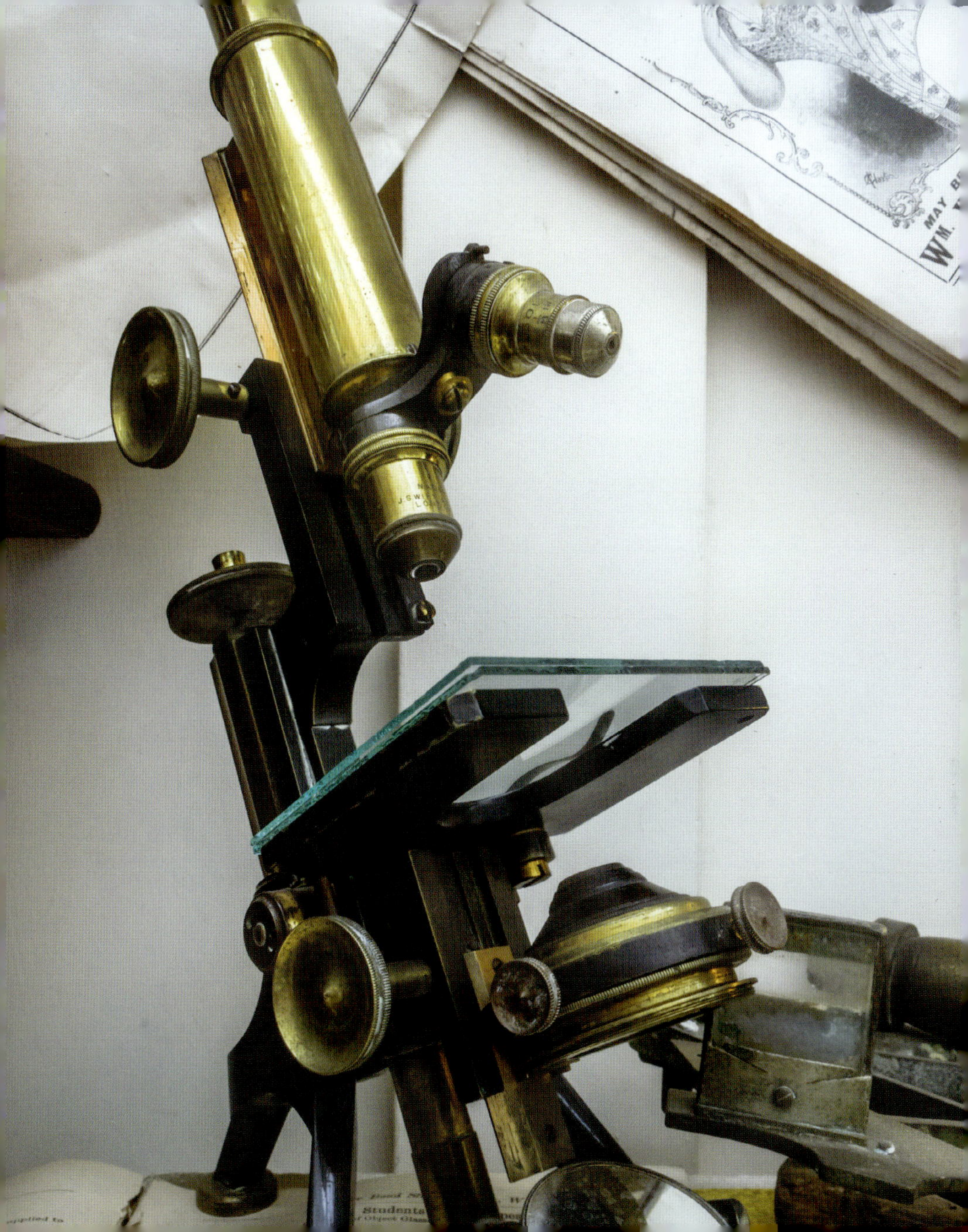

7 » USING ❀

Shooting close-up images on the G16 is essentially the same as "normal" shooting, and the same controls (such as exposure and white balance) are all available, provided that shooting mode would normally allow you to alter these controls. The main difference is that the optics of the lens are set slightly differently to allow closer focusing.

The minimum focusing distance is dependent on the focal length the lens is set to: at 🌲🌲🌲, the focusing distance is 0.4in.–1.6ft. (1–50cm), while at the 🌲 setting, the focusing distance increases to 1.3ft.–∞ (40cm–∞).

❀ mode is also not available in all of the G16's shooting modes and is detected automatically in others. See chapter 2 for further details.

Setting the G16 to ❀

1) In shooting mode press ◀, followed by (FUNC. SET).

2) ❀ will be displayed at the top right corner of the LCD screen.

3) Press halfway down on the shutter-release button to focus (you can also use MF in ❀ for more control over focus, particularly when peaking is activated).

4) Press ◀ again to cancel ❀.

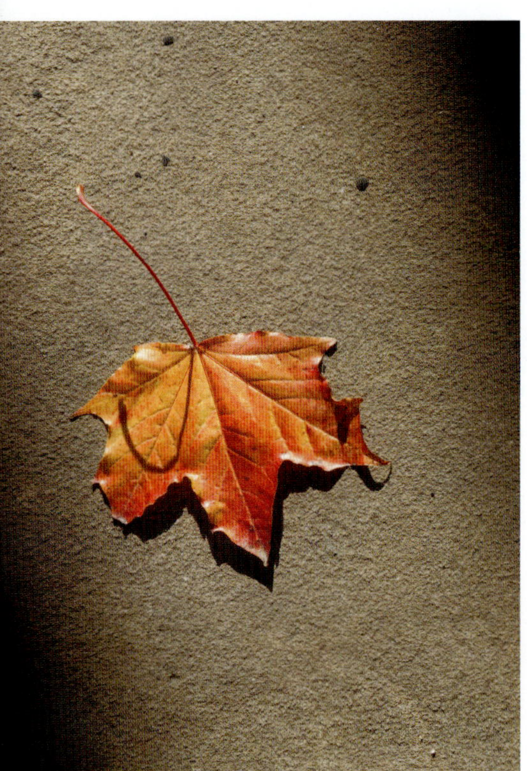

LOOKING DOWN «
Interesting close-up details can be found everywhere, sometimes literally at your feet.

› ❀ Shooting in practise

The G16's lens can focus far more closely when set to ▤ than when set to ▯. However, the best results are often achieved when using the lens set to ▯. This means you have to move back from your subject to deal with the increased focusing distance, but this is offset by the fact that moving back will result in a more natural perspective.

By comparison, shooting ❀ with the lens set to ▤ can produce strangely distorted images because you often have to get very close to your subject, making it relatively large in the frame.

If you're shooting JPEGs, another option to consider is to use ❀ in conjunction with the Digital Zoom or Digital Tele-Converter. Although there is a slight degradation in image quality, both of these options will allow you to achieve much greater magnification by digitally increasing the focal length of the lens. Of the two, Digital Tele-Converter is the most useful if you're handholding your camera.

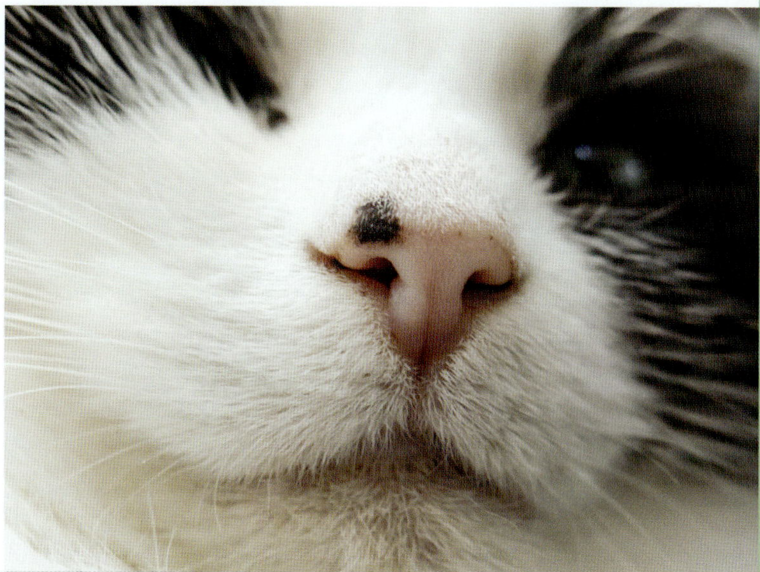

TOO CLOSE »
Shooting ❀ when the lens is set to ▤ means that you have to get very close to your subject in order to fill the frame. The perspective this creates is not flattering though!

» ILLUMINATING YOUR SUBJECT

The simplest way to illuminate macro subjects is with direct sunlight. However, you can't always rely on the sun shining and it also changes position over the course of the day. You may also find that contrast is too strong, in which case you might want to use a reflector to push light back into the shadows. Reflectors can be bought commercially or you could use a sheet of white card or paper.

Another solution is to use a softer light source to reduce the contrast. This occurs naturally on overcast days, when the sun is covered by cloud, and it also occurs when your subject is in shade.

The light in both cases will be naturally bluer so you may need to adjust the white balance before you begin shooting. Light levels will also be lower than when your subject is in direct sunlight so a tripod may be needed, particularly if you're using the lens set to ▮ (camera shake becomes more of a problem as the focal length of a lens increases).

Unfortunately, the G16's built-in flash isn't an ideal light source for ❀ shooting. This is partly because the lens can cause a shadow when shooting close up, and partly because camera-mounted flash is a hard, frontal light source that is not flattering to any subject. As an alternative, Canon produces the MT-24EX Macro Twin Lite and MR-14EX Macro Ring Lite lighting units, both of which are compatible with the G16. These two lights fit around the camera's lens and provide a subtler, softer illumination for macro subjects.

> **Note:**
> When using **AUTO** there is an automatic IS mode (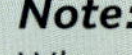) that is optimized to reduce camera shake when shooting close-up.

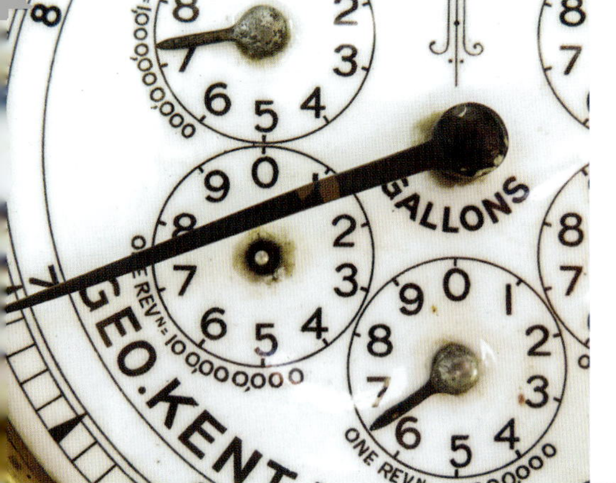

UNEVEN »
This dial was frontally lit, which meant that I cast a partial shadow over the face. This was solved by asking a friend to block the light completely.

» DEPTH OF FIELD

Depth of field with the lens set to ⬤ is also reduced compared to ▲▲▲. This means that you will need to focus precisely on the area of the subject that you want to be sharp. Switching to FlexiZone AF will make focusing more precise, although with practise **MF** can be more precise still (particularly when focus peaking is activated). To shoot this image I focused precisely on the iguana's eye.

Settings
> Focal length: 30.5mm
> Exposure: 0.3 sec. at f/4.5
> ISO: 200

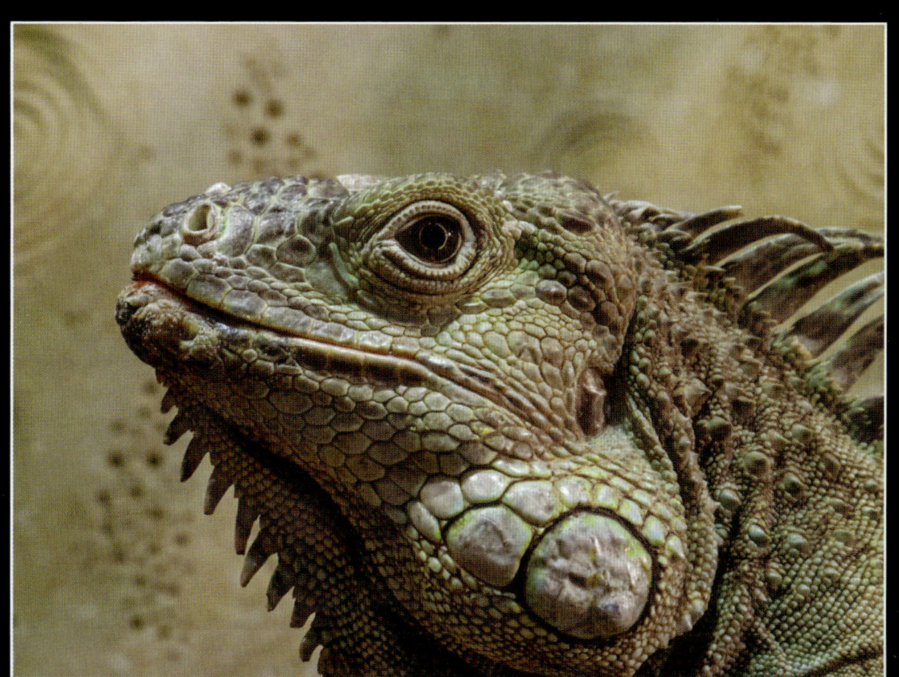

» MACRO TIPS

Use a tripod to keep your G16 steady when you're shooting ✿. If your tripod has a center column you may be able to remove it and reinsert it upside down. This is a very useful way of getting your camera down to ground level, although it does mean that the LCD screen will be upside down. This makes it trickier to compose your shots, but it's surprising how quickly you adapt!

If you shoot ✿ in **Av** (or even **M**) mode you have more control over the aperture (and therefore the depth of field) of your ✿ images. For even greater control use FlexiZone AF and move the focus point to the area of the subject that you want to be critically sharp.

Common macro subjects are flowers and plants, but both tend to be delicate and will move in even the slightest breeze. A piece of card held on the windward side of your subject will help to shelter it, and you can also use a larger aperture or increase the ISO to allow a faster shutter speed if movement is still a problem.

Macro doesn't have to involve shooting your subjects in a literal, documentary way. If you can get close enough, shoot patterns and textures for a more abstract approach. Even ordinary household objects can take on a new meaning when shot in an abstract way. Repetitive patterns can be soothing to look at if there is no break in the pattern across the image. However, by breaking the pattern with another picture element you can add a note of interest or tension to the image.

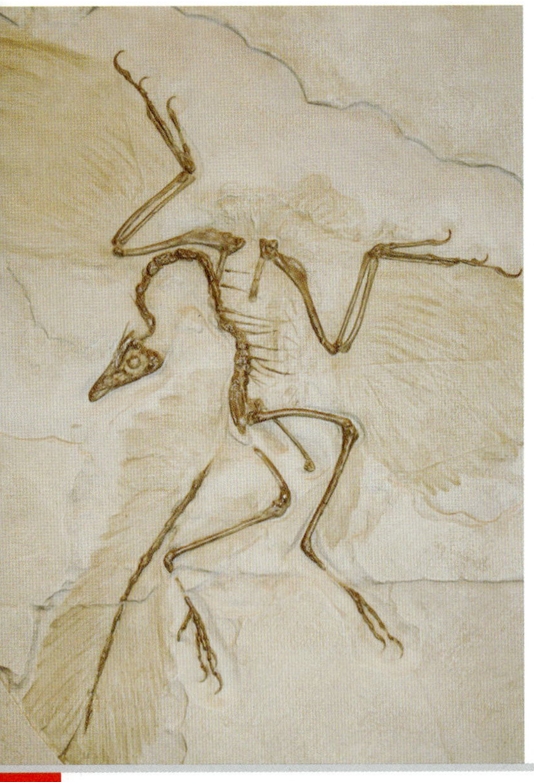

FILLED　　»

I used the G16's zoom to fill the frame with the subject and exclude distracting details around the edge.

» CLOSE-UP LENSES

With the FA-DC58D filter adapter fitted to your G16 you can add close-up attachment lenses to your camera. These essentially act like a magnifying glass, allowing you to focus much closer than you could otherwise. They're not perfect, as they degrade image quality, but they're fun to use and can help you create images that would otherwise be impossible with the G16.

Settings
> Focal length: 30.5mm + close-up attachment lens
> Exposure: 0.6 sec. at f/8
> ISO: 200

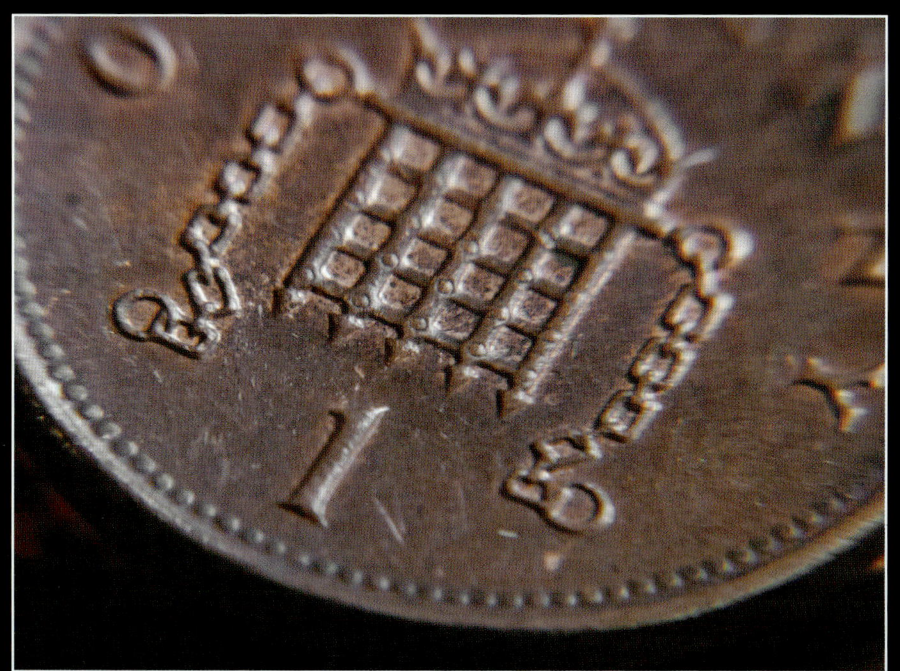

8 ACCESSORIES

The Canon G16 is one part of a camera system: although it's perfectly possible to use your G16 on its own, it really begins to shine with the addition of extra optional equipment.

There is a bewildering range of accessories compatible with the G16 (many of which are also compatible with previous G-series models). Some of these accessories are useful and will help to improve your image making, while others are less useful and will probably be used only once before they are put at the back of a drawer and forgotten about. The key to navigating your way through all this choice is to critically assess how you work and decide where an accessory would truthfully make your photographic life easier.

Arguably the two most useful additions to your G16 equipment are a spare battery and a spare memory card: all the other accessories (and your G16) are useless if your camera is no longer able to shoot and record images.

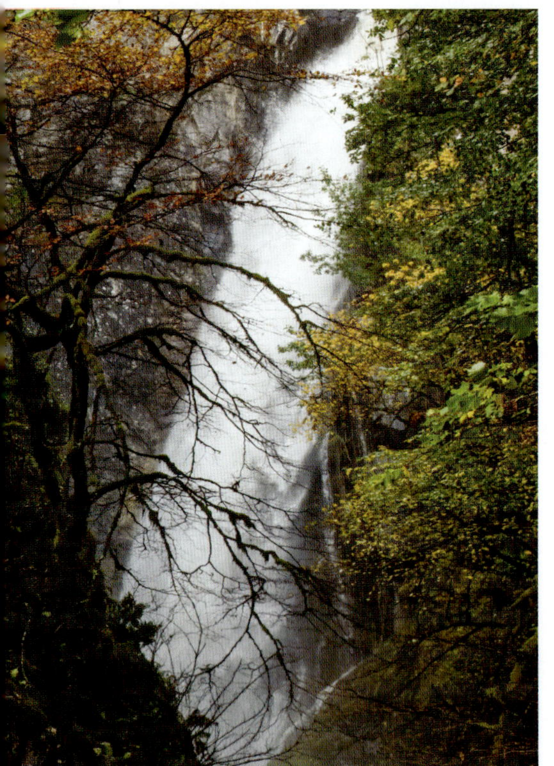

UMBRELLA «

Useful accessories don't just include those made by camera equipment manufacturers. I keep a small umbrella in my camera bag to shelter my camera when shooting in rain or close to waterfalls.

TRIPOD »

After sunset (or before sunrise) the light levels are generally so low that the use of a tripod is imperative. This is particularly true when using the G16's ▨ mode.

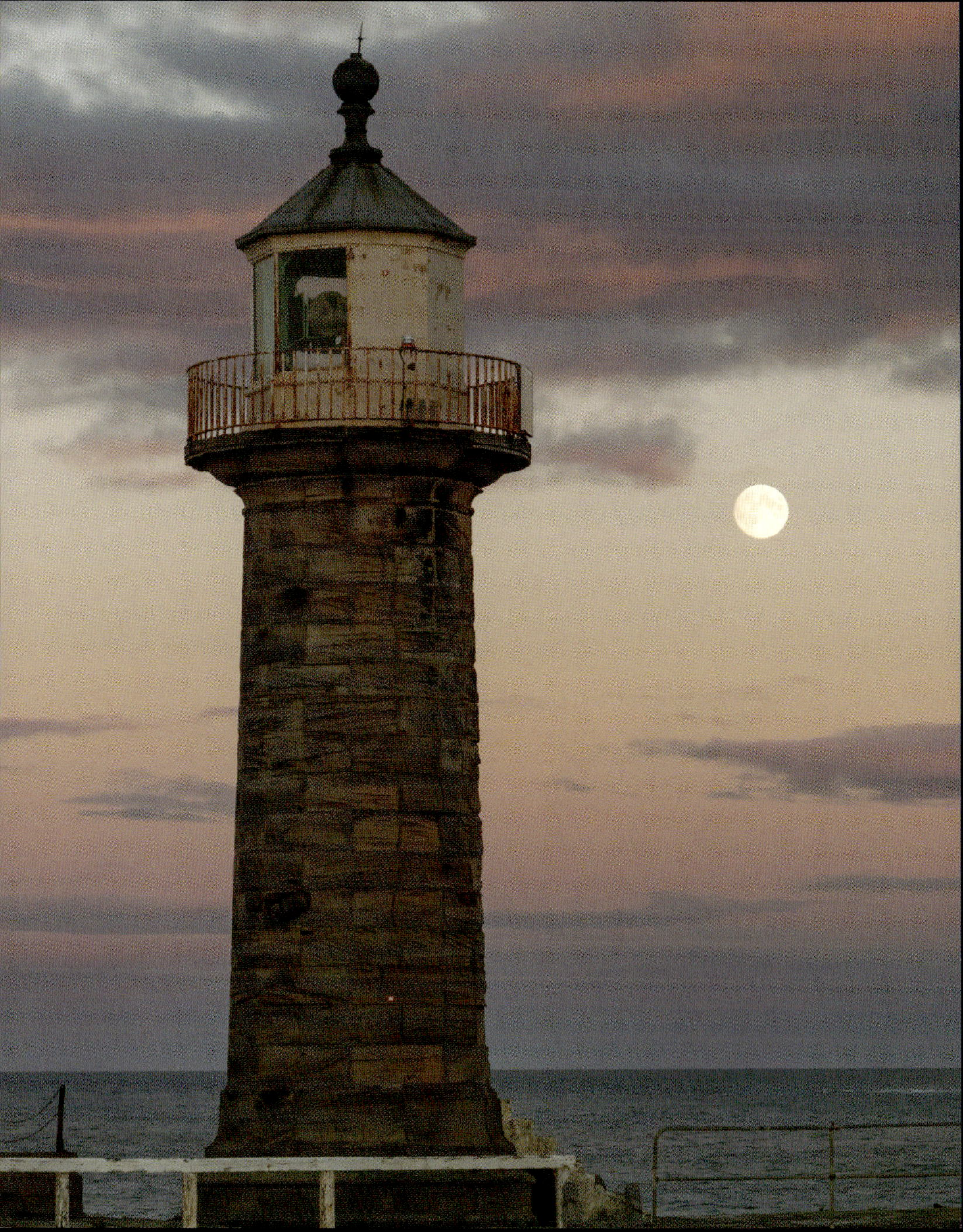

» CANON ACCESSORIES

There's an extensive range of accessories for the G16 that will add to the camera's capabilities and make your photography more enjoyable and rewarding. It's only natural to favor official Canon accessories, as these are guaranteed to work with your G16, but there's absolutely no need to stick to Canon—it's possible to find third-party equivalents of the following items, often at a lower price.

AC adapter kit (ACK-DC80)

The adapter pack replaces the G16's battery and powers the camera from a wall socket. This is particularly useful if you are using your camera to display images or movies on a TV, or when transferring a large number of files to your computer.

Filter adapter (FA-DC58D)

This adapter replaces the lens ring and can be used to attach filters with a 58mm diameter thread.

Remote switch (RS60-E3)

This remote switch allows you to fire the shutter remotely, reducing the risk of camera shake. It is almost essential if you use a tripod on a regular basis.

Conversion lens adapter (LA-DC58L)

Like the FA-DC58D filter adapter, this adapter replaces the lens ring. It can be used to attach the Tele-converter TC-DC58E and Macro Ring Lite/Macro Twin Ring Lite.

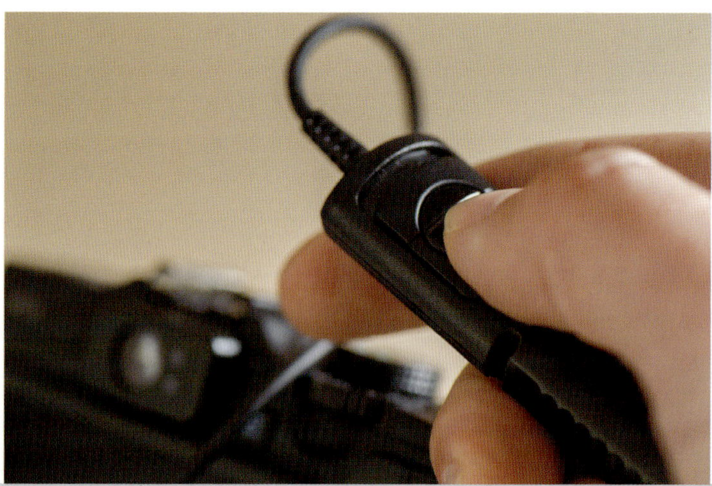

REMOTE «
The RS60-E3 remote switch.

Tele-converter (TC-DC58E)

This is an optical tele-converter that increases the maximum focal length of the G16's lens by 1.4x. Unlike the built-in digital tele-converter, it doesn't interpolate images, so image quality will be higher. When the tele-converter is fitted, set **Converter** on the  Shooting menu to TC-DC58E. The tele-converter requires the LA-DC58L conversion lens adapter.

Interface cable (IFC-400PCU)

If your computer or printer does not have a built-in SD memory card slot you'll need this USB cable to connect your G16 to your PC or printer.

HDMI cable (HTC-100) and Stereo A/V cable (AVC DC400ST)

These cables enable you to connect your G16 to a television, for still image and video playback.

Waterproof case (WP-DC52)

This waterproof case will protect the G16 underwater to depths of up to 130ft (40m). The case will also protect your camera from wet weather and foreign particles such as sand. It features a built-in flash diffusion plate, which helps to prevent glare when using flash underwater, reducing the risk of backscatter and ensuring even flash illumination.

Speedlite bracket (SB-E2)

The SB-E2 bracket allows you to mount your Speedlite flash at the side of the G16. This can help to reduce red-eye and provides more scope for creating interesting lighting effects. The bracket is supplied with Canon's Off-camera shoe cord (OC-E3).

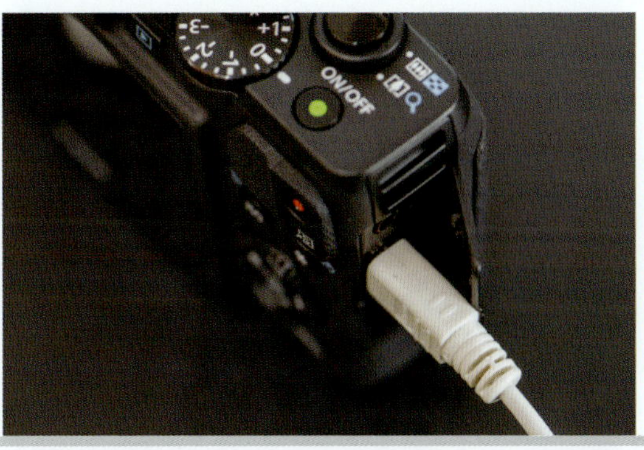

USB »

If you want to connect your G16 to a computer or printer you'll need to buy a USB cable if you don't already have one (or use the G16's built-in Wi-Fi connection).

» FILTERS

A filter is a piece of glass, gelatin, or optical resin that is placed in front of a camera lens to affect the light in some way before it reaches a camera's sensor. There are filters that are purely gimmicks and some that are almost indispensable (a polarizing filter is arguably one such essential filter). One filter that you won't need is a neutral density (ND) filter, as there is one built into the G16.

To use filters you will have to buy the optional FA-DC58D filter adapter. This will allow you to attach 58mm circular filters directly to the lens, or use a filter holder system such as the Cokin A system. The following list features a range of filters that you may find useful.

> **Note:**
> One disadvantage to using a filter holder system is that it may block the view through the viewfinder.

Filter type	Effect
Polarizer	Eliminates polarized light, cutting down reflections from non-metallic surfaces (water, paint, foliage, and so on).
ND graduate	Darkens one half of your image to help balance exposure. Typically used to balance the exposure of a bright sky with a darker foreground.
UV	Cuts out excessive Ultra Violet (UV) light. Typically used at high-altitude. Has no effect on exposure.
Soft-focus	Softens the image, reducing sharpness and contrast. Has no effect on exposure.
Strong ND	Provides up to 10-stops of light elimination to allow ultra-long shutter speeds to be used.
IR	Cuts out visible wavelengths of light, allowing you to create infrared (IR) images.
Colored	Yellow, orange, red, or green; used when shooting monochrome in-camera.

› Filter tips

Apart from those that are essentially clear (such as UV filters) most filters reduce the amount of light that reaches the sensor. This is useful if you want to extend shutter speeds or use a wider aperture for a certain effect, but be aware that if you set the G16 to ISO AUTO, the ISO will increase automatically to take account of the reduction in light. This can lead to more "noise" in your images, so consider using a fixed ISO setting to avoid this.

ND graduate filters are most often used to darken skies to match the exposure of the foreground. Using evaluative metering with an ND graduate can cause exposure problems. Instead, use spot metering with **Spot AE Point** on the Shooting menu set to **AF Point**. When you focus, move the AF point to the foreground, so the exposure is biased to the foreground rather than the filtered sky.

There are two types of polarizing filter: linear and circular. This isn't to do with the shape, but the method of construction. The G16 can use either type, although circular polarizers (which are generally the more expensive of the two) are necessary when using cameras with phase-detection AF systems, such as most DSLRs.

If you plan to share your filters between cameras, or think you may upgrade in the future, it's safer to buy the circular type. In both cases, the front element of a polarizing filter can be turned to vary the strength of its effect.

POLARIZED
A polarizing filter is useful for adding contrast to the sky.

8

» SUPPORT

The G16 has built-in lens stabilization, so you may think that a tripod isn't necessary. However, a tripod is just as useful as it would be for a larger format camera like a DSLR. The maximum shutter speed you can set on the G16 is 250 seconds (over 4 minutes!), and there's no way you could handhold your G16 for this length of time without causing camera shake.

The bad news about tripods is their weight and the time they take to set up. Fortunately, the G16 is light and therefore a suitable tripod doesn't need to be too heavy. The advantage of a tripod is that it allows you to be experimental with shutter speeds and lighting conditions. Tripods also make you think more about your photography: they slow you down, giving you time to consider each shot. And, if you've carried a tripod around all day, you'll be more inclined to get the shot right!

Tripods vary in weight and in the height to which they can be erected: the simple rule is that the taller a tripod, the more it will inevitably weigh. It is a good idea to buy a tripod that will bring your camera close to eye-level without the use of the center column. This is because extending the center column will raise the center of gravity, which increases the likelihood of the tripod toppling over if there is any wind, or if it is knocked. It is also less stable. Some tripods come with a hook on the center column from which you can hang your camera bag. This will help to stabilize your tripod, as long as the bag is resting on the ground, rather than swinging around.

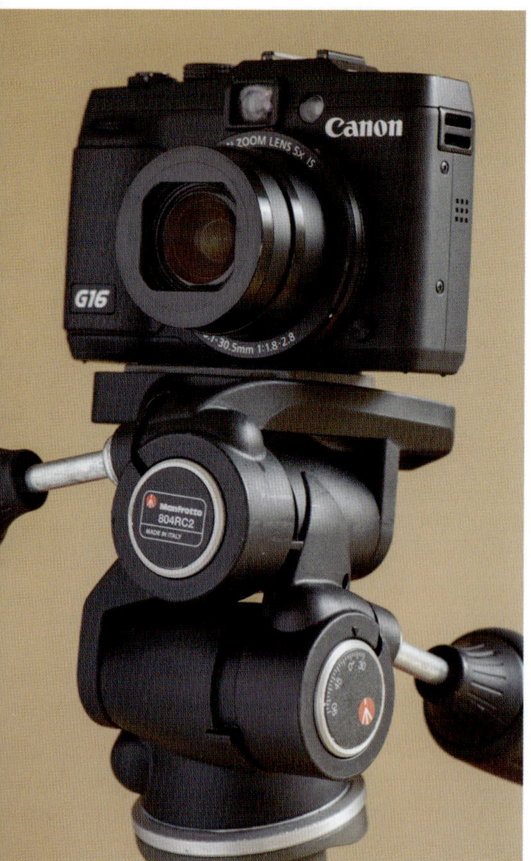

» BEANBAG

Some venues don't like you to use a tripod, and these are usually places there they are most needed. This shot required some support for the camera, but it wasn't possible to use a tripod. Instead, the G16 was nestled into a beanbag placed onto a flat surface. I used the G16's self-timer to avoid knocking the camera out of position.

Settings
> Focal length: 6.1mm
> Exposure: 1 sec. at f/4.5
> ISO: 80

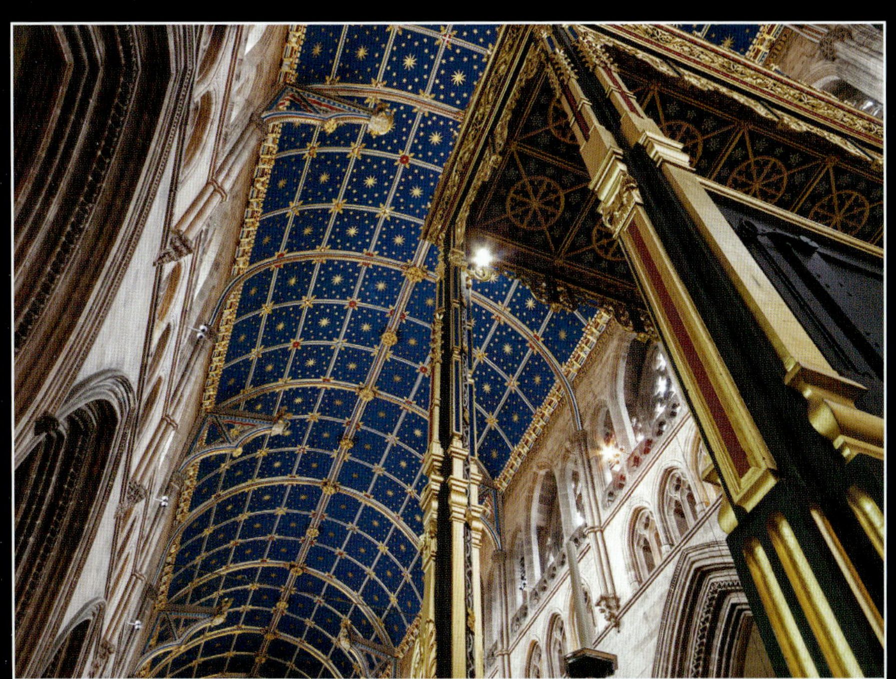

CONNECTION

Eventually there will come a time when you'll need to connect your G16 (or memory card) to an external device, such as a computer, printer, or television to archive, review, edit, and/or print your images.

› Color calibration

Maintaining accurate colors from camera to print via a computer means calibrating your computer monitor and using a relevant profile for the paper you want to use with your printer (using PictBridge bypasses the first of these requirements). The most accurate way to profile a monitor is to use a hardware color profiler (you could use a software color profiler, but these rely on a subjective judgement of color, brightness, and contrast and so are generally less accurate). Hardware color profilers are now reasonably priced and available from most good retail and online electronics stores.

Different papers have different qualities when it comes to how ink is absorbed and how colors are reproduced. A printer profile specifies how the printer needs to modify its output so that the paper receives the correct amount of ink in the right proportions, so an image's colors are reproduced correctly. For total accuracy you will need to use a hardware printer profiler, but manufacturers often supply profiles for popular papers and printers that work perfectly well.

CALIBRATION «
Calibrating a monitor using a hardware color profiler.

ON THE RIGHT LINES »
Make the right connections with your G16 to extend your photographic journey.

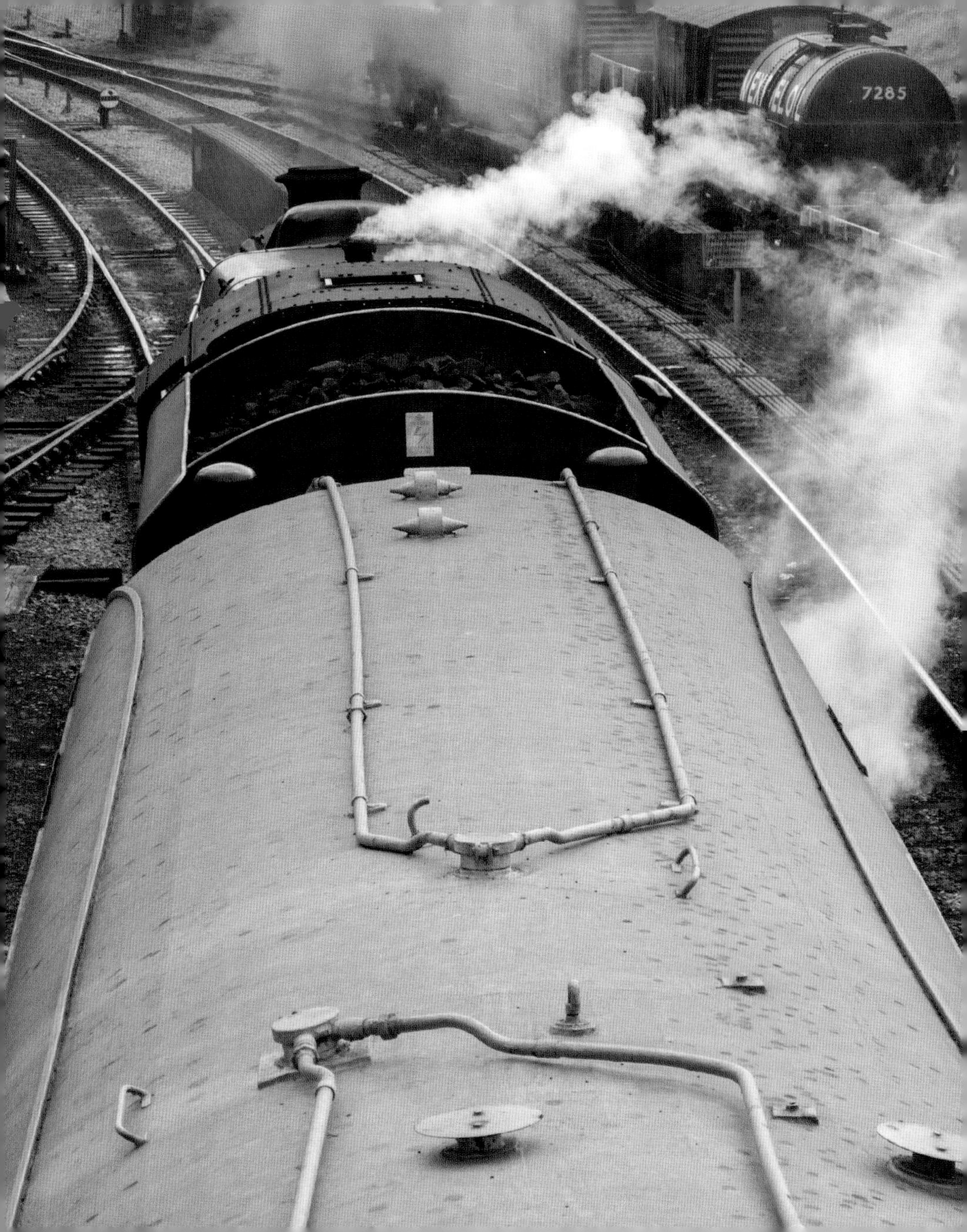

7285

» CANON SOFTWARE

The G16 isn't supplied with any imaging software, so if you want to use any of Canon's software you must first download a software bundle to your Windows PC (XP SP 3, Vista SP 2, 7 SP1, or 8) or Mac (OS X 10.6–10.8) from Canon's web site.

It's not obligatory to do this, but the software is free and useful—Digital Photo Professional (DPP) in particular is a very powerful and professional piece of software. You can also download CameraWindow, ImageBrowser, and PhotoStitch. Unfortunately, there's not enough space in this book to give an in-depth guide to all this software, but Canon supplies comprehensive notes for each package as a PDF document (also available via its web site).

WEB SITE

The software for the G16 has to be downloaded from Canon's web site—no CD is supplied with the camera.

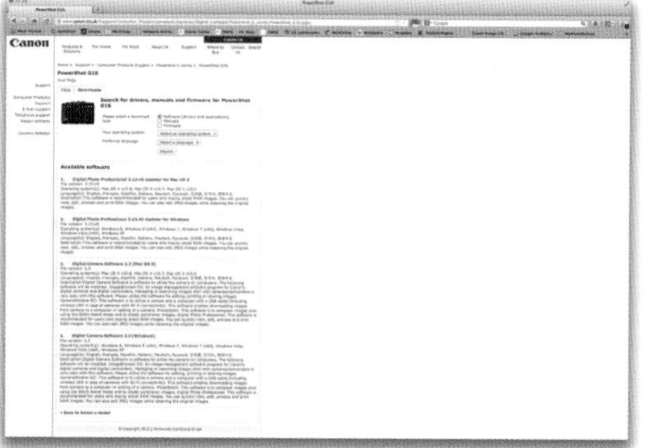

Downloading the software

1) Go to www.canon.com/icpd

2) Select your country of residence.

3) Click on **PowerShot** under the **Cameras** column.

4) Under the **PowerShot G Series** column select **PowerShot G16**.

5) Click on the **Downloads** tab and select **Software (drivers and applications)**.

6) Select your computer's operating system and preferred language from the drop-down menus and click on **Search**.

7) Click on **Digital Software 2.3** followed by **Accept & Download**.

8) When prompted, enter the serial number of your G16. You can find this on the base of the camera.

9) Downloading should begin. The length of time it takes will depend on the speed of your Internet connection.

Installing the software

1) Double-click on the downloaded software file.

2) The Canon software installation screen should appear automatically. Click on **Easy Installation** to install all the software automatically, or click on **Custom Installation** to select which of the programs you want to install. Follow the instructions on screen to continue.

3) Attach your G16 to your computer when prompted.

4) When the installation is complete click on either **Finish** or **Restart** as required.

5) Either archive or delete the downloaded file. As you can download the software—including updates—at any point, it is arguably just as easy to delete the file and save hard drive space.

> **Note:**
> Once you've bought your G16, you're eligible to join the CANON iMAGE GATEWAY. This is a free service that gives you 10GB of online storage space to host images and videos. These can then be viewed by other members or shared with family and friends through social web sites such as Facebook or Twitter.

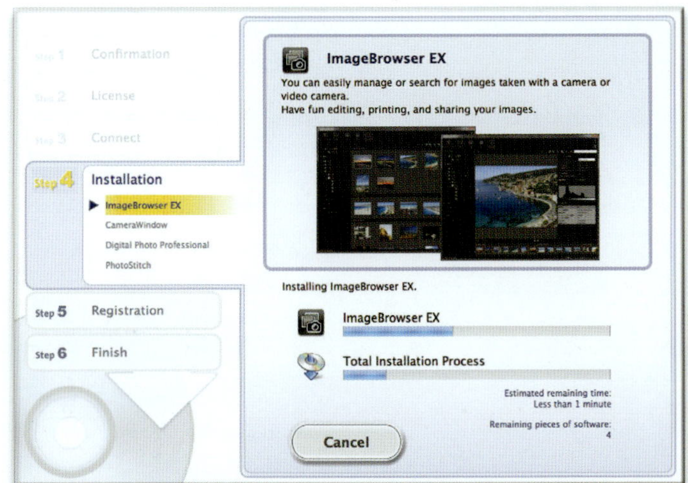

INSTALLATION «
Installing the downloaded software.

CameraWindow

This nifty application enables you to import your images automatically from your G16 onto your Windows PC or Mac, organize the images on the memory card, and set options such as the startup image and sounds on your camera.

PhotoStitch

PhotoStitch allows you to merge a number of images shot with the intention of creating a panoramic image. This usually means shooting a sequence of images from left to right or up and down, allowing an overlap between each image.

ImageBrowser EX

ImageBrowser EX is an image database application that can be used to import, sort, and manage your images on your Windows PC or Mac. Using the simple interface you can view shooting details in image metadata, copy, duplicate, move, rename, or delete your photographs. You can also rate your images using a star system to rank them for editing.

Digital Photo Professional

Digital Photo Professional (DPP) is an easy way to convert the G16's Raw files, and is capable of extracting a high level of detail from them. Adjustments such as altering color, contrast, and sharpening can be quickly made, before saving the result in an easier to use format such as TIFF or JPEG.

CANON DPP SOFTWARE ⌄

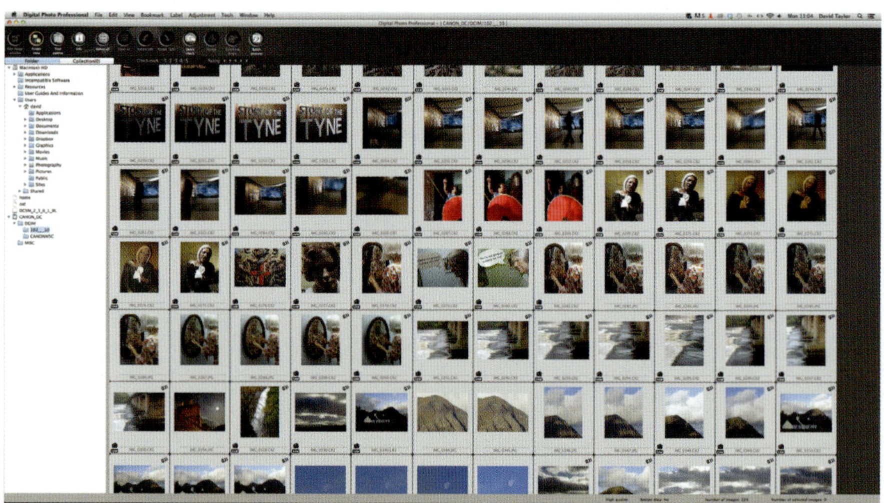

» CONNECTING TO A PC

To copy the still images and movies from your G16 to a computer, you'll either need to remove the memory card and insert it into a card reader, or connect your camera directly to your computer using a Mini-B USB cable.

Unfortunately, neither a card reader nor USB cable is supplied with your G16. If you already have one or the other you're ready to go, otherwise you'll need to buy either one from a photography or online store. If you're connecting your G16 directly to a computer you will also first need to install the Canon software described previously.

> **Warning!**
>
> *Before connecting your G16 to your computer, make sure that it is switched off and that the battery is fully charged.*

Attaching your G16 directly to a computer

1) Attach the Mini-B connector to the A/V OUT / Digital port on your G16.

2) Insert the other end of the USB cable into a USB 2.0 port on your computer.

3) Press ▶ to turn on your G16.

4) On a Windows PC click on **Downloads Images From Canon Camera using Canon CameraWindow**. CameraWindow should now automatically appear. Always do this for this device if you want to make this a default action when you connect your G16. On Mac OS X, CameraWindow should run automatically when the camera is connected to your Mac and switched on.

5) Follow the on-screen instructions for CameraWindow.

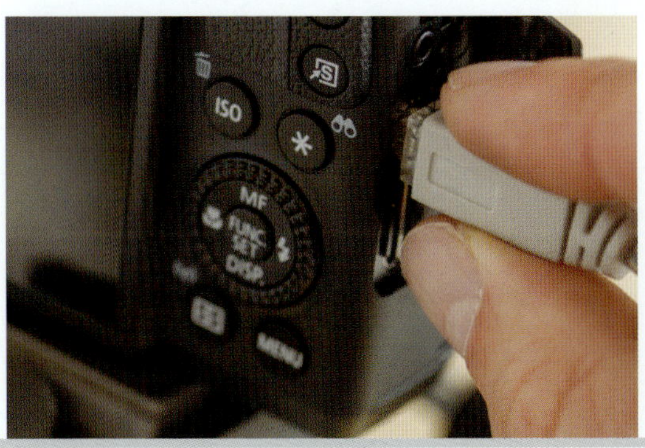

» CONNECTING TO A TV

Another cable omitted by Canon when you buy a G16 is the A/V cable that would allow you to connect your G16 to a compatible TV and view still images and movies without a PC. Canon currently sells two types of cable: the Stereo A/V Cable AVC-DC400ST and HDMI Cable HTC-100. The former uses standard RCA video terminals for use with analog TVs, while the latter (a type C mini-pin HDMI) is needed for HDMI-compatible sets. Either cable (or a suitable third-party equivalent) will open up a new world, enabling you to show off your images and movies to family and friends on a TV.

Connecting your G16 to an analog television

1) Ensure that both your G16 and TV are switched off. Open the G16's terminal cover and connect the A/V cable plug into the A/V OUT / Digital port.

2) Plug the three RCA plugs into the relevant connections on your TV. The connectors are color-coded: yellow for video, and white and red for the left and right audio inputs respectively. Match the correct color plug to the correct connection. If the connectors on your TV are not color-coded, check the TV's instruction manual before proceeding.

3) Turn on your TV and switch to the correct channel for external devices.

4) Turn on your camera by pressing the ▶ button. The image from the G16 should now be displayed on the TV, rather than the LCD.

5) When you are finished, turn off the G16 and TV before disconnecting.

VIEWING IMAGES ON A TELEVISION ⟱

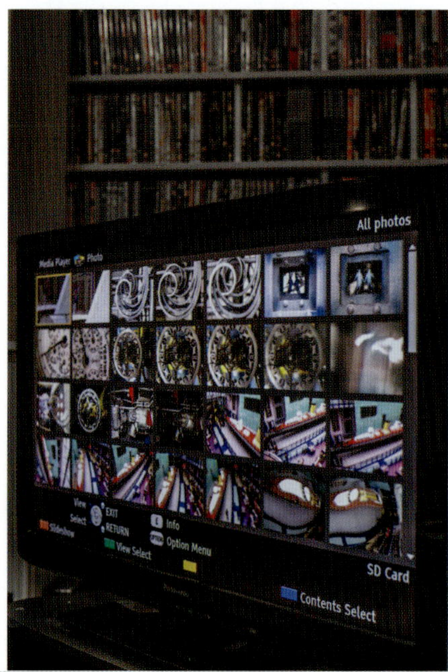

Connecting your G16 to an HDTV

1) Ensure that both your G16 and TV are switched off.

2) Open the G16's terminal cover and connect the HDMI cable to the HDMI port.

3) Plug the other end of the HDMI cable into a free slot on your TV.

4) Turn on your TV and switch to the correct channel for external devices.

5) Turn on your G16 by pressing the ▶ button. The image from the G16 should now be displayed on the TV rather than the LCD.

6) When you are finished, turn off the G16 and TV before disconnecting.

HDMI TV remote control

If you own an HDMI CEC-compatible television, the G16 can be controlled using the TV's remote control when connected to the television using an HDMI cable.

1) Set **Ctrl via HDMI** to **Enable** on the ⚙ Settings menu.

2) Follow steps 1 to 5 for *Connecting your G16 to an HDTV*.

3) Press the TV's remote control ◀ / ▶ buttons to select an image.

4) Press the OK/Select button on the remote control to display the G16's control panel. Press ◀ / ▶ to choose an item and then press OK/Select once more.

Camera control panel on TV

↩ **Return**	Closes the menu.
▣ **Group playback**	Displays sets of images shot using continuous shooting or individual image shot using ✦ mode.
▶ **Movie playback**	Plays movie when movie is selected.
⬙ **Slideshow**	Plays back images automatically. You can use ◀ / ▶ to skip more quickly through the slideshow.
▨ **Index**	Displays an index of images.
DISP. Change display	Switches the G16's screen display.

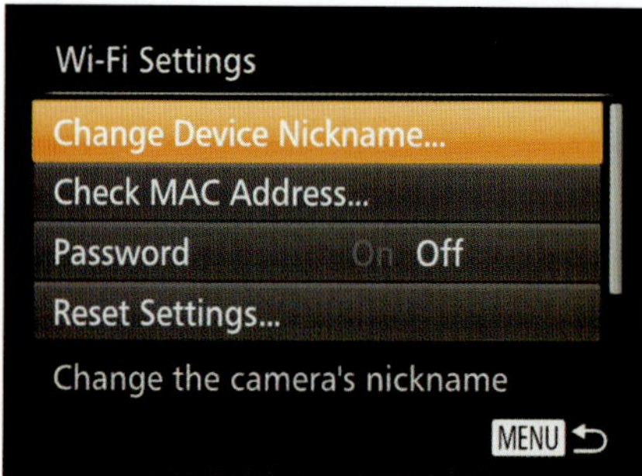

The G16 is the first G-series camera to feature built-in Wi-Fi capability (previous models required the use of an Eye-Fi memory card). There are two basic ways of connecting wireless devices. The first is to make a direct connection between two Wi-Fi-enabled devices. This method would typically be used to connect your G16 to a smartphone or printer.

Alternatively, you can use a wireless access point (such as a wireless router) as a bridge to connect the two devices. If you wanted to send your images to a web service, this type of connection is the one that is generally used, allowing you to send your images via a wireless router to an internet-enabled computer.

Enabling Wi-Fi

1) Select **Wi-Fi Settings** on the ![menu icon] menu.

2) You'll first need to give your G16 an easily recognizable nickname of up to 16 characters in length. Select **Change Device Nickname...**, press ![FUNC SET], and use the G16 keyboard to enter a nickname. Press **MENU** when you're done.

3) If your Wi-Fi network requires you to enter a MAC address to allow your G16 to connect to the network select **Check MAC Address...**. Enter the string of characters shown into network access point and press **MENU**.

4) If you want to set up a password-protected direct connection set **Password** to **On**.

5) If you want to start again from scratch select **Reset Settings...** followed by **OK** when prompted.

6) Finally, you can save the **Target History** (a list of devices and web services the G16 has previously connected to) by setting this option to **On**.

Using Wi-Fi

1) Press ![play] followed by ![Wi-Fi] / ![grid].

2) Press ![up/down] to highlight a connection option, and then press ![FUNC SET] to begin the connection process.

› Wi-Fi options

There are five connection options when using Wi-Fi: (1) Connecting to Another Camera; (2) Connecting to Smartphone (and other devices such as iPad/iPod or tablet); (3) Connecting to a Computer; (4) Connecting to a Printer; (5) Connecting to a Web Service. The connection process—such as whether a password needs to be entered—will depend on how your device or wireless network is configured.

If you want to connect your G16 to a smartphone (or iPad/iPod or tablet) you will need to download Canon's free CameraWindow app. This app is available for Apple iOS and Android devices. Once the app is installed and a connection made you can send images to your smartphone. If your smartphone is GPS-enabled you can use it to add location information to images on your camera.

Connecting to your smartphone

1) Install CameraWindow on your smartphone.

2) On your G16 select **Connecting to smartphone** at step 2 of *Using Wi-Fi.*

3) Select **Add a Device...**

4) On your smartphone, add a new Wi-Fi network and use the information on the G16's LCD to connect to your G16 (the network name is SSID information shown on the LCD; the password uses the WEP standard). Every time you connect to your G16 using your smartphone you'll need to switch to this network rather than your default network.

5) Run CameraWindow on your smartphone and select the correct device on your G16 (which should be highlighted by default and be shown as the nickname you previously set up).

6) Select **Yes** when **Allow images on camera to be viewed on target device** is shown on screen.

7) Select **View images on camera** on your smartphone.

8) Tap on a thumbnail to view the image full screen on your smartphone. If you want to save the image to your smartphone, tap on ➦ and follow the on-screen instructions.

» PRINTING

There's nothing more satisfying than seeing an image as a print—it's a more tactile way of looking at an image than viewing it on a screen. The G16 offers two ways to make the printing process easier.

› PictBridge

You can connect your G16 directly to a PictBridge compatible printer, so that images can be printed without using a PC as a "go-between." This can be done either wirelessly or using a USB cable (some printers also have SD memory card slots, although you can only print JPEGs using this method).

Connecting to a printer (USB):

1) Check that the camera's battery is fully charged, or connect your G16 to mains power, before beginning to print.

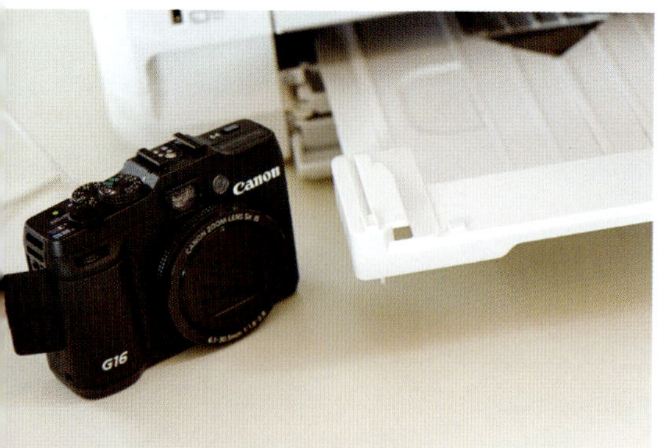

2) Make sure that both the camera and printer are switched off. Insert the memory card of images you want to print into the G16 if it is not already installed.

3) Open the G16's terminal cover and connect the USB cable to the A/V OUT / Digital port.

4) Connect the other end of the cable to the printer's USB port. Follow any instructions about PictBridge printing in the manual supplied with the printer.

5) Turn on the printer, followed by the G16 (using the ▶ button).

6) Find the image you want to print and then press (FUNC/SET) to view the detailed print settings screen (see table on next page).

7) Highlight **Print** and press (FUNC/SET) again.

8) Repeat steps 6 and 7 to print out additional images.

9) Turn off the G16 and printer and disconnect the USB cable.

Printing options

Option	Description
Default	The print will be made using the printer's standard setup.
Date	The date the image was shot on will be added to the print.
File No.	The image file number will be added to the print.
Both	Both the date and file number will be added to the print.
Off	–
Default	Color setup uses default printer settings.
Off	No automatic correction applied.
On	Colors corrected using shooting information.
Red-eye 1	Corrects red-eye automatically.
No. of Copies	Select number of copies to be printed.
Cropping	Allows you to crop your image before printing.

Paper settings

Paper Size	Select the size of the paper loaded in the printer.
Paper Type	Select the paper type.
Page Layout	Select how the image will look on the printed page.

Page layout	Description
Default	Print will be made using the printer's standard setup.
Bordered	The print will be made with white borders.
Borderless	The print will go to the edge of the page if your printer supports this facility.
N-up	Choose how many images to print on a single sheet.
ID-photo	Prints images that can be used for ID purposes (only images shot using **L** and a 4:3 aspect ratio can be used).
Fixed Size	Choose the print size (either 3.5 x 5in., postcard, or wide-format print).

Movie printing	Description
Single	Prints the current frame.
Sequence	Prints a series of frames a certain time interval apart on the same page.

› Digital Print Order Format (DPOF)

DPOF is an industry standard set of printing instructions that cameras, including the G16, can add to a memory card. These instructions include the number of prints to be made from a particular image, the paper size to be used, and whether title text is to be printed over the image.

The DPOF instructions can be read by compatible printers or by a photographic printing service so that you get exactly the prints required. There are a few caveats though: DPOF only works with JPEGs and DPOF instructions stay tagged to images after printing, so you'll need to remove them once the printing is complete.

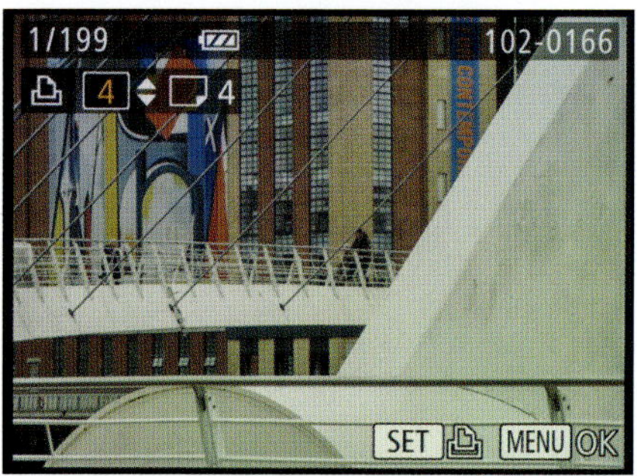

DPOF selection during playback

1) Press **MENU** and choose **Select images & Qty** from the 🖳 tab.

2) Find the image you want to tag DPOF instructions to.

3) Press 🔘 to start tagging the image. Press ▲ / ▼ or turn 🔘 to increase or decrease the number of prints to be made of the image, up to a maximum of 99.

4) Press 🔘 to continue searching through your images and repeat step 3.

5) Press **MENU** to save the DPOF list of tagged images to the memory card.

> **Notes:**
> You cannot add images to the DPOF list if your G16 is already connected to a printer.
>
> Once you've added an image to the DPOF list you can remove it by following steps 1–2 and setting the number of prints to 0.

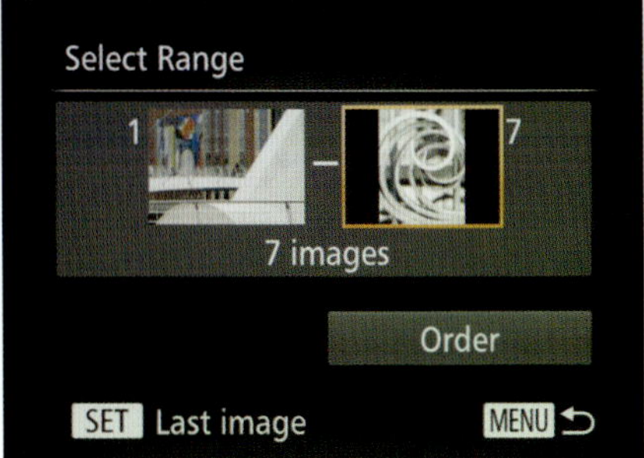

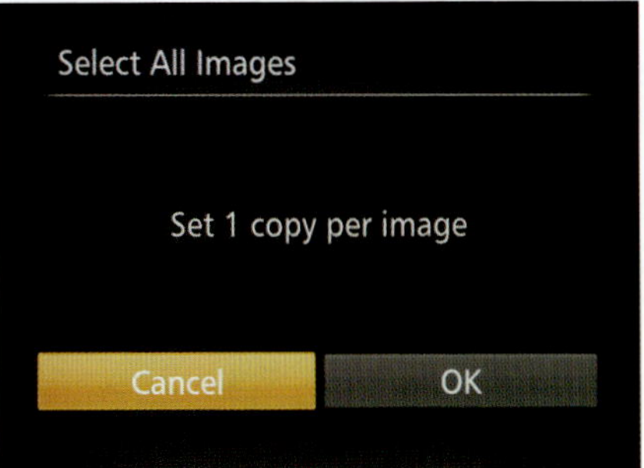

Selecting a range of images for DPOF

1) In Playback mode press **MENU**, highlight 🖨, and choose **Select Range**.

2) Turn ⚙ to navigate to the desired starting image in the range. Press (FUNC SET) once to view the image full screen and again to return to the **Select Range** screen.

3) Press ▶. Turn ⚙ to navigate to the last image in the range that you want to print. Press (FUNC SET) once to view that image full screen and then again to return to the **Select Range** screen. You will not be allowed to choose an image that comes before the first image chosen in step 2.

4) Press ▼ to highlight **Order** and then press (FUNC SET) to add the selected range to the DPOF list, or press **MENU** to return to the main 🖨 menu without adding any images to the DPOF list.

Selecting all images

1) In Playback mode press **MENU**, followed by 🖨, and then choose **Select All Images.**

2) Select **OK** and one print will be specified for all of the JPEG images on your memory card. Select **Cancel** to return to the 🖨 menu without adding any images to the DPOF list.

Clear all DPOF instructions

1) In playback mode press **MENU** and highlight 🖨.

2) Select **Clear All Selections**.

3) Choose **OK** and all the DPOF instructions on the memory card will be cleared. Select **Cancel** to return to the main 🖨 Print menu without clearing the DPOF instructions.

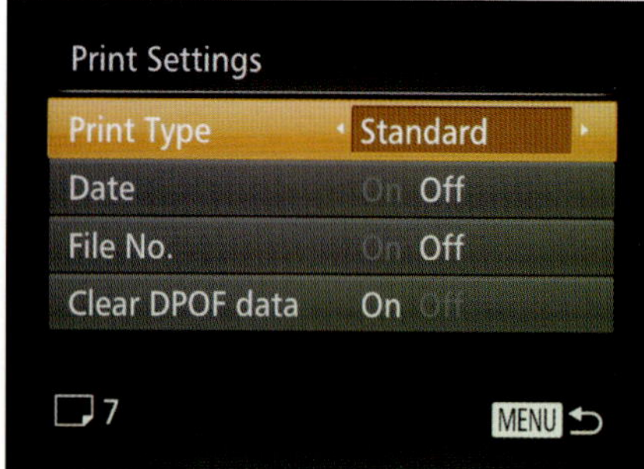

DPOF Print Settings

1) In playback mode press **MENU** and highlight 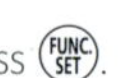.

2) Highlight **Print Settings** and press (FUNC SET).

3) Highlight the setting you want to alter and use ◄ / ► to make the required changes. See the table below for the setting options.

4) When you're finished press **MENU** to save the altered settings and return to the main menu.

Printing DPOF images on a PictBridge printer

1) Follow steps 1–5 on page 228 to connect your G16 to a PictBridge printer.

2) Highlight **Print** and then press (FUNC SET).

3) The printer will now print out images according to the DPOF settings.

> **Note:**
> If you want to delay printing, highlight **Print Later** and then press (FUNC SET).

Setting	Options	Description
Print type	Standard	One image is printed per page.
	Index	Several images are printed per page at a reduced size.
	Both	Prints both Standard and Index pages.
Date	On	Shooting date is printed over the image.
	Off	–
File no.	On	File number is printed over the image.
	Off	–
Clear DPOF data	On	Removes all print settings after printing.
	Off	–

» KEEPING IT SIMPLE

It's all too tempting to throw everything into a photograph. However, what you exclude is almost as important as what you include when composing. Ask yourself what the simplest image is that you can produce from the scene in front of you, while still saying exactly what you want to say.

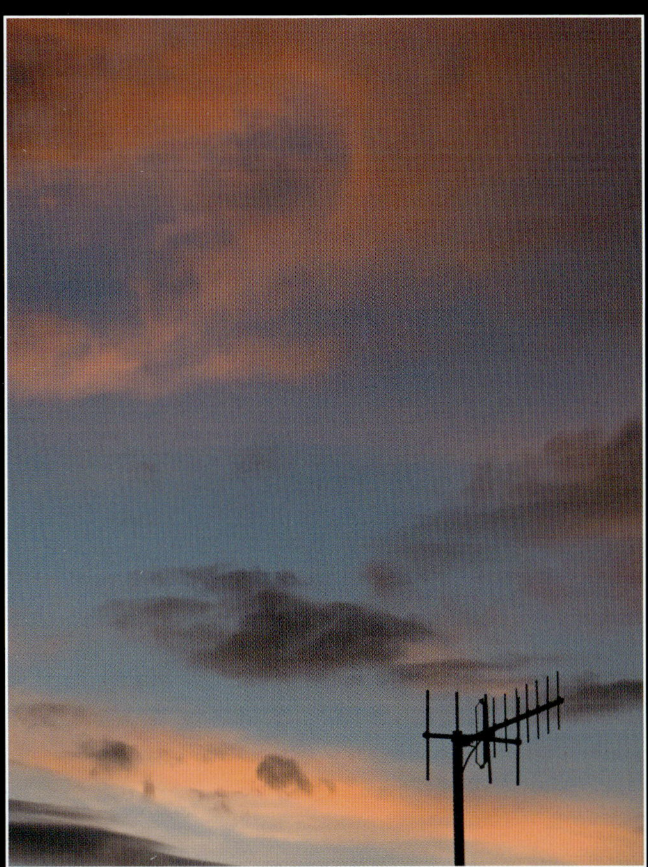

» GLOSSARY

Aberration An imperfection in a photograph, usually caused by the optics of a lens.

AEL (automatic exposure lock) A camera control that locks in the exposure value, allowing a scene to be recomposed.

Angle of view The area of a scene that a lens takes in, measured in degrees.

Aperture The opening in a camera lens through which light passes to expose the sensor. The relative size of the aperture is denoted by f-stops.

Autofocus (AF) A reliable through-the-lens focusing system allowing accurate focus without the photographer manually turning the lens.

Bracketing Taking a series of identical pictures, changing only the exposure, usually in $1/3$-, $1/2$-, or 1-stop increments.

Buffer The in-camera memory of a digital camera.

Center-weighted metering A metering pattern that determines the exposure by placing importance on the lightmeter reading at the center of the frame.

Chromatic aberration The inability of a lens to bring spectrum colors into focus at a single point.

CMOS (Complementary Metal Oxide Semiconductor) A type of imaging sensor, consisting of a grid of light-sensitive cells. The more cells, the greater the number of pixels and the higher the resolution of the final image.

Color temperature The color of a light source expressed in degrees Kelvin (K).

Compression The process by which digital files are reduced in size. Compression can retain all the information in the file, or "lose" data usually in the form of fine detail for greater levels of file-size reduction.

Contrast The range between the highlight and shadow areas of a photo, or a marked difference in illumination between colors or adjacent areas.

Depth of field This is controlled primarily by the aperture: the smaller the aperture, the greater the depth of field.

Diopter Unit expressing the power of a lens.

dpi (dots per inch) Measure of the resolution of a printer or scanner. The more dots per inch, the higher the resolution.

DPOF Digital Print Order Format.

Dynamic range The ability of the camera's sensor to capture a full range of shadows and highlights.

Evaluative metering A metering system where light reflected from several subject areas is calculated based on algorithms.

Exposure The amount of light allowed to hit the digital sensor, controlled by aperture, shutter speed, and ISO. Also, the act of taking a photograph, as in "making an exposure."

Exposure compensation A control that allows intentional over- or underexposure.

Fill-in flash Flash combined with daylight in an exposure. Used with naturally backlit or harshly side-lit or top-lit subjects to prevent silhouettes forming, or to add extra light to the shadow areas of a well-lit scene.

Filter A piece of colored or coated glass, or plastic, placed in front of the lens.

Focal length The distance, usually in millimeters, from the optical center point of a lens to its focal point.

fps (frames per second) A measure of the time needed for a digital camera to process one photograph and be ready to shoot the next.

f/stop Number assigned to a particular lens aperture. Wide apertures are denoted by small numbers (such as f/1.8 and f/2.8), while small apertures are denoted by large numbers (such as f/16 and f/22).

HDR (High Dynamic Range) A technique that increases the dynamic range of a photograph by merging several shots taken with different exposure settings.

Histogram A graph representing the distribution of tones in a photograph.

Hotshoe An accessory shoe with electrical contacts that allows synchronization between a camera and a flash.

Hotspot A light area with a loss of detail in the highlights. This is a common problem in flash photography.

Incident-light reading Meter reading based on the light falling on the subject.

Interpolation A way of increasing the file size of a digital image by adding pixels, thereby increasing its resolution.

ISO The sensitivity of the digital sensor measured in terms equivalent to the ISO rating of a film.

JPEG (Joint Photographic Experts Group) JPEG compression can reduce file sizes to about 5% of their original size, but uses a lossy compression system that degrades image quality.

LCD (Liquid crystal display) The flat screen on a digital camera that allows the user to preview digital photographs.

Macro A term used to describe close focusing and the close-focusing ability of a lens.

Megapixel One million pixels is equal to one megapixel.

Memory card A removable storage device for digital cameras.

Noise Interference visible in a digital image caused by stray electrical signals.

PictBridge The industry standard for sending information directly from a camera to a printer, without the need for a computer.

Pixel Short for "picture element"—the smallest bit of information in a digital photograph.

Predictive autofocus An AF system that can continuously track a moving subject.

Raw The file format in which the raw data from the sensor is stored without permanent alteration being made.

Red-eye reduction A system that causes the pupils of a subject's eyes to shrink, by shining a light prior to taking the main flash picture.

Remote switch A device used to trigger the shutter of the camera from a distance, to help minimize camera shake. Also known as a "cable release" or "remote release."

Resolution The number of pixels used to capture or display a photo.

RGB (red, green, blue) Computers and other digital devices understand color information as combinations of red, green, and blue.

Rule of thirds A rule of composition that places the key elements of a picture at points along imagined lines that divide the frame into thirds, both vertically and horizontally.

Shutter The mechanism that controls the amount of light reaching the sensor, by opening and closing.

Soft proofing Using software to mimic on screen how an image will look once output to another imaging device. Typically this will be a printer.

Spot metering A metering pattern that places importance on the intensity of light reflected by a very small portion of the scene, either at the center of the frame or linked to a focus point.

Tele-converter A supplementary lens that is fitted between the camera body and lens, increasing its effective focal length.

Telephoto A lens with a large focal length and a narrow angle of view.

TIFF (Tagged Image File Format) A universal file format supported by virtually all relevant software applications. TIFFs are uncompressed digital files.

TTL (through the lens) metering A metering system built into the camera that measures light passing through the lens at the time of shooting.

USB (universal serial bus) A data transfer standard, used by the Canon EOS 70D (and most other cameras) when connecting to a computer.

Viewfinder An optical system used for composing and sometimes for focusing the subject.

White balance A function that allows the correct color balance to be recorded for any given lighting situation.

Wide-angle lens A lens with a short focal length and, consequently, a wide angle of view.

» USEFUL WEB SITES

CANON

Canon Worldwide
www.canon.com

Canon US
www.usa.canon.com

Canon UK
www.canon.co.uk

Canon Europe
www.canon-europe.com

Canon Middle East
www.canon-me.com

Canon Oceania
www.canon.com.au

GENERAL

David Taylor
Landscape and travel photography
www.davidtaylorphotography.co.uk

Digital Photography Review
Camera and lens review site
www.dpreview.com

Photonet
Photography Discussion Forum
www.photo.net

EQUIPMENT

Adobe
Image-editing software (Photoshop, Photoshop Elements, and Lightroom)
www.adobe.com

Apple
Hardware and software manufacturer
www.apple.com/uk

PHOTOGRAPHY PUBLICATIONS

Photography books & Expanded Camera Guides
www.ammonitepress.com

Black & White Photography magazine
Outdoor Photography magazine
www.thegmcgroup.com